Sober Celebrations

Lively Entertaining Without the Spirits

Liz Scott

Sober Celebrations: Lively Entertaining Without the Spirits

Cleveland Clinic Press
All rights reserved
Copyright ©2007 by Liz Scott

Contact:
Cleveland Clinic Press
9500 Euclid Ave. NA32
Cleveland, OH 44195
216-445-5547
delongk@ccf.org
www.clevelandclinicpress.org

Scott, Liz, 1957-
Sober Celebrations: Lively Entertaining Without the Spirits / by Liz Scott.
p. cm.
Includes bibliographical references and index.
ISBN 978-1-59624-028-5 (alk. paper)
1. Cookery. 2. Entertaining. 3. Alcoholism--Diet therapy. I. Title.
TX714.S39244 2006
641.5--dc22   2006028962

Book Design by Whitney Campbell & Karen Diekmann
Photography by Steve Travarca, the Center for Medical Art and Photography, Cleveland Clinic

Printed on chlorine-free, environmentally friendly paper

Contents:

For Mom

Acknowledgments

The number of talented, dedicated, and supportive people it has taken to put together *Sober Celebrations* is vast and far-reaching. I can only hope to acknowledge a very special few here for all their hard work, enthusiasm, and commitment.

I would like to thank everyone at the Cleveland Clinic Press, most especially Larry Chilnick, for the privilege of working under your auspices and direction – your belief in the value of this project is unmatched and I am grateful to have had the opportunity to be a part of your outstanding organization. Thanks also to Kathryn DeLong, Dr. John Clough, Peter Studer, Julianne Stein, Laurie Weiss, and the Department of Nutrition for its seal of approval.

No book sees the light of day without painstaking production, for which I must thank Whitney Campbell, Matt McManus, and most especially Karen Diekmann, whom I will be personally nominating for sainthood. Thanks also to Beth Shepard, Gail Bellamy, and Steve Travarca of the Cleveland Clinic Center for Medical Art and Photography. Steve has proved to possess an outstanding eye as well as a bottomless supply of patience and integrity. The wonderfully warm and generous Jones family of the Chef's Garden and the Culinary Vegetable Institute who welcomed me with open arms will forever be in my prayers. The Joneses allowed us to use their amazing and breathtaking facility in Huron, Ohio for our photo shoot. To Chef Greg Claus – what can I say? If not for you I doubt we'd have made it through our cooking and photo sessions without a few casualties – you are the best! Thanks also to all the talented students at EHOVE Career Center in Milan, Ohio, who worked tirelessly all week.

Personal thanks go to Anna, Jimmy, Sherri, and of course Jennifer, whose friendship has gotten me through more than one difficult time. Rich, Nancy, Connie, and "Baby" afforded the warmth of family. Although my mother never saw the final result of this work, she enjoyed reading it as it was created, and I know she would have been proud and thrilled with the outcome. Thanks for everything, Mom – I miss you.

Hosting a holiday celebration or a special occasion party without a drop of alcohol might at first conjure up a dull affair, but with the help of *Sober Celebrations*, your next alcohol-free party may just end up being the liveliest and most exuberant affair you've ever given. After all, what makes for a memorable party, and how do you turn a good gathering of friends and family into a great one? The answer is simple: good company, great food, and a warm and winning atmosphere. These are always the main ingredients of any successful event you are hosting, whether it's Thanksgiving dinner for the relatives or a cozy birthday dinner for two. The truth is, the availability of alcoholic beverages at social events means very little to most people. Surprised? So was I.

When I gave up drinking eight years ago, I discovered a remarkable fact: There are a lot of folks out there who, for whatever reason, simply don't drink. And it's not just because they got sober or are medically restricted – it's because they actually choose not to. Maybe they dislike the taste or the effect, or both. Perhaps they adhere to certain religious protocols or their current diets preclude it. Did you know that less than 10 percent of the entire population consumes 100 percent of the alcohol sold in America? What does the other 90 percent drink?

Abstainers are all too often offered boring beverages at parties and functions – beverages they could easily get from a vending machine. As a former drinker as well as a busy caterer, I know that a refreshment with a little pizzazz is much preferred and graciously appreciated. Mocktails of traditional drinks can be fun and festive to imbibe, while alcohol-free beverages perfectly paired to accompany a terrific meal can be downright delicious. That's why you'll find plenty of beverage recipes in this book as well as recommended purchased refreshments that enhance every menu. (All purchased beverage and food selections appear italicized on each menu page.) From delectable palate-teasing aperitifs to creative coffee and tea concoctions, every course is covered with an answer to the question "What to pour?" It is a trend we are beginning to see more of in the restaurant and culinary professions, with inspired creations and delicious results.

On a similar note, we are now aware that cooking alcohol does not somehow magically make it disappear. Depending on the choice of liquor (beer and wine included) and the cook's method of preparation, up to 85 percent of the original alcohol added to a recipe may remain. For people who are on medication that carries alcohol warnings (there are more than 9,000 medicines that do), a small amount could prove problematic. Newly sober individuals on the drug Antabuse, for example, could become severely ill, while even the smell or taste of alcohol in food could trigger unwanted brain chemical recognition for those in early recovery and lead to a craving for a drink. But we needn't abandon our favorite recipes because of this fact. Throughout the book, I offer appropriate substitutes for wine and other alcoholic beverages that often appear in the ingredient list of many popular recipes, particularly during the holidays. Without sacrificing flavor and appeal, dishes we routinely associate with alcohol can be made sober and safe for any celebration.

Finally, as with recipes that contain alcohol, if you are taking something away, I believe you need to replace it with something just as good if not better, so I've applied this to the theme of each celebration by adding some extra-special touches that won't go unnoticed by your guests. Whether it's toasting the new year with the Spanish tradition of eating grapes or celebrating the 1920s in quirky Prohibition style, from the first to the last menu, you'll find all the creative tips and suggestions you'll need to host an unbeatable bash that will be "high-spirited" and long remembered.

Liz

Part One

Holidays and Traditions

Chapter 1

A New Year, A New Beginning

*Pomegranate Ratafia
with Sicilian Olives, Taralli,
and Asiago Nibbles*

As a new year begins, we are filled with the anticipation of the future and the excitement of making a fresh start in our lives. We may resolve to be healthier, more successful in our work, or more focused on making a difference in our community and the world we live in. And in the company of friends and family, we toast these new beginnings while saying "so long" to the old and familiar, enjoying a tradition of plentiful food, drink, and frivolity.

New Year's celebrations and resolutions date back to Babylonian times, when festivities lasted 11 days and people wholeheartedly resolved to return borrowed farming equipment to their neighbors! Although today we may take only one special night and the following day for celebrations, and promise ourselves quite different things like losing weight or looking for a new job, our desire for fun and our resolve to improve are just the same. But can an atmosphere of "high spirits" be reached without the inclusion of alcohol? You bet. When you are the host of these two exceptional get-togethers, no one will even notice or care that the menu is "sober safe," although they may remember that you haven't yet returned their hedge-trimmer!

Whatever our hopes and wishes for the upcoming year may be, one thing is certain: We could all use a little extra luck to assist us in carrying out our resolutions! And this party's menu is guaranteed to provide just that for all your guests. Borrowing from a medley of European traditions, the food selections symbolize wealth, prosperity, and happiness in delicious and satisfying opulence. Not unlike our Southern U.S. tradition of serving black-eyed peas on New Year's, lentils represent the "coins" of our future wealth and are a must at every Italian New Year's celebration. Round or ring-shaped foods, such as the Roman-Style Gnocchi and taralli, symbolize the completion of the year passed and are considered to hold us in good stead for the future, while eating grapes, one each at the 12 strokes of midnight, is a long-standing Spanish tradition believed to guarantee 12 months of the best life has to offer.

Pomegranate Ratafia and refreshing citrus sodas complement your menu, while a finale of the classic Greek Vassilopita cake, where a coin lies hidden for the luckiest of your guests to find, provides a sweet ending for a fabulous evening. Offering a selection of the highest-quality European chocolates with coffee will take this menu over the top and make your guests feel truly lucky and special!

A Good Luck New Year's Eve Party

MENU
Buffet for Eight

APPETIZER:

Sicilian Olives, Taralli, Asiago Nibbles

MAIN COURSE:

Fortuna Lentils with Italian Chicken Sausage
Roman-Style Gnocchi
European Greens with White Balsamic Vinaigrette
Italian Ciabatta

AT MIDNIGHT:

Sugared Grape Clusters

DESSERT:

Lucky Vassilopita Cake
Assorted European Chocolates

BEVERAGE PAIRINGS:

Appetizer: Pomegranate Ratafia
Main Course: *Variety of Italian Sodas*
Dessert: *Italian Roast Coffee*

Tips on Purchased Ingredients

Sicilian olives are robust and meaty – a perfect choice for teasing the palate. However, any type of olive will do, according to availability and preference. Good substitutes are Kalamata, oil-cured, Spanish queens (often stuffed with pimiento or garlic), or a Mediterranean medley. Just watch out for those that are "spiked" with vodka or vermouth.

Taralli are the Italian cousins of the common pretzel and often come flavored with fennel, black pepper, or sun-dried tomatoes in addition to the plain versions. Authentic taralli are often made with wine, so be sure to read the ingredient list before purchasing. Good alternatives would be crostini, cracklebread, or lavash.

Asiago cheese comes in two varieties: *morbido* (soft) and *duro* (hard). Either one would be delicious here. Other intensely flavored cheeses you could use are Manchego, Kasseri, or Parmigiano-Reggiano. Dice or crumble the cheese for easy handling and nibbling.

Ciabatta is a delicious traditional Italian bread, somewhat crispy on the outside and moist on the inside. As with nearly all breads, fresh is best, so plan on purchasing your ciabatta loaves or rolls on the day of your party. Alternatives might be French baguettes, focaccia, or another Italian bread, but refrain from choosing a semolina or other heavy bread, which would detract from your semolina-based Roman-Style Gnocchi.

European chocolates such as Perugina's Baci (kisses) and Gianduia (hazelnut creams) are superb choices, although any Swiss or Belgian variety will certainly fit the bill. If your guests offer to bring something, a box of any of these delights would be a great suggestion. Watch for liqueur-filled chocolates, however, and those that mimic the flavors of alcohol, like rum truffles, which could spark some unwanted recognition in the newly sober.

Italian sodas have become quite popular in American grocery stores and tend to be a little less sweet than our own versions. Refreshing choices like Orangina, Limonata, and Pompanello (a grapefruit variety) are ideal. Offer a good-quality sparkling water as well for those who prefer a sugar-free drink. If you have trouble finding these imported drinks, offer a sparkling lemonade or make your own citrus sodas by combining two parts fruit juice and one part sparkling water.

Italian roast coffee is an excellent, full-bodied, and flavorful dessert choice, although if you have access to an espresso or cappuccino maker, your guests would probably enjoy these specialties as well. Be sure to offer decaffeinated versions for those who must or choose to refrain from this stimulant. Preparation in a large, European-style coffee press would be a nice touch.

Pomegranate Ratafia

A Mediterranean specialty, ratafia is a sweet, aromatic drink that is meant to be sipped before a meal as an aperitif. Traditionally red wine based, ratafia is made by infusing alcoholic beverages with seasonal fruits and spices. Variations are numerous, and in this alcohol-free rendition, we use pomegranate juice as the base – a wonderfully flavorful and healthy alternative (pomegranate juice contains more antioxidants than red wine!).

If you cannot find a sweetened pomegranate juice such as Pom Wonderful®, you will need to add a touch of sugar to taste while simmering. A 32-ounce bottle will provide the perfect amount to serve eight people, but if you think your ratafia will prove a particular hit or you expect extra guests, you can certainly double the recipe. Keeping the vanilla bean whole will allow you to use it for another purpose after it has dried.

Ingredients:

One 32-ounce bottle sweetened pomegranate juice

1 whole vanilla bean, uncut

1 small orange or clementine, cut into pieces, pulp and skin included

Juice of half a lemon

1 bay leaf

1 cinnamon stick

1 teaspoon whole coriander seeds

½ teaspoon whole black peppercorns

1. In a large saucepan, combine all the ingredients and bring to a boil. Reduce the heat to low and let simmer for 3 minutes. Remove from the heat and allow to sit, uncovered, for 2 hours or until the ratafia is at room temperature.

2. Pour through a fine-mesh strainer into a glass container (or the original juice bottle fitted with a funnel) and chill. Can be prepared up to 2 days ahead. Serve well-chilled in port or juice glasses.

Serves 8

Casting a New Role for Your Old Drinking Glasses

For the newly sober or those who rarely drink alcohol, specialty glasses accumulated over the years as gifts and whims tend to gather dust on the shelf or end up on the garage-sale table. But with a little creativity, many of these pretty pieces of crystal can be used for surprisingly perfect presentations quite apart from their original purpose. Before you give away those old flutes or snifters, consider some of the following ideas:

Tall "highball" or "collins" glasses (12 to 14 ounces) are the obvious choice for soda, iced tea, and sparkling water. But smoothies, ice-cream floats, and milk shakes are also ideal fillers, and if they are particularly decorative, these glasses make attractive mini-vases for dinner-table floral arrangements.

Short "old-fashioned" glasses (6 ounces) are great for fruit juices and anything "on the rocks," such as alcohol-free mocktails. They also make excellent votives for tea lights, especially if they are heavy-bottomed and full lead crystal.

"Martini" or similar cocktail glasses used for "cosmopolitans" (4 to 10 ounces) are ideal for serving appetizers and desserts, depending on their size. Shrimp cocktail, cold soup, and fruit salad are just a few of the many foods that can be artfully presented in them. Ice cream and sorbet are also great fillers.

Champagne flutes (8 ounces), the quintessential toasting glasses, can of course be filled with any sparkling alcohol-free beverage for this purpose. But don't discount their use at dessert time for rich mousses and parfaits. Traditional champagne glasses, round and shallow, are great for floating candles or after-dinner mints.

Wineglasses come in various shapes and sizes (8 to 12 ounces) and have unlimited uses for a variety of alcohol-free drinks and punches, as well as dessert selections such as puddings and ice cream. Large, balloon-shaped wineglasses are perfect for nibbles such as nuts, olives, and candies.

Beer mugs and steins are perfect for heady sodas like root beer and birch beer, but they also make sturdy containers at the table for breadsticks or cutlery. Brandy snifters of all sizes can be used to hold fragrant potpourri or seasonally colored glass pebbles for party decorations.

Small cordial, port, and sherry glasses are ideal for alcohol-free aperitifs such as Pomegranate Ratafia (page 8), but could also make for elegant additions to the dinner table when used to prop up place cards and hold a single flower or herb sprig.

A Note to the Newly Sober:

We know from scientific studies called "cue reactivity" that the mere sight of a wineglass or bottle can trigger unwanted cravings in those struggling to maintain initial sobriety. If you or your guests fall into this category, it's best not to "tease the tiger." Keep potential "cues" such as drinking glasses out of sight for the time being. The longer sobriety is sustained, the less likely that these triggers will pose any difficulty.

Fortuna Lentils with Italian Chicken Sausage

Based on the classic *cotechino con lenticchie* (pork sausage with lentils), an Italian New Year's Eve dish representing the coins of our future wealth (lentils) and next year's richness of life (sausages), this version makes convenient use of the many types of delicious precooked chicken sausages now available on the market. In addition to making this recipe a snap (they are simply browned in the oven), the lower fat content allows us to be a bit more extravagant with our lentils by finishing them with a touch of heavy cream, a technique I saw a Bolognese chef do and have loved ever since.

The common brown lentil is fine here, although the tiny gourmet French *de puy* lentils would also work nicely. Be sure to pick over your dried lentils for pebbles and dirt, and rinse well under cold running water before cooking. You can prepare the lentils a day ahead and reheat in the microwave or stovetop on the night of your party.

For a slightly larger (or hungrier) crowd, simply add more sausages to your roasting pan; the amount of lentils below will be more than sufficient for everyone to have a "lucky" spoonful.

Lentils:

1. In a large, heavy-bottomed pot, combine all the ingredients except the cream, add enough cold water to cover, stir well, and bring to a gentle boil over medium heat.

2. Reduce heat to low and simmer uncovered, stirring occasionally, until lentils are tender, about 25 minutes. Add water if necessary to prevent sticking. The mixture should be thick, not soupy.

3. Remove from heat and discard vegetables and herbs. Stir in the heavy cream and taste for seasoning before serving on a large, heated platter.

Sausages:

1. Preheat the oven to 400 degrees.

2. Place the sausages in a medium-size roasting pan, prick them several times with a fork, drizzle a little olive oil over, and bake in the oven until golden brown and heated through, about 35 to 40 minutes. Periodically shake the roasting pan to brown the sausages evenly.

3. To serve, place the sausages on top of the lentils and sprinkle with the parsley.

Serves 8

Ingredients

Lentils:

One 16-ounce package dried brown lentils, picked over and rinsed

1 medium-size onion, peeled and quartered

1 medium-size carrot, peeled and quartered

2 garlic cloves, peeled

1 bay leaf

3 sprigs fresh thyme

One 4.5-ounce can tomato sauce

½ cup heavy cream, heated

Salt and pepper to taste

Sausage:

8 Italian chicken sausages, precooked

Extra virgin olive oil for drizzling

2 tablespoons chopped fresh Italian parsley leaves

Roman-Style Gnocchi

Unlike its more famous potato-based cousin, gnocchi prepared in the Roman style is really polenta in disguise. Semolina flour, which resembles a fine yellow cornmeal and is sometimes found simply as "semolina," is the key ingredient while whole milk, egg yolks, and butter add an undeniable richness, elevating a traditional peasant dish to regal status fit for a New Year's celebration.

You can set up this dish earlier in the day (or even the night before) and then bake alongside the chicken sausages on the night of the party. Be sure to wear a long-sleeved top when stirring the semolina mixture since it spits and splatters as it cooks. Keep in mind that the gnocchi will go from oven to table, so choose a decorative baking dish (or two) for layering the rounds.

This recipe makes more than enough to accommodate any unexpected additional guests, but don't worry if leftovers abound. New Year's Day early risers will relish a repeat performance for breakfast, topped with a fried egg – a real Italian treat!

Ingredients:

6 cups whole milk

2 cups semolina flour

2 teaspoons salt

8 tablespoons (1 stick) unsalted butter, softened

1 cup finely grated Parmigiano-Reggiano cheese

3 large egg yolks, lightly beaten

1. Butter a large, rimmed baking sheet.

2. In a large saucepan, whisk together the milk, semolina, and salt and bring to a boil over medium heat, whisking constantly to avoid lumps. When the mixture begins to thicken, reduce the heat to low, switch to a wooden spoon, and stir constantly until very thick and stiff, about 2 minutes. Remove from the heat and stir in 5 tablespoons of the butter and ½ cup of the cheese, stirring until well combined. Beat in the egg yolks. Spread the gnocchi mixture onto the prepared baking sheet to an even thickness and chill, uncovered, until very firm, about 1 hour or more.

3. Butter a large oval casserole or gratin dish (or 2 smaller baking dishes of any shape).

4. Use a 2½-inch round cookie cutter or an inverted drinking glass and cut out circles from the chilled gnocchi mixture, arranging them in the prepared baking dish, overlapping slightly. Combine scraps, flatten evenly, and continue to cut rounds until the gnocchi mixture is used up. Sprinkle the remaining cheese over the gnocchi and dot with the remaining butter. (You may cover and refrigerate the gnocchi at this point, if desired, to bake later.)

5. Bake in a preheated 400-degree oven until the top is very lightly browned, about 30 minutes. Let stand 5 minutes before serving.

Serves 8

EASY DOES IT: The world of modern food convenience has not bypassed polenta. Precooked logs are available in many grocery stores and can be substituted in a pinch for the gnocchi mixture above, although they will be decidedly less rich in flavor and texture. Simply slice the logs into ½-inch rounds, layering and baking as above.

European Greens with White Balsamic Vinaigrette

A salad of crisp greens is always a welcome addition to any meal and here, a medley of European lettuces provides the perfect complement to your menu. You can prepare the greens ahead of time by washing, patting dry (or drying in a salad spinner), and storing the leaves in a plastic bag in the fridge. Insert a dry paper towel into each bag to absorb any excess moisture and retain crispness.

White balsamic vinegar is slightly sweet, not unlike its darker-colored counterpart, and has the added advantage of not discoloring your salad greens. Consequently, you can dress your salad before bringing it to the buffet table or, if you prefer, offer the vinaigrette in a cruet *alongside* the salad bowl for guests to help themselves.

1. To make the dressing, whisk together all the ingredients in a small mixing bowl, cover, and chill until ready to serve. The vinaigrette can be prepared a day ahead.

2. Tear all the lettuce leaves into bite-size pieces and place in a large salad bowl.

3. Toss with half of the vinaigrette to begin with, tasting and adding more as needed. Or serve with the dressing on the side.

Serves 8

Ingredients

Vinaigrette:

3 garlic cloves, peeled and minced

1½ teaspoons dried oregano

½ teaspoon dried mustard

½ cup white balsamic vinegar

1 cup extra virgin olive oil

Salt and pepper to taste

Greens:

1 head romaine lettuce, leaves washed and dried

5 cups assorted European greens (such as frisée, radicchio, endive, and escarole), leaves washed and dried

Sugared Grape Clusters

When midnight arrives, you and your guests will relish munching on these tasty treats, one grape at each stroke of the clock. Even theater productions and movies in Spain are interrupted to carry out this long-standing custom. No one will even notice the absence of a champagne toast when you present this delightful (and delicious!) way to welcome in the New Year.

Choose red or green seedless grapes (or a combination of both); seasonal globe grapes, although tasty, are a bit large and always heavily seeded. You will need between 1 and 2 pounds of grapes depending on their size and quality. Sugared grape clusters are a common garnish for dessert platters and are well worth knowing how to make for future party hosting. The alternative freezing method mentioned below is a popular summer presentation, but feel free to serve your grapes this way if you prefer.

If raw egg whites are an issue for you or any of your guests (pregnant women, the elderly, and those with compromised immune systems), there are a couple of solutions: Pasteurized eggs can be found in your grocery and are safe to use. Otherwise, reconstituted meringue powder (found in baking specialty stores) could be substituted. Egg whites in some form are necessary, however, because the protein they contain dries the sugar onto the fruit and creates the distinctive shell.

1. Wash the grape clusters and pat dry with paper towels.

2. Beat the egg whites until slightly foamy or prepare the meringue powder according to package directions. Pour the sugar on a rimmed baking sheet lined with waxed paper.

3. Using a pastry brush, lightly and evenly coat the grapes with the egg whites and immediately roll in the sugar. You can check for missed spots and reapply the whites and sugar if necessary.

4. Transfer the clusters to a cake rack and allow to set at room temperature. Keep them in a cool, dry place (do not refrigerate) until you're ready to serve. Can be prepared several days ahead. Alternatively, you can freeze the clusters on a clean tray, covered lightly with plastic wrap, and serve frozen.

Serves 8

Ingredients:

1½ pounds red or green seedless grapes, cut into 8 clusters of 12

3 large egg whites (or 3 tablespoons meringue powder and 6 tablespoons lukewarm water)

2 cups granulated sugar

15

Lucky Vassilopita Cake

This delicious Greek dessert has its origin in the folklore of St. Basil, whose celebrated feast day is January 1. It is said that St. Basil convinced a tax collector to refrain from taking away a pile of coins that had been collected from the villagers of his parish. To return the money to its rightful owners, Basil had a divine inspiration and instructed his parishioners to bake lots of cakelike breads, into which he inserted the coins. When the "cakes" were distributed to the villagers, everyone miraculously received the original coins! Every year since, Vassilopita, or St. Basil's bread, is baked in this tradition on December 31, and coins inserted in the cakes are found by the luckiest people, ensuring a prosperous new year.

There are two distinct versions of Vassilopita: one that is yeast-based and breadlike, the other here, which is similar to a pound cake and much easier to prepare. Although they are traditionally flavored with exotic aromatics like *mahlepi* and *mastic*, here we use almond and lemon as the featured flavors. Just about any small coin will do for luck, although something of European origin would be novel. These days, most bakers will wrap the coin in foil before inserting it into the batter because of the high nickel content; however, silver, gold, or aluminum coins are certainly safe to insert unwrapped. Make your cake a day ahead and when cooled, wrap tightly in plastic wrap to keep moist. You can even freeze it this way up to 2 weeks in advance. Before serving, dust liberally with confectioners' sugar and cut slices with a serrated knife.

Ingredients:

1 cup (2 sticks) unsalted butter, softened

2½ cups granulated sugar

6 large eggs

1 cup self-rising cake flour

2 cups all-purpose flour

½ teaspoon baking soda

1 cup whole milk

2 teaspoons grated lemon rind

1 tablespoon fresh lemon juice

2 teaspoons alcohol-free almond extract

1 coin, wrapped in foil

½ cup sliced almonds

1. Preheat the oven to 350 degrees. Lightly butter a 10- or 11-inch springform pan.

2. In a large mixing bowl, combine the butter and sugar and, with an electric mixer at medium-high speed, beat until light and fluffy. Add the eggs, one at a time, and beat until well combined.

3. In a medium-size mixing bowl, whisk together the flours and baking soda. Alternating between the flour mixture and the milk, add to the butter-sugar-egg mixture, beating briefly on medium speed to combine after each addition. Stir in the lemon rind, lemon juice, and almond extract. Pour the batter into the prepared pan. Insert the coin.

4. Bake for 30 minutes, sprinkle the sliced almonds on top, and return to the oven for another 30 to 40 minutes, or until golden and a toothpick inserted in the center comes out clean. Let cool on a cake rack for 15 minutes. Run a clean knife around the edges, unlock the spring, and remove the side of the pan. Cool completely before serving or wrapping in plastic wrap.

Serves 8

What better way to start off the new year than with an elegant, "pull out all the stops" dinner for your closest friends or family? Your guests will think they've stepped into a five-star restaurant when they hear the menu, but you won't let on how easy this classy meal was to prepare. Bring out your finest linens and china for this memorable affair that will be talked about for the rest of the year!

The menu, in addition to its show-stopping presentation, is an excellent exercise in the ease of substituting for alcohol in a variety of cooking methods (see Cooking with Alcohol: Busting the Myth, pages 26-27, for the facts and figures). From the delectable Shrimp and Fennel Bisque to the Olde English Trifle, you'll see how it's done with flavor and flair, while a variety of alcohol-free beverages highlights each course to perfection.

You can easily accommodate two more guests if need be since these recipes provide generous portions. Prepare the bisque and trifle ahead to marry the flavors and free your attention for the main course as well as for your guests.

A Classy New Year's Day Dinner

MENU
Dinner for Six

HORS D'OEUVRES:
Selection of Hot Miniatures

APPETIZER:
Shrimp and Fennel Bisque

MAIN COURSE:
Outstanding Rib Roast au Jus
Whole Roasted Potatoes
Sautéed Snow Peas and Baby Carrots
Warm Rolls with Whipped Butter

DESSERT:
Olde English Trifle

BEVERAGE PAIRINGS:

Hors d'Oeuvres and Appetizer:
Sparkling Lemonade
Main Course: Cranberry Iced Tea
Dessert: *Café Noir*

Tips on Purchased Ingredients

A selection of *hot miniature hors d'oeuvres* is a classy way to start things off for your guests while you put the finishing touches to the main event. But don't think for a second that you need to prepare these yourself when there are delicious varieties to be had in the frozen food section that simply require a few minutes in a hot oven. Or, if you prefer, contact some local caterers who will sell ready-to-bake trays of their own frozen selections for a reasonable price. Just be sure to choose varieties that don't compete with your dinner menu – mini mushroom quiches, *gougères* (pastry cheese puffs), or phyllo-wrapped chicken are a few suggestions. Allow no more than two of each per person so as not to spoil your guests' appetites for the stellar dinner to come.

Warm rolls with whipped butter are always a nice touch at the table. You probably will be buying your rolls the day before, so choose soft varieties that will remain fresh overnight, rather than crusty types. Wrap them together in a large piece of aluminum foil and heat them in the oven while your roast is resting. Petite balls of whipped butter are easy to make with a melon baller dipped in hot water to prevent sticking. Make the butter balls the day before, chill in a ramekin or butter dish, and bring to the table about an hour before dinner to soften them up.

Sparkling lemonade and other types of sparkling alcohol-free beverages add a festive touch to holiday entertaining. Whether corked or simply screw-topped, bottles should be well chilled before serving. Flavored sparkling waters are also a good thing to have on hand for those who prefer no added sugar.

Splurge on a good-quality, flavorful coffee to make after-dinner *Café Noir* (strong black coffee with or without sugar). Use twice the amount of ground coffee normally called for to create a rich and robust accompaniment to dessert. In general, people who do not drink alcohol tend to relish a good cup of coffee so serve it up elegantly in a small urn or filtered press with some classy cups and saucers. Although black coffee is the perfect ending for a stomach overtaxed by a hearty meal, keep milk and cream on hand for those who may request it.

Shrimp and Fennel Bisque

A thick and rich soup, usually made of puréed seafood and cream, bisque always brings elegance to any dinner table. However, traditional methods tend to be too tedious and labor-intensive, discouraging most home cooks from adding it to their repertoire. Not so here! This recipe will surprise you with its ease of preparation and depth of flavor.

Pernod, an anise-flavored liqueur, is a common ingredient in seafood bisques, but the inclusion of fennel, also licorice in flavor, fits in nicely as a subtle substitute. Leeks, rather than onions, also add a delicate layer of flavor, allowing the shrimp to reign as the star. Beautifully pink and smooth when blended, your bisque can be garnished with a whole shrimp and fennel frond before it's served in heated soup bowls.

1. In a heavy-bottomed soup pot, melt the butter over medium heat and add the shrimp. Cook gently, stirring frequently, until the shrimp have turned pink, about 3 to 4 minutes, reducing the heat if necessary to prevent the butter from browning. Using a slotted spoon, transfer the shrimp to a bowl and set aside.

2. Add the fennel, leek, and carrot to the pot, sprinkle with salt and pepper, and over medium heat, cook, stirring, until the vegetables are softened, about 10 minutes. Add the remaining ingredients, stir well, and bring to a simmer. Place all but 6 of the shrimp in the pot and cook over low heat, stirring occasionally, until the rice is tender, about 20 minutes.

3. Carefully transfer the hot bisque in batches to a blender and purée until smooth. Transfer to a clean pot. Taste for salt, pepper, and lemon juice, and adjust if necessary. If made ahead, cover and refrigerate soup, and chill remaining shrimp separately. Reheat over a low flame – do not boil – and thin with a touch of milk or water if too thick. Garnish and serve immediately.

Serves 6

Ingredients:

2 tablespoons unsalted butter

1 pound large, uncooked shrimp, peeled and deveined

1 medium-size fennel bulb, trimmed of stalks, cored, and chopped (fronds reserved)

1 medium-size leek (white part only), end trimmed, washed well, and chopped

1 small carrot, peeled and sliced

Salt and pepper to taste

Two 8-ounce bottles clam juice

2½ cups water

½ cup heavy cream

3 tablespoons long-grain white rice, uncooked

2 tablespoons tomato paste

Juice of half a lemon

Cranberry Iced Tea

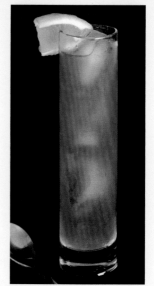

Ingredients:

3 quarts water

⅓ cup sugar

15 tea bags

One 12-ounce can frozen cranberry juice concentrate

Sometimes called Boston Iced Tea, this combination is the perfect complement to beef since it contains the same tannins found in red wine that refresh the palate with each sip. These astringent substances are what create the characteristic "puckering" of the mouth, and the longer the tea is steeped, the more tannin is produced.

Use a strong black tea like Orange Pekoe or English Breakfast, regular or decaffeinated. You can make this unsweetened if you like, and allow your guests to add their own sugar to taste. Make ahead and serve well-chilled in a decorative pitcher with plenty of ice. Pour into tall highball glasses or large wineglasses.

1. In a large pot, bring the water to a boil and stir in the sugar, stirring until dissolved. Remove from the heat, add the tea bags, and steep for 5 to 7 minutes.

2. Remove the tea bags, stir in the cranberry juice concentrate, and allow to cool. Chill in a covered container until ready to serve.

Serves 6

Outstanding Rib Roast au Jus

Standing rib roast may be more familiar to you in a restaurant setting as prime rib, a truly delicious and tender choice and a real showstopper when brought to the table for slicing. If you have never prepared a roast such as this, you'll be surprised at how little labor is involved – this elite cut needs little enhancement. During the holiday season, you will find a good selection in your grocer's meat department, or you can purchase straight from the local butcher. A roast of 3 or 4 ribs will easily serve up to 8 guests.

As with other roasts, you should allow it to sit at room temperature an hour or two before putting it in the oven to help speed the cooking process. Beginning with a very hot oven temperature will help to seal in the juices. You will need an instant-read thermometer to determine doneness and a sturdy roasting pan to make the jus on top of the stove. Your roast should rest for at least 30 minutes before carving to allow the juices to be reabsorbed, which will free you up to finish last-minute touches to the side dishes and table setting. A standing rib roast is usually served medium rare, but one with a more pronounced slope will provide some slices that are medium well if desired.

Au jus means that the meat is served with its pan juices, which are thin in consistency and usually embellished with a touch of wine and beef stock. Here, instead of wine, we use a small amount of cranberry juice to deglaze the roasting pan and provide a bit of necessary acidity and flavor.

1. Preheat the oven to 475 degrees.

2. Place the roast, ribs side down, on a rack in a large flameproof roasting pan and rub all over with the oil. Use the cut side of the garlic cloves to rub into the meat areas and set aside for later. Season generously with coarse salt and freshly ground pepper, and roast in the oven for 30 minutes.

3. Reduce the oven to 350 degrees and continue roasting for about 1½ hours (15 minutes per pound) or until an instant-read thermometer inserted in the thickest part of the roast reaches 130 degrees. Transfer to a platter and let rest for at least 30 minutes.

4. To make the jus, skim the fat from the pan juices, add the cranberry juice, bay leaf, thyme, and reserved garlic cloves, and on top of the stove over medium-high heat, bring to a simmer and stir, scraping up the browned bits from the roast. Add the beef broth and any juices that have accumulated on the platter, and gently simmer for 10 minutes.

5. Pour through a fine-mesh strainer into a small saucepan, taste for the addition of salt and pepper, and keep warm over the lowest heat. Serve in a warmed gravy boat.

Serves 6 to 8

Ingredients:

3- or 4-rib standing beef rib roast (about 7 to 8 pounds), all but ¼ inch of fat removed

1 tablespoon canola oil

6 garlic cloves, peeled and cut in half

Salt and pepper to taste

⅓ cup cranberry juice

1 bay leaf

2 small sprigs fresh thyme

2 cups low-sodium beef broth

How to Carve a Standing Rib Roast

After you have presented the roast in standing position on its platter for all to admire, use a carving fork and knife to place the roast on its side. If necessary, slice a small piece from one of the ends so the meat rests flat on the platter. Insert the fork below the first rib from the top and slice sideways from the outside toward the rib side as close to the bone as possible, making half-inch slices or thicker if desired. After making several cuts, slice down along the inner side of the rib bone to release each slice. Use your knife underneath and fork on top to lift the prime rib slices to individual plates.

Whole Roasted Potatoes

Although a traditional accompaniment to many an English roast dinner, potatoes roasted whole rather than cut are less frequently seen in the United States but always add a special touch to any dinner. Any type of potato can be used, but I prefer a russet, Idaho, or Yukon Gold variety for better outside crisping and inner creaminess. A size somewhere between a standard baking potato and a baby potato is ideal, about 4 ounces in weight. One per person is probably enough, but they're so tasty that it's a good idea to make at least 2 for each guest.

Shaking the potatoes in a covered pot to create surface texture is a method I learned in England, which guarantees an extra-crispy crust. You can certainly roast the potatoes alongside the beef, but using a separate roasting pan will provide more control over even crisping and avoid heavy lifting from the oven. It is the fat from the roast that provides the potatoes with a superb flavor, but canola oil will also crisp them nicely if you prefer. Preheating the pan and fat will facilitate browning.

Ingredients:

Twelve 4-ounce Idaho, russet, or Yukon Gold potatoes (about 3 pounds), peeled

½ cup rendered fat from roast, canola oil, or a combination of both

Salt and pepper to taste

1. Place the potatoes in a large pot, cover with cold, salted water, and bring to a simmer. Cook uncovered until barely fork-tender on the outside but still firm in the center, about 12 to 15 minutes. Do not overcook.

2. Drain the potatoes in a colander, allow them to sit for 5 minutes, and return them to the empty pot. Cover with a tight lid and shake the pot sideways and up and down for a few seconds. Check to see whether the potatoes have developed a slightly fluffy exterior. Shake again if necessary.

3. Have ready a preheated 350-degree oven and a hot medium-size roasting pan containing the beef fat or oil. (You can remove the fat from the rib roast pan using a bulb baster – add oil, if necessary, to make ½ cup.) Place the potatoes in the prepared pan, coat well with the fat, and roast in a single layer, occasionally turning to brown evenly, until golden, crispy, and tender on the inside, 30 to 40 minutes. Sprinkle with salt and pepper before serving.

Note: If you have used only the beef fat to roast the potatoes and have generously seasoned the rib roast, you may not need to add much salt and pepper, if any. Taste before adjusting.

Serves 6

Sautéed Snow Peas and Baby Carrots

The delightful crunch of snow peas and sweetness of baby carrots are the ideal complement to the Outstanding Rib Roast and Whole Roasted Potatoes. A simple presentation is all that is needed. If you happen to see bunches of fresh baby carrots in the produce section, you could use these instead of the packaged carrots for an extra-special touch. You'll need 3 or 4 per person, depending on the size of the carrots. Trim all but 1 inch of the green stems and peel them gently, then continue as instructed below.

You can prepare these somewhat ahead of time by parboiling and refreshing in cold water to stop the cooking process, ensuring that they will be fresh and crisp when served. Have a large bowl of ice water ready, and after draining and patting dry, transfer them to a covered pan for a quick reheat later.

1. In a medium-size pot of boiling salted water, cook the carrots until tender-crisp, 8 to 10 minutes. Add the snow peas and continue to cook for 30 seconds. Drain the vegetables through a strainer. Refresh as above if preparing in advance.

2. Transfer the parboiled vegetables to a large sauté pan or skillet, add the remaining ingredients, and cook covered over medium-low heat for 3 to 4 minutes, gently stirring once or twice to evenly coat with the butter and thyme. Season with salt and pepper, and serve immediately in a heated bowl.

Serves 6

Ingredients:

One 16-ounce bag peeled baby carrots

1½ cups snow peas,
ends and tough strings removed

2 tablespoons unsalted butter

2 tablespoons water

1 teaspoon finely chopped fresh thyme leaves

Salt and pepper to taste

Olde English Trifle

Sometimes called the "tipsy cake," traditional trifles are usually loaded with booze. Sherry is most common, but often fruit-flavored liqueurs are used to complement the fruit that is used in the layering of cake, custard, and whipped cream. The alcohol is applied by a method known as "punching" – drizzling or lightly dabbing with a pastry brush to moisten the cake. In this alcohol-free recipe, we'll be using a piquant syrup that is derived from the raspberries themselves to "punch" the cake. And to add extra intrigue in lieu of alcohol, the custard will be flavored with a hint of bay leaf and lemon.

A trifle dish is a straight-sided glass dessert bowl set on a pedestal. It is surprisingly inexpensive to buy and is usually 8 inches wide and tall, holding between 3 and 4 quarts by volume. Punch bowls or other types of tapered glass bowls will also work well: One with a 9- to 10-inch diameter is a good choice as long as you are able to see the beautiful layering of this dessert from all sides.

Raspberries are the classic fruit of choice, and frozen ones are fine for the layering, but invest in a small box of fresh raspberries to decorate the top. Since the custard requires a bit of work, we can cut corners elsewhere by using a purchased pound cake, rather than making the traditional trifle sponge cake. I find that the pound cake holds up much better anyway when the trifle is prepared a day or two ahead. Finish with the whipped cream and decorative garnishes the day of your dinner party, however, for a clean and pristine presentation at the table. Use a long-handled spoon to serve and dig down so each guest receives every delectable layer!

Ingredients
Custard:

2½ cups whole milk

1 bay leaf

Rind of half a lemon, white pith removed

6 egg yolks, at room temperature

½ cup granulated sugar

4 tablespoons cornstarch

1 teaspoon alcohol-free vanilla extract
(see Resources)

Other Ingredients:

Two 10-ounce packages frozen raspberries in syrup, thawed, drained, and syrup reserved

1 tablespoon raspberry vinegar

¾ cup raspberry preserves

One 16-ounce frozen or store-baked pound cake, cut into ½-inch-thick slices

1 cup whipping cream

2 tablespoons confectioners' sugar

⅓ cup sliced almonds, lightly toasted

1 cup fresh raspberries

1. To prepare the custard, heat the milk, bay leaf, and lemon rind in a medium-size stainless steel pot to just under a boil. Set aside for 5 minutes, then remove the bay leaf and lemon with a slotted spoon.

2. In a medium-size mixing bowl, whisk together the egg yolks, sugar, and cornstarch until smooth and ribbony, about 2 minutes. Slowly whisk in half the hot milk, then pour the egg mixture back into the pot and bring to a very low boil over medium heat, whisking constantly until the custard thickens. Immediately pour through a strainer into a clean mixing bowl and stir in the vanilla. Cover the surface with plastic wrap (to prevent a skin from forming), poke a few holes in the wrap to vent, and allow to cool to room temperature.

3. In a small bowl, combine all but 1 tablespoon of the raspberry syrup with the vinegar. In another small bowl, whisk together the remaining syrup and the raspberry preserves.

4. Begin assembling the trifle by placing the cake slices, cut to fit, on the bottom of the bowl. Brush lightly with the syrup-vinegar mixture and spread ⅓ of the preserve mixture over the slices. Sprinkle ⅓ of the defrosted raspberries over and pour ⅓ of the custard on top. Be sure each addition is touching the sides of the trifle bowl so that the layers are visible and attractive. Repeat layering twice more, ending with the custard. Cover the surface with plastic wrap and refrigerate at least overnight.

5. To finish the trifle, whip the cream with the confectioners' sugar to soft peaks. Spread evenly over the custard, and sprinkle the almonds and fresh raspberries decoratively on top. Return to refrigerator; chill until ready to serve.

Serves 6 to 8

Note: Almonds can be toasted quickly in a dry frying pan over medium-high heat. Shake the pan frequently and toast until the edges are lightly golden.

EASY DOES IT: In a pinch, you could replace the homemade custard with a vanilla pudding or custard mix, or a tub of prepared vanilla pudding (about 4 cups will be needed). Thin with ½ cup of cream to improve the consistency.

Cooking with Alcohol: Busting the Myth

Prompted by an increased interest in cooking with wine and spirits to cut back on calories and fat, food scientists commissioned by the United States Department of Agriculture (USDA) discovered that, contrary to popular belief, alcohol does not burn off or evaporate completely during cooking. Needless to say, this surprising finding has important implications for alcoholics and those with alcohol-related illnesses.

How much alcohol are we unknowingly consuming at the dinner table in dishes that have been prepared with wine, beer, or spirits? Potentially, quite a bit, as the following table shows:

Cooking Method	Percent Alcohol Remaining
Simmered (1 to 2 minutes)	85
Flamed	75
Refrigerated (overnight)	70
Baked (25 minutes)	45
Boiled (10 minutes to 2½ hours)	between 60 and 4 percent

In practical terms, a serving of traditional English trifle could provide several sips of sherry, while a Grand Marnier sauce could contain a good swig of liqueur. When total abstinence is required, these amounts, as small as they may seem, could jeopardize our health in serious ways. In addition, for those struggling to stay sober, the smell and taste of alcoholic beverages used in cooking could pose further problems by triggering recognition through neurochemicals in the brain. These triggers, combined with physical withdrawal, psychological stress, and visual cues, may spark dangerous cravings and could lead ultimately to relapse.

So do we simply leave out the alcohol when we run across recipes that include it as an ingredient? No, because the outcome and taste may depend on it, so we need instead to safely substitute for these amounts to provide whatever layer of flavor or texture the wine or spirit was contributing. And this is easy to do using any number of ingredients such as fruit juices, vinegars, and teas, which offer a good balance of acidity, sweetness, and thickening power, mimicking the role that alcohol plays in many recipes we encounter (see page 73, Alcohol-Free Substitutes for Wine and Spirits, and page 177, Substituting for Liqueurs).

For those who, by choice, do not consume alcohol, small amounts in food may not pose a problem. However, more often than not, people who do not care to drink are usually put off by the taste, and if that taste is evident in their food, it may be similarly off-putting. If you are not sure of your guests' preferences, using alcoholic-free substitutions will resolve this without a glitch.

Chapter 2

Orange Marmalade-Glazed Corned Beef with Cabbage, Baby Red Potatoes and Carrots, Irish Soda Bread, and Iced Green Tea

When the Saints Go Marchin' In

In between the lingering chill of winter and the official arrival of spring lie two of our most popular, saintly holidays – Valentine's Day and St. Patrick's Day. Whether it's the wearing of the green or your heart on your sleeve, marking these occasions has become an annual tradition of fun, food, and celebration.

Both holidays have their origin in "feast days," an early Christian tradition begun to commemorate each saint's day of martyrdom; indeed, early festivals sometimes included reenactments of a saint's demise. Happily, however, as time passed, saint-day celebrations became lighter-hearted in tone and began to be characterized by specific foods, drink, and other customs (rightly or wrongly) associated with each saint. Today, for instance, we celebrate St. Valentine for his supposed connection to romance, love, and chocolate, rather than his unfortunate beheading.

Both Valentine's Day and St. Patrick's Day have come to have strong connotations of alcohol, from champagne to green beer, but with a little creativity we can start our own alcohol-free traditions that are anything but staid. Sumptuous ingredients categorize *A Passionate Valentine's Day Dinner*, while *A Saint Patrick's Day Feast for Family and Friends* combines traditional hearty fare with inspired new drink ideas. After you have served up these two heavenly menus, don't be surprised if you're nominated for your own sainthood!

Wine and roses pale in comparison to the passion stirred up by this romantic menu for two. From the first sensuous bite of Tuna Carpaccio to the last delectable nibble of Bittersweet Chocolate Fondue, you'll be adored and cherished for your gastronomic gift of "wining and dining" without a drop of alcohol.

Most of this dinner is make-ahead easy, allowing you to attentively entertain at your own pace. Preparing many of the components in advance will help you serve smoothly and effortlessly. Only the angel hair pasta for the Angel Hair with Saffron Alfredo Sauce and Lobster Medallions requires immediate focus, and fortunately, it's the quickest of all pastas to cook. Keep a pot of simmering water on the back burner for when you are ready to proceed with your entrée. And make good use of the microwave to quickly reheat the lobster and the fondue. Simple tricks like these will keep you out of the kitchen and beside your dinner partner where you belong.

A simple passion fruit-based beverage to accompany both the appetizer and the entrée will make it easy to top up refills, while a surprise sorbet course will provide a special touch and allow you to linger a bit longer at the table. By the time dessert is served, you'll be well into an evening of delicious romance and enchantment. Don't forget to dim the lights!

A Passionate Valentine's Day Dinner

MENU

Dinner for Two

APPETIZER:

Tuna Carpaccio with Wasabi Caper Sauce
Breadsticks

MAIN COURSE:

Angel Hair with Saffron Alfredo Sauce
and Lobster Medallions

SORBET COURSE:

Pink Grapefruit Granita

DESSERT:

Bittersweet Chocolate Fondue
Miniature Biscotti

BEVERAGE PAIRINGS:

Appetizer and Main Course:
Passion Fruit Potion

Dessert: *Peppermint Tea*

Tips on Purchased Ingredients

Breadsticks are an excellent light alternative to bread and rolls. Choose the pencil-thin Torinese style, also called *grissini*, and set them vertically in a decorative glass or vase on the table. For added appeal, lightly brush about 3 or 4 inches of each top with softened unsalted butter, and wrap delicately with a thin slice of *prosciutto di Parma*.

Miniature biscotti, hard little twice-baked dunking cookies, are a great addition to your chocolate fondue spread or as an accompaniment to your tea. Look for authentic *biscotti di Prato*, which are studded with almonds, or select an assortment package that includes the traditional anise-flavored and chocolate versions as well. Some even come individually wrapped with little fortunes and words of wisdom tucked inside.

Peppermint tea is a decaffeinated herbal beverage popularly consumed after rich meals as it is believed to aid digestion and freshen the breath. You could use bags or loose tea leaves to brew. A small teapot with matching cups would add a distinctive flair to the end of your meal. Serve "straight up" without sugar or milk. Good alternative teas include chamomile, rose hips, or a fruity infusion.

Tuna Carpaccio with Wasabi Caper Sauce

Traditional *carpaccio*, thinly sliced raw beef fillet, first arrived on the restaurant scene in Venice, where the owner of Harry's Bar created it as homage to the painter Vittore Carpaccio. But the technique and presentation have found their way to the raw fish world as well, thanks in part to the popularity of Japanese sushi and sashimi.

Here, ahi tuna becomes the base for this luxurious appetizer, while a garnish of mâche, also known as lamb's lettuce, adds color and tang. If you can't find mâche, baby arugula or mesclun (also called spring mix) will fit in nicely. The tuna should be the freshest possible and of the highest quality. Buy it at your local seafood store if your grocer cannot guarantee sushi grade. Wasabi is Japanese horseradish and the usual accompaniment to *maguro* (raw tuna), while capers are a traditional garnish for carpaccio. Look for wasabi paste in a tube, or a jar of wasabi powder, which can be reconstituted into paste with a bit of water. Depending on your "heat" threshold, add more or less wasabi paste to the sauce.

For those who prefer not to consume raw fish for health reasons or are simply not enticed by sushi-like appetizers, pieces of smoked salmon work extremely well as a substitute. Unlike with the tuna, no flattening will be necessary – just lay the salmon slices evenly on the center of the plate.

This is a delicate and beautifully presented dish that is deceptively easy to prepare. Having all the components set to go for assembly when the time is right is the key to success.

Ingredients

Wasabi Caper Sauce:

⅓ cup mayonnaise

2 tablespoons heavy cream

1 tablespoon rice vinegar (unseasoned)

1 heaping tablespoon drained capers, chopped

2 teaspoons wasabi paste (or more to taste)

Tuna Carpaccio:

6 ounces sushi-grade tuna

Extra virgin olive oil

Salt and pepper to taste

2 cups mâche or baby greens, washed and patted dry

1 small celery stalk, trimmed, peeled, and diced

1 teaspoon finely chopped, fresh chives

1. Prepare the sauce by whisking the ingredients together in a small mixing bowl. Cover and chill until ready for assembly.

2. Using a very sharp knife, slice the tuna horizontally into 3 pieces. Place 1 piece between 2 lightly oiled sheets of plastic wrap, and using the side of a cleaver or the flat part of a tenderizing mallet, gently flatten the tuna into a thin disk about 6 inches in diameter. Carefully transfer the wrapped disk to a chilled appetizer plate and set in the refrigerator. Repeat with the second piece of tuna. Dice the remaining tuna into ½-inch pieces. Transfer to a small bowl, coat lightly with olive oil, season with salt and pepper, and set aside to chill.

3. To assemble the carpaccio, remove the tuna and plates from the refrigerator. Peel off the top layer of plastic wrap and place the disk, tuna side down, onto each plate. Remove the remaining plastic.

4. Drizzle the wasabi caper sauce over the tuna and place the mâche in a circle around each disk. Scatter the diced tuna, celery, and chives over all, and serve immediately.

Serves 2

Passion Fruit Potion

Toast each other with this seductively fragrant drink made from the enticing juice of the passion fruit and sparkling fruit seltzer. Not too sweet and not too tart, it complements beautifully the opulence of your appetizer and entrée.

Passion fruit nectar is available in grocery stores and generally comes in 12-ounce cans or larger-sized cartons. Choose a seltzer like lemon-lime or a tropical fruit blend and garnish with the matching fruit. Both the nectar and seltzer should be well chilled in advance, then kept nearby in an ice bucket at dinner for quick refills and top-ups.

Have ready two well-chilled champagne flutes or wineglasses. Pour enough nectar to fill a third of each glass. Add seltzer to fill and garnish with fruit.

Serves 2

Ingredients:

One 12-ounce can passion fruit nectar, chilled

One 32-ounce bottle fruit-flavored seltzer water, chilled

Fruit garnish of lemon or lime twist, orange slice, or pineapple wedge

Pink Grapefruit Granita

Granita is a classic Sicilian cousin of sorbet and easy to prepare without the aid of an ice-cream maker. The mixture is simply poured into a metal bowl or pan and stirred up to make it granular, not smooth (hence its name – *granita*). It's a palate cleanser of gourmet proportions and a decidedly delicious and refreshing treat to present after the richness of your entrée.

Ingredients:

⅓ cup water

½ cup granulated sugar

2 cups pink grapefruit juice

Red or pink grapefruit juice will produce a lovely pink-colored granita, but if you prefer, you can use white grapefruit juice or even substitute orange, tangerine, or pineapple juice if medical reasons prohibit grapefruit consumption (grapefruit can interfere with various prescription drugs, including statins – check with your doctor). You can make granita up to 1 week ahead and keep it covered in the freezer. It serves up elegantly in chilled martini glasses or any small crystal dessert dishes.

1. In a small saucepan, bring the water and sugar to a boil, stirring until the sugar is dissolved. Remove from the heat, add the grapefruit juice, and stir to combine.

2. Pour into a medium-size metal bowl or baking pan and transfer to the freezer. Stir occasionally (about every 40 minutes) with a fork until the liquid is frozen and granular, about 6 hours total. Cover with plastic wrap and keep frozen.

3. To serve, scrape the granita with a fork to break up any lumps and spoon into dessert dishes.

Serves 2

Angel Hair with Saffron Alfredo Sauce and Lobster Medallions

Ingredients:

One 10-ounce frozen
lobster tail, thawed

6 tablespoons unsalted butter,
melted

¼ teaspoon crumbled
saffron threads

1¼ cups heavy cream

½ teaspoon grated lemon rind

Dash cayenne pepper

Pinch of salt

8 ounces angel hair pasta

¾ cup freshly grated Parmesan
cheese

2 sprigs fresh Italian parsley
(optional)

The mere title of this dish suggests luxury at its finest and tells that certain someone, "You're special." Yet, as extraordinary as this entrée may be, it will no doubt rank as one of the most easily prepared pasta dishes you have ever cooked. Organization is again the name of the game, and with everything prepped and ready, it will be no time at all before you're serving up this most elegant of dishes.

Saffron threads, though pricey, go a long way in small amounts. A mortar and pestle are the ideal tools for crushing these tiny stigmas from the purple crocus but not at all necessary since a quick crumbling between your fingers will crush most of the threads. The beautiful color it adds to the sauce and the fragrant aroma it imparts are the reasons that saffron is considered such a culinary delicacy. It is usually readily found in the spice section of many grocery stores.

Angel hair is the most delicate of pastas and is sold either dried or fresh. Either is fine to use here, but be aware that it cooks very quickly so overcooking is a real danger. For that reason, it is not recommended that you cook it ahead of time and refresh in cold water as is possible with many other types of pasta. Everything else can be prepared in advance the day of the dinner.

Frozen lobster tails are uncooked and usually weigh between 8 and 12 ounces (in the shell). If you are a particularly big lobster fan, by all means go for the larger size and add a minute or two to its cooking time. If lobster is not your favorite shellfish, large shrimp (about 5 or 6 per person), shelled and deveined, can be substituted.

1. Bring a medium-size pot of water to a boil, add the lobster tail, and simmer covered for 6 minutes. Remove the lobster from the pot and set aside on paper towels to drain. When cool enough to handle, remove the shell and cut the tail into ½-inch-thick slices. Wrap in plastic and refrigerate until needed (can be done up to a day ahead).

2. Bring a large pot of salted water to a boil, cover, reduce heat to low, and keep on the back burner until ready to cook the pasta. In a small bowl, stir together the melted butter and crushed saffron threads. Set aside.

3. Whisk together the cream, lemon rind, cayenne, and salt in a large stainless or nonstick skillet, and bring to a simmer over medium heat. Cook, whisking occasionally, until the cream mixture is slightly reduced and is able to coat the back of a spoon, 2 to 3 minutes. Cover with a lid and set aside.

4. When you're ready to assemble the dish, bring the large pot of water back to a boil, add the pasta, and cook according to the package directions, stirring occasionally. Meanwhile, reheat the cream mixture over low heat, whisk in all but 1 tablespoon of the saffron butter, and stir in the cheese. Using tongs, immediately transfer the cooked angel hair to the skillet and toss well to coat. Add a spoonful of the hot pasta cooking liquid if the sauce becomes too thick, and taste for the addition of salt.

5. Warm the wrapped lobster in a microwave oven for 1 minute. Divide the pasta between 2 heated plates, distribute the lobster in equal portions over each serving, and brush them lightly with the remaining saffron butter. Garnish with the parsley sprigs, if desired, and serve immediately.

Serves 2

Bittersweet Chocolate Fondue

What could be more romantic than ending a passionate Valentine's Day dinner by sharing a warm and delectable chocolate "dip" with your special someone? Fondues have happily returned to the scene – if you don't have a fondue pot up in the attic, you can easily purchase a small dessert-size one or use a gravy warmer with a candle source.

Many fondues will include a liqueur for added flavor, but here a touch of cherry juice is the secret ingredient that will provide an added layer of flavor. The most important part is always the chocolate, so don't skimp in this department. Using the finest dark chocolate you can find will make all the difference.

Whole strawberries are an obvious choice for dipping and you could certainly serve only them, but don't discount other seasonal fruits for varied color, texture, and flavor. If lingering is your intention, the more tastes there are to savor, the longer you'll be delighting in each other's company. P.S. Don't forget the biscotti!

Ingredients:

8 ounces good-quality bittersweet or semisweet chocolate, roughly chopped

½ cup heavy cream

1 tablespoon maraschino cherry juice

Assorted fruit (such as whole strawberries, 1-inch-thick slices of peeled banana, apple, and pear wedges, 1-inch chunks of peeled kiwi, and sliced star fruit)

1. Place the chocolate in a medium-size glass or ceramic bowl. In a small saucepan, bring the cream to a simmer, then pour over the chocolate and whisk until melted. Add the cherry juice and stir to combine.

2. Immediately transfer to a fondue pot set to low heat, and serve with the fruit and fondue forks or skewers for dipping.

Serves 2

Note: The fondue can be made several hours ahead. Cover and store at room temperature, then reheat on top of the stove over low heat, or set in the microwave and heat in 10-second intervals, stirring occasionally until warm and glossy.

Passion and Romance: Addicted to Love?

If you've been feeling euphoric, irrational, anxious, and intoxicated lately, you just might be addicted … to love, that is. New neuroscientific studies have found that the initial passion and romantic love we feel for someone at the beginning of a relationship are born in the brain's addiction center, where craving, desire, and drive for reward originate. And dopamine, the main neurochemical responsible for the "high" induced by cocaine as well as other drugs and alcohol, is at work here too. Indeed, people smitten by passion tend to behave a lot like addicts — they need that person more and more, act and think compulsively and obsessively, and experience painful withdrawal when apart or rejected.

Perhaps this is why newly sober alcoholics and addicts are often advised to refrain from entering into intimate relationships too soon, since the possibility exists of trading one addiction for another. It is also possible that, due to many common physiological symptoms experienced in early recovery (called "post-acute withdrawal"), which can wreak havoc on hormones, nerves, and the overall ability to feel pleasure, any chance of developing a healthy new relationship is minimal at best. In reality, whether you're married or single, your love life in sobriety will probably get worse before it gets better, but the good news is that, sooner or later, greater fulfillment and satisfaction will arrive in all areas of life — passion and romance included.

So, when the time is right, should nondrinkers date only nondrinkers? And more generally, should those who, for whatever reason, choose not to drink, steer clear of heavy drinkers? We can never be sure in what direction Cupid may aim his arrow. What seems to be the more important question is whether a potential partner is willing to understand why you choose not to imbibe or, at the very least, respects your decision without question or coercion. Although alcohol is always touted as a great enhancement to romance, in reality it is a depressant that interferes with sexual drive and response and is more often than not the primary cause of rifts, abuse, and unhappiness between the sexes.

Perhaps Shakespeare summed it up best in *Macbeth* when he warned of the effects of drinking: "It provokes the desire, but takes away the performance." Former chronic drinkers and their partners know this all too well. But as modern science seems to indicate, Mother Nature has already provided us with all the "provocation" we need to stir passion and experience love. You just need to put yourself in Cupid's path, and the rest will take care of itself. And as the song goes, "That's amore." Although a dozen roses and a sumptuous, romantic dinner (did anyone mention chocolate?) wouldn't hurt either.

Whether Irish or not, everyone loves to celebrate St. Patrick's Day. Today more of a secular holiday than a religious one, March 17 is synonymous with the wearing of the green, shamrocks, and leprechauns. But it has also become strongly associated with drinking – everything from green beer to whiskey-laden Irish coffee. So, how do we subtract the alcohol and still maintain the high spirits? Easy!

There's no other saintly day more closely linked to a specific dish than St. Patrick's Day, the holiday when no Irishman worth his salt would pass up a plate of corned beef and cabbage. If your experience with this most famous of Irish meals has been less than wonderful, Orange Marmalade-Glazed Corned Beef with all the fixings will quickly change your mind. Surprisingly, it was the most popular and frequently requested meal I prepared for my clients when I was a personal chef. I guarantee that once you prepare this menu for your family and friends, you too will be asked to make it an annual tradition.

Nibbles of traditional cheeses and cream crackers will keep folks at bay until the hearty main event arrives, while pitchers of refreshing iced green tea "spiked" with time-honored Rose's® Lime Juice answer the question of "What to drink?" When the Mock Irish Coffee and cookies arrive, everyone will agree that you've created a feast fit for kings and saints alike!

A Saint Patrick's Day Feast for Family and Friends

MENU

Dinner for Eight

APPETIZER:

Cheese Platter with Cream Crackers

MAIN COURSE:

Orange Marmalade-Glazed Corned Beef with Cabbage, Baby Red Potatoes, and Carrots

Irish Soda Bread

DESSERT:

Shamrock Sugar Cookies

BEVERAGE PAIRINGS:

Appetizer and Main Course:

Iced Green Tea

Dessert:

Mock Irish Coffee

Tips on Purchased Ingredients

A ***cheese platter*** of traditional varieties from the British Isles is a great choice for appetizer-nibbling. Irish cheddar is particularly smooth and creamy, with a hint of sweetness. It is white in color as opposed to the more common orange cheddars, which are colored with a natural dye called *annatto*. Gloucester (sometimes called Double Gloucester) and Cheshire varieties are close cousins of cheddar and would also be good choices. Derby is a milder and less tangy cheese that is often sold as Sage Derby when flavored with the herb. The sage also adds interesting green color markings to the cheese, making it perfect for St. Patrick's Day. Another good addition to your cheese platter would be the spreadable "pub cheeses" that are available in tubs and are flavored with ingredients like horseradish, garlic, and herbs. Rarely do they contain any alcohol, but it's always a good idea to check the label for ingredients like wine, port, and stout. Firm and semi-firm cheeses should be served at room temperature, where their flavor is at its best.

Cream crackers are the most popular cracker or "biscuit" (as they are called in Britain and Ireland) across the pond and are deliciously flaky and somewhat rich compared to the better-known English water cracker that we see pretty much everywhere here in the U.S. If you can find them, they are the ideal accompaniment to your cheese platter. Some companies also make an assortment box called "Biscuits for Cheese," in which you'll find a few cream crackers tucked inside along with other traditional varieties like Bath and Digestives. For a truly authentic presentation, purchase a jar of Branston Pickle®, a brand of condiment that is a cross between relish and chutney, and is traditionally served with cheese and cold meats.

Irish soda bread can be found in many supermarkets and bakeries when March 17 arrives, and although not very hard to make yourself, it is nearly always extremely tasty and reasonably priced, so saving time and energy on this front makes sense. Baked in rounds and studded with raisins or currants, Irish soda bread gets its name from the inclusion of baking soda as a leavening agent. It is somewhat sweet and particularly delicious when slathered with butter. Slice it into wedges with a serrated knife and serve with the corned beef.

Orange Marmalade-Glazed Corned Beef with Cabbage, Potatoes, and Carrots

A brisket cured in a seasoned brine, corned beef is bright rosy-red, and generally comes packaged as "first cut" or "flat cut," although a "second cut" or "point cut" can sometimes be found (more flavorful but fattier). Any one will do here. I recommend buying those that come with a seasoning packet that you add to the water, since it makes life easier and really enhances the flavor of your vegetables. A tender corned beef requires a few hours of simmering, and the remaining liquid is key to the success of your cooked vegetables, so plan on prepping the cabbage, potatoes, and carrots but not actually cooking them until the beef is done and ready to glaze. Because of this, it is probably better to plan on cooking the beef the day of your dinner rather than beforehand, although, if you are prepared to save and chill the cooking liquid, you can certainly get a head start the day before – something I have done out of necessity on more than one occasion. Keep the beef moistened in a little of the liquid and store in an airtight container in the fridge. When dinnertime approaches, just give it a quick reheat in the hot cooking liquid before glazing.

Corned beef should be sliced thin against the grain of the meat. Have a large, heated platter ready to receive the slices and the well-drained, cooked vegetables. If you like, you can brush everything just before serving with a little melted butter for a truly glistening presentation.

Ingredients:

One 4- to 5-pound corned beef, with seasoning packet

½ cup orange marmalade

2 tablespoons light brown sugar

1 tablespoon spicy brown mustard

1 large green cabbage, cored, tough outer leaves removed, and cut into thick wedges

24 baby red potatoes, peeled or unpeeled

5 medium-size carrots, peeled and cut into 2-inch pieces

2 tablespoons unsalted butter, melted (optional)

1. Remove the corned beef from its package, rinse under cold water, and place in a large pot. Add the seasoning packet and enough water to cover well, and bring to a boil over medium-high heat. Reduce to a low simmer and cook, partially covered, until fork-tender, about 3 hours. Turn the beef over every 40 minutes to cook evenly and skim off any foam that appears.

2. Transfer the beef to a flameproof pan and cover with foil. In a small bowl, combine the marmalade, brown sugar, and mustard.

3. Bring the cooking liquid back to a boil, add the vegetables, and cook at a medium simmer uncovered, until fork-tender, 25 to 30 minutes. Drain well in a colander.

4. Meanwhile, spoon the glaze over the corned beef and place the meat under the broiler, set to high heat until bubbly and caramelized, about 3 minutes. Turn the pan to brown evenly. Transfer the beef to a cutting board, slice thin, and serve surrounded by the vegetables on a heated platter. Brush with melted butter, if using, just before serving.

Serves 8

Shamrock Sugar Cookies

It is said that St. Patrick used the shamrock to illustrate the Trinity concept of Christianity: three leaves joined by a common stem. Today, we find shamrocks decorating everything from greeting cards to earrings, and without these little green gems, St. Patrick's Day just wouldn't be the same. So, it seems appropriate to finish our feast with these delectable cookies that commemorate Ireland's best-known emblem.

Sugar-cookie dough that requires rolling out does best when very well chilled, so making this the day before would be a good idea as well as a time-saver. A shamrock cookie cutter measuring about 2 inches is ideal and will yield about 3 dozen cookies, but you could just as easily use smaller or even larger shamrock cutters if you have them, being sure to adjust the baking time up or down. Keep this recipe on hand for other holiday cookie-cutter baking as the results are always deliciously crisp yet chewy.

Ingredients:

1 cup (2 sticks) unsalted butter, softened

1 cup granulated sugar

2 large eggs

1 teaspoon alcohol-free vanilla extract

3 cups all-purpose flour

2 teaspoons baking powder

1 teaspoon salt

1 egg white, lightly beaten

Green sugar or sprinkles for decorating

1. In a large mixing bowl, using an electric mixer, beat together the butter and sugar until smooth and fluffy. Add the eggs and vanilla, and beat to combine well.

2. In a medium-size mixing bowl, whisk together the flour, baking powder, and salt. With the mixer speed set on low, add the dry ingredients to the butter-and-egg mixture a little at a time until well blended.

3. Divide the dough in two, wrap in plastic, and chill for at least 3 hours or overnight.

4. Preheat the oven to 350 degrees. Roll out the dough to ¼-inch thickness, cut the shamrock shapes, and carefully transfer to an ungreased cookie sheet. Brush lightly with the beaten egg white and decorate with the green sugar or sprinkles. Bake until the edges are lightly golden, 8 to 12 minutes, depending on the size of the cookie. Transfer to a wire rack to cool.

Makes about 3 dozen cookies

EASY DOES IT: Ready-to-go sugar cookie dough found in the refrigerated section of your grocery will save you time, if necessary. Roll it out, decorate as above, and bake according to the package directions.

Baking with Extracts That Contain Alcohol

If we look in our kitchen pantries, we'll find alcohol lurking in a number of places, not least of which is in bottles of baking extracts, where it is used as a preservative. Extracts such as vanilla and almond can contain up to 35 percent alcohol by volume (lemon extract can contain up to 80 percent). These little bottles of concentrated flavor, so commonly used in everything from cookies to ice cream, can be potential triggers for the alcohol-addicted. In fact, addicted and desperate individuals have been known to down a bottle or two for immediate relief of withdrawal symptoms — an illustration of how strong the pull of addiction can be. So what are the alternatives and how important is it, in actual fact, to omit the use of these extracts in cooking?

For those whose health relies on total abstinence, eliminating and substituting for alcohol-laden extracts is a must. Fortunately, many companies now offer alcohol-free alternatives, often using glycerin as a base. Although these products are not yet commonly found in the supermarket, many health food stores and baking outlets carry them. They are full-flavored and excellent to use in place of traditional extracts. There are also flavored oils available, primarily in the citrus family, which make excellent alternatives and even contribute a truer and more natural flavor to the final product. For vanilla aficionados, the fragrant vanilla bean offers a wonderful alternative when used to make vanilla sugar, powder, or paste and is, in fact, preferred by most pastry chefs because of its intense aromatic qualities and characteristic "speckles" of vanilla bean, which appear in such treats as ice cream, crème brûlée, and vanilla sauces.

In most recipes calling for the use of extracts, some of the alcohol, but not all (see Cooking with Alcohol: Busting the Myth, pages 26-27) will dissipate in the cooking process. If you simply wish to abstain from alcohol consumption, but are not averse to using small amounts of products that contain alcohol, it is not critical to worry about trace amounts of alcohol. However, if you are newly sober and are baking with alcohol-containing extracts, remember that the mere smell might trigger brain cells into unwanted recognition and, ultimately, craving. For this reason, steer clear of them, at least until sobriety is well established. Personally, on mere principle, I cook only with alcohol-free products and always read labels to prevent any surprises. When you're embracing a new, sober lifestyle, it's not a bad idea to do the same and, in the process, create definitive lines between what you will and will not accept as a part of your recovery plan. When the lines are fuzzy, they unfortunately become easier to cross and allow us to wander into questionable territory. To err on the side of caution is always a good idea.

Do we sacrifice flavor when we skip the alcohol? A recent taste test of vanilla ice creams found that those made with vanilla bean were preferred by most participants. In fact, the tasters commented that some of the French vanilla varieties (those that use vanilla extract instead of vanilla bean) had a "boozy" aftertaste that masked the true vanilla flavor.

Iced Green Tea

Ingredients:

8 cups boiling water

16 green tea bags

8 cups cold water

One 12-ounce bottle Rose's® sweetened lime juice

Forget the green beer and offer up pitchers of this delightful and refreshing alternative. Choose a good-quality tea and steep well to obtain rich color and flavor. This recipe makes one gallon, which should certainly suffice, but make more if there are a number of tea "guzzlers" present. Rose's® sweetened lime juice, an alcohol-free bar staple famous for its inclusion in lager and lime, adds just the right touch of zing. It's usually found in the beverage aisle of your supermarket.

Make the iced tea ahead of time and keep cold, with a minimum of ice. Serve in chilled 16-ounce beer mugs or Pilsner glasses, and always pour the lime juice into the tea as it is heavier in weight. A 1½-ounce jigger or standard shot glass is perfect for this. Remember, however, that the sight of bar paraphernalia might actually pose a trigger to the newly sober, in which case a tall soda glass and a small measuring cup will do the trick.

In a large saucepan, pour the boiling water over the tea bags and allow to steep for 10 minutes. Remove the tea bags, add the cold water, and chill in 2-quart pitchers or beverage containers. Serve as instructed above.

Serves 8

Mock Irish Coffee

This famous drink was invented in the early 1940s at Shannon Airport in Ireland to warm the chilled bones of weary passengers. Traditionally composed of strong coffee, Irish whiskey, sugar, and cream, it has a flavor that has become universally recognized and reproduced in everything from baked goods and candy to nondairy creamers and ice cream. But for those who may be in the early stages of sobriety, even alcohol-free copycat products could pose a trigger through familiarity of taste and smell. If this is not a problem and you happen to enjoy the taste of Irish Cream-flavored products without the buzz, you can use the appropriate flavored coffee or creamer in this recipe.

What is truly unique about Irish coffee is its all-important method of preparation and presentation, and it is that which we'll be replicating below. Connoisseurs will insist on Irish coffee mugs, but any tall, heat-proof glass that allows you to see the wonderful cream as it floats atop the dark coffee will work nicely. The coffee is meant to be sipped through the cream layer, not mixed in. The fresh cream used in Ireland and Britain is much less pasteurized and doctored with additives, so it naturally floats without whipping. Here, we'll beat the cream ever so slightly to obtain the right consistency. I've chosen a vanilla cream-flavored coffee, but you could certainly choose another flavor if you prefer, or simply use your favorite unflavored strong roast. Make these at the table for your guests to appreciate the technique and applaud your skill!

1. In a medium-size mixing bowl, beat together the cream and confectioners' sugar until very slight, soft peaks form and the cream is still pourable. Keep well chilled until ready to use.

2. To serve, drop 3 sugar cubes into warmed Irish coffee mugs or tall glasses and add 1 cup of hot coffee. Pouring over the back of a spoon, gently add the prepared cream, floating it on top of the coffee. Serve immediately.

Serves 8

Ingredients:

1 cup heavy cream

2 tablespoons confectioners' sugar

24 sugar cubes

8 cups vanilla cream-flavored coffee, strongly brewed

Chapter 3

The Rites of Spring

*Herb-Roasted Leg of Lamb with
Blood Orange Balsamic Reduction*

With the arrival of spring come two of our most important religious holidays: Easter and Passover. They are typically celebrated in the company of family generations – from grandparents to grandchildren – and tradition plays a key role not only in the festivities but also in the menu selections. Specialty dishes from handed-down recipes appear at the table to delight us and remind us of the importance of family and continuity. And in keeping with that all-important custom, you will be hailed for adding your own touches to tradition when you host either of these extraordinary meals.

With religious holidays and the accompanying rituals comes the inevitable question of the role of alcohol. For those who must abstain, like the newly sober, these special occasions can sometimes create cause for concern, especially when we are enmeshed in a family affair of expected behavior and sometimes uncomfortable situations. As the host, remember that you have the ability to create an atmosphere of comfort and serenity in every way, from your demeanor to your choice of food and drink. And with the help of these menus and the tips and advice they contain, you will no doubt be lovingly appreciated for your thoughtfulness and attention to every detail. Not to mention, of course, the fabulous array of food you've prepared!

When Easter Sunday finally arrives, marking the end of the 46-day period of Lent, it's time to celebrate spring and enjoy a hearty, rich meal with our family. And who better than the Italians to show us how! If the idea of another baked ham and string-bean casserole is leaving you less than inspired, try your hand at this extraordinary menu that will wow even the most skeptical relatives into a round of "Bravo!" by the time dessert is served.

This menu highlights ingredients that are quintessentially spring – artichokes, leg of lamb, fresh herbs, baby peas, and soft wheat berries – celebrating rebirth and renewal in delicious style. An easy Primavera Antipasto Platter starts things off and primes the palate for the sumptuous entrée to follow. Nothing truly signifies spring like a leg of lamb, and this recipe, with its flavorful, alcohol-free reduction sauce, will definitely steal the show while the exceptionally creamy Mascarpone Mashed Potatoes will provide unmatchable side support. Perfectly paired alcohol-free beverages, including a simple White Cranberry Cordial to begin, will complement the flavors and textures of each dish. But be sure to have your guests hold their applause until you surpass all expectations with Nonna's Easter Wheat Pie and your gorgeous mountain of Lavender Honey-Drenched Struffoli. Then take your bows and know that the "rights" of spring entertaining belong to you!

Italian Easter Sunday Lunch

MENU
Lunch for Eight

FIRST COURSE:

Primavera Antipasto Platter

Sautéed Baby Artichokes

Pane Rustica

ENTRÉE:

Herb-Roasted Leg of Lamb with Blood Orange Balsamic Reduction

Mascarpone Mashed Potatoes

Baby Peas and Pearl Onions

DESSERT:

Nonna's Easter Wheat Pie

Lavender Honey-Drenched Struffoli

BEVERAGES:

First Course: White Cranberry Cordials

Entrée: *Sparkling Orange Spring Water*

Dessert: *Espresso*

Tips on Purchased Ingredients

There is much debate among Italian cooks over what belongs on a proper antipasto platter, the most important considerations being availability of seasonal ingredients and how substantial the entrée is that follows. Platters that include hot selections, meats, or seafood in addition to a variety of vegetables, olives, and cheeses – all of which can quickly weigh down diners – are best served before a light pasta or poultry dinner. For this menu, however, the ingredients you purchase for the *Primavera Antipasto Platter* should be light palate-pleasers that will complement your stellar first-course dish, Sautéed Baby Artichokes, and leave room for the hearty leg of lamb entrée that follows. Refrain from including traditional sliced meats and keep cheeses at a minimum. If you feel you'd like to add something a bit more substantial, your best bet would be large shrimp served cocktail-style, clams, or oysters on the half shell, or a purchased seafood salad. Pull out the largest platter you own, or two medium-size platters for each end of the table, and arrange an assortment of the following, finished with a generous drizzle of good-quality extra virgin olive oil for soaking up with the bread: spring greens, radishes, marinated sun-dried tomatoes, roasted peppers, pickled beet slices, bocconcini (miniature fresh mozzarella balls), assorted olives, and canned cannellini beans (drained and rinsed). Other fine additions are steamed or roasted asparagus spears or grilled zucchini or eggplant if time allows for their preparation. Everything should be served at room temperature for peak flavor. If your platter is large enough, you can pile the baby artichokes in the center, arranging the other components around them; otherwise, serve them on their own platter.

Pane Rustica, a delicious variety of Italian bread with a crispy, thick crust, generally comes in very large oval-shaped loaves and is perfect for eating antipasto. You can pre-slice it or present it on a cutting board at the table for guests to tear or slice themselves. Spring wouldn't be spring without "petit pois" at the table – choose frozen, not canned peas for a crisp, clean contrast to the heavier lamb and potato dishes. *Baby peas* and *pearl onions* are a classic combination and often can be found together in frozen bags or boxes. Otherwise, simply buy and cook them separately, and serve mixed together (aim for three times the amount of peas to onions) with a little butter.

To best complement the blood orange balsamic reduction that accompanies the lamb and to cut the richness of the potatoes, a simple unsweetened *sparkling orange spring water* will fit the bill. Keep several bottles in an ice bucket near the table for easy refills, and garnish each glass (wine or highball glasses are ideal) with an orange slice.

No Italian meal is complete without *espresso*, and lunchtime is perfect for serving the real thing. It's generally agreed that stovetop espresso pots like the ones used in Italy make the best-tasting coffee – they come in 3-, 6-, 9-, and 12-cup sizes (each cup being 1½ ounces). Two medium-size pots will allow you to make both caffeinated and decaffeinated at the same time if necessary. The filter must always be tightly packed with the finely ground espresso beans. It is then placed in the bottom portion of the pot containing the water; when the water boils, it is forced up through the coffee and up the inner spout into the top section. When the characteristic hissing ceases, your espresso is ready. Sugar and perhaps a lemon-rind twist are the only accompaniments you'll need. Offer anisette sugar (naturally alcohol-free) as a substitute for traditional anisette liqueur. Italians usually serve their espresso after dessert and gulp it down in one or two sips, but you can serve it alongside the pie and struffoli if you like.

White Cranberry Cordial

White cranberry juice is made by harvesting the berries before they become red and is a bit smoother and less tart than its traditional counterpart. If you can, look for brands that are 100 percent juice, not watered-down varieties. Kedem® brand white grape juice, with no added sugar, is always my choice of grape juice in the kitchen as it has a clean, authentic flavor, but any similar brand will work just as well. The combination of acidity and sweetness in these ingredients complements the artichokes, antipasto, and most important, the rich extra virgin olive oil. You can make these up individually or in a large pitcher for the table. Serve extremely well chilled in small juice or cordial glasses for sipping.

Have all ingredients well chilled. For individual glasses, combine 4 ounces white cranberry juice, 2 ounces white grape juice, and a quick splash of the vinegar. For serving from a pitcher, stir to combine the juices, then add a few splashes of vinegar to taste. If preparing ahead of time, wait to add the vinegar until just before serving.

Ingredients:

32 ounces white cranberry juice

16 ounces white grape juice

Splash white balsamic vinegar

Sautéed Baby Artichokes

These wonderful little gems come around a few times during the year, but in spring, they tend to be at their smallest and most tender. They're usually sold packaged in quantities from 9 to 16, depending on their size; you'll want to provide at least 2 or 3 per person as part of your antipasto platter. Although a bit labor-intensive, they are well worth the effort, and for those who have tasted only the usual antipasto type of artichoke hearts from a jar, you're in for a real gourmet treat. Making this the highlight of your first course will definitely start things off with style. You can prepare them a day ahead and keep refrigerated. Bring to room temperature before serving.

Ingredients:

1 lemon

16 to 24 baby artichokes

5 tablespoons extra virgin olive oil

Salt and pepper to taste

12 garlic cloves, trimmed, peeled, and left whole

¼ cup white grape juice

⅓ cup water

1 tablespoon chopped fresh Italian parsley leaves

1 teaspoon chopped fresh mint leaves

1. Halve the lemon and squeeze the juice of one half into a large bowl of cold water. Reserve the remaining half.

2. Prepare the artichokes one at a time by bending back the dark green outer leaves and snapping them off at the base until only the pale yellow-green leaves remain. Cut about ½ inch off the tip and trim the stem to 1 inch long or less.

Mascarpone Mashed Potatoes

Rich and creamy mashed potatoes are the perfect accompaniment to the leg of lamb and its piquant reduction sauce. Mascarpone is a soft-textured, delicate-tasting Italian cheese, best known for its use in the rich dessert tiramisu but often underused in the savory kitchen. Here, it combines beautifully with the fluffiness of high-starch potatoes to create a delectable side dish that will have your guests asking for seconds and thirds.

Idaho and russet potatoes are the best to use here, and a potato ricer will definitely make your job a lot easier as well as produce optimal smoothness. Drying out the cooked potatoes is a necessary step to avoid a watery result. You can prepare these a few hours ahead and carefully rewarm on top of the stove over low heat, stirring often.

Ingredients:

5 pounds russet potatoes, peeled and cut into 2-inch pieces

1 tablespoon kosher salt

8 ounces mascarpone cheese at room temperature

½ cup (1 stick) unsalted butter, softened

¼ cup whole milk or light cream, warmed

Salt and pepper to taste

1. Place the potatoes and the kosher salt in a large pot. Add enough cold water to cover, bring to a boil, and cook until the potatoes are fork-tender, about 25 minutes. Pour into a large colander and allow to drain until the edges look dry but the potatoes are still warm, about 20 minutes.

2. In a large mixing bowl, combine the mascarpone, butter, and milk, and using a hand-held electric mixer, beat until smooth. Working in batches, rice the potatoes into the mixing bowl over the mascarpone mixture and blend well with a wooden spoon. Alternatively, you may transfer all the cooked, dried potatoes to the mixing bowl and mash them with a potato masher to desired smoothness. Season to taste with salt and pepper, and serve immediately, or set aside and reheat on top of the stove before serving.

Serves 8

With a sharp paring knife, carefully whittle around the base of the artichoke to remove any dark green areas as well as any discolorations. Halve lengthwise and drop in the acidulated (lemon) water.

3. Heat the olive oil in a large skillet over medium-high heat and add the well-drained artichokes. Sprinkle with salt and pepper, and sauté, stirring frequently until lightly browned at the edges, about 5 minutes. Add the garlic cloves and cook a further minute. Add the grape juice, water, and the juice of the remaining lemon half, stir well, and bring to a boil. Cover, reduce the heat to low, and cook until the artichokes are tender and most of the liquid has been absorbed, about 8 minutes. Stir in the parsley and mint, and continue cooking, uncovered, a further 2 minutes. Remove from the heat and allow to come to room temperature before tasting for seasoning. Drizzle a little olive oil over all before serving.

Serves 8

Herb-Roasted Leg of Lamb with Blood Orange Balsamic Reduction

Ingredients

Lamb:

One 7- to 8-pound semi-boneless leg of lamb, all but ¼ inch fat removed

4 garlic cloves, peeled and minced

1 tablespoon each finely chopped, fresh rosemary, parsley, thyme, and mint leaves

Olive oil to moisten (1 to 2 tablespoons)

Salt and pepper to taste

There is little to match the festive spring splendor of bringing a perfectly roasted leg of lamb to the table. Garlic and herbs always bring out the best that lamb has to offer, and here, the paste that is rubbed on the outside of the meat provides an undeniably delectable layer of flavor. The accompanying reduction sauce is sublimely pungent and heady, in spite of the absence of any alcohol in the usual form of red or fortified wine. This dish will make you a culinary star in no time, and surprisingly, it's extremely easy to prepare.

Quality ingredients are particularly key: First, it would be a good idea to make friends with your local supermarket butcher. Although leg of lamb is usually found already semi-boneless with the aitchbone (rump bone) removed to ensure even cooking, it wouldn't hurt to ask your butcher to prepare one especially for you, trimming the excess fat and tying if necessary. This will save you time better spent on other parts of the menu. In addition, be sure to choose an excellent-quality balsamic vinegar for the reduction – the price will no doubt reflect the flavor. Sometimes you can find blood orange juice in bottles, which is fine to use here. If, however, you can't locate either the juice or the oranges themselves, substitute Florida juicing oranges as they are somewhat similar in size and sweetness.

Although it is generally agreed that lamb should be served medium rare, the nice thing about a leg of lamb is that there will always be parts cooked to medium or well-done simply because of its shape, so every preference can be satisfied. As with all roasts, you will need to rest the lamb before carving so the juices can be reabsorbed. Finishing up the reduction sauce at this time is the ideal last-minute task.

1. Pat the lamb dry and score the fat just down to the meat with the tip of a sharp paring knife. In a small mixing bowl, combine the garlic, herbs, and olive oil to create a paste. Place the lamb in a large, heavy roasting pan, season well with salt and pepper, and rub the paste all over. Let stand at room temperature for 30 minutes.

2. Preheat the oven to 450 degrees.

3. Begin the reduction: In a small saucepan, melt the butter over medium heat, add the shallots, and cook without browning, until soft, about 5 minutes. Stir in the vinegar and orange juice, bring to a boil, and continue cooking until the volume is reduced by half and the liquid coats the back of a spoon, about 20 minutes. Remove from the heat and set aside.

4. Roast the lamb for 30 minutes, reduce the oven temperature to 350 degrees, and continue roasting for about 1 hour and 15 minutes more, until an instant-read thermometer inserted in the thickest part of the meat registers 135 to 140 degrees (for medium rare). Transfer to a platter, cover with foil, and let stand for at least 20 minutes.

5. Finish the reduction: Skim off any excess fat from the roasting pan. Place the pan over 2 burners and add the beef broth. Bring to a boil over high heat and, using a wooden spoon, deglaze the pan by scraping up any brown bits. Reduce the liquid by half and add to the small saucepan of the orange-balsamic mixture. Bring to a simmer and strain through a fine-mesh strainer into a clean saucepan. Taste for seasoning and serve in a warmed gravy boat alongside the lamb.

Serves 8

How to Carve a Leg of Lamb

Impressive carving at the table is easy to do with the right tools. A *manche à gigot*, designed specifically for carving lamb, grips the leg bone nicely, but you can accomplish the same steadying of the roast by inserting a meat fork into the small end of the leg. Grip the fork, raise the leg slightly off the platter, and with a sharp slicing knife, cut ¼- to ½-inch slices parallel with the bone, beginning with the fat side up. When you reach the rump bone, turn over the leg and continue carving in the same manner. For guests who prefer a greater degree of doneness, cut slices farther up toward the shank bone. Place the slices on a warmed plate for passing or serve on individual plates.

Reduction:

¼ cup (½ stick) unsalted butter

1 medium shallot, peeled and roughly chopped

½ cup balsamic vinegar

Juice of 8 blood oranges (about 2 cups)

1½ cups low-sodium beef broth

Salt and pepper to taste

Lavender Honey-Drenched Struffoli

Although struffoli, also called "honey balls," are a typical addition to the Christmas season dessert table, many Italian families enjoy serving them on nearly every holiday, including Easter. Sweet, gooey, and piled up into a mountain of scrumptious little nibbles, struffoli always encourage lingering at the table and can be impossible to resist. Here, we'll give a twist to the classic recipe by using lavender honey instead of the more common types to coat the struffoli, along with ground culinary lavender (see Note) in the dough to add a lovely fragrance and subtle taste – perfect for the spring table.

If you don't have a deep-fryer, you can easily set up a makeshift version on top of the stove with a saucepan and frying basket. A clip-on thermometer will help you determine temperature. Sometimes you'll find the addition of wine, sherry, or brandy in these types of fried dough recipes to contribute a layer of flavor, but here, since we want the lavender honey to predominate, we needn't substitute for any liquor; a little less flour will keep the dough at the proper consistency.

Depending on your level of patience and how many extra hands you're able to enlist to roll the balls, this recipe will make either 3 to 4 dozen 1-inch balls or twice as many smaller balls – smaller being best and most impressive at the table. You can make these a day ahead and wrap the mounded plate tightly in lightly buttered plastic wrap to prevent sticking.

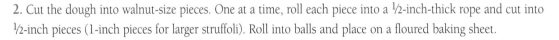

Ingredients:

3 large eggs

1 tablespoon unsalted butter, melted

2 teaspoons granulated sugar

½ teaspoon baking powder

½ teaspoon culinary lavender, finely ground

2 cups all-purpose flour

4 cups light olive oil
or canola oil

1½ cups lavender honey

1 tablespoon each purple, yellow, and white sprinkles, for garnish (optional)

1. In a large mixing bowl, whisk together the eggs, butter, and sugar until well combined. In a medium-size mixing bowl, whisk together the baking powder, ground lavender, and flour. Add the dry ingredients to the wet, and stir with a wooden spoon. With your hands, work the mixture into a soft dough, cover, and refrigerate for at least 30 minutes.

2. Cut the dough into walnut-size pieces. One at a time, roll each piece into a ½-inch-thick rope and cut into ½-inch pieces (1-inch pieces for larger struffoli). Roll into balls and place on a floured baking sheet.

3. Heat the oil in a deep-fryer or saucepan to 375 degrees. Working in batches, shake off any excess flour and fry the dough balls until puffy and golden brown. Transfer to paper towels or brown paper to drain.

4. Heat the honey in a large, wide skillet until it appears thinner in consistency. Add the drained struffoli and, using a wooden spoon or heat-proof rubber spatula, gently turn them to coat on all sides. Pour onto a large, round plate and shape into a pyramid, wetting your hands first to prevent sticking. Decorate with the colored sprinkles and serve.

Serves 8

Note: Culinary lavender has been certified organic and safe for cooking. A little bit goes a long way, so don't over-do. See the Resource section for ordering lavender products online.

Cooking Wines and Alcohol-Free Wine and Beer – Why Not Use Them?

Cooking wines found in the supermarket (including sherry and vermouth) actually contain up to 17 percent alcohol – even more than normal table wines. And since we know that the alcohol does not burn off during cooking (see Cooking with Alcohol: Busting the Myth, pages 26-27), they fall into the same category when it comes to the amount of alcohol retained – and so does the dangerous familiarity of their smell and taste. If total abstinence is required, steer clear of them. Speaking of taste, cooking wines also contain an inordinate amount of salt and chemical preservatives, which for any good cook, sober or not, is a definite turnoff.

"Alcohol-free" wine and beer are not, in reality, alcohol-free. Why? Because the FDA allows any product that contains 0.05 percent or less alcohol to be labeled as such, and all of them, regardless of the extraction process used, contain trace amounts of alcohol. We already know that small amounts can still trigger recognition in the newly sober, but there's more. The ritual of opening a wine bottle or popping a beer can is an activity that our brains can vividly recall and, with this recollection, we will expect the outcome to be the same as if we were handling and drinking the real thing. But when the outcome (intoxication) is not attained, the reward system feels deprived and cravings take place. Not a comfortable place to be, particularly when other stress factors may be present as is the case during family holiday gatherings. So, for those in recovery, so-called alcohol-free drinks should be avoided at the table and in the kitchen.

When complete abstinence is not the issue and small amounts are either medically permissible or personally unimportant, using these alcohol-free products to cook with is probably not risky. However, if you have ever tasted nonalcoholic wine, it's really nothing more than a glorified, expensive grape juice and, because of its high sugar content and taste, would still require the addition of an acidic element to replicate the role of wine in cooking. Save your money and opt for a good-quality "no sugar added" grape juice instead. Nonalcoholic beer is a different matter; if the characteristic taste is not a problem, it can be used in recipes that call for malt beverages. Bear in mind that often beer is added in cooking, particularly in marinades, because the properties of the alcohol will break down the proteins and tenderize the food. Without the alcohol present, the use of the substitute product becomes irrelevant.

Nonna's Easter Wheat Pie

Ingredients

Pasta Frolla:

2 cups all-purpose flour

½ cup granulated sugar

1 teaspoon baking powder

½ teaspoon salt

Grated rind of ½ lemon

½ cup (1 stick) unsalted butter, chilled and cut into chunks

1 large egg

1 large egg yolk

1 teaspoon alcohol-free vanilla extract

Filling:

½ cup hulled wheat berries or 1 cup canned cooked wheat

1 pound fresh ricotta cheese

⅔ cup granulated sugar

3 large eggs

1½ teaspoons alcohol-free vanilla

Grated rind of ½ lemon

Dash of ground cinnamon

When I was growing up, Easter dinner was unthinkable without my grandmother's (Nonna's) wheat pie, a traditional Italian dessert made from ricotta cheese and soft wheat berries meant to celebrate the rebirth of spring. Neapolitan in origin, this pie is now made all over Italy with regional variations and can include the addition of pastry cream, candied cherries, cinnamon, orange flower water, and candied orange peel. Over the years, I've dabbled with my grandmother's recipe by adding a number of these ingredients but have always returned to her simple-tasting rendition as the best version I know.

Years ago, whole wheat or wheat berries were hard to find and sometimes required a special trip to an Italian market. I remember my grandmother taking the time to soak them overnight and then cook them for what seemed hours before she was able to begin her pies. These days, many markets carry cans of cooked wheat for this popular Italian American dessert and often stock shelled wheat berries as well, which cook up in less time than the harder varieties. Making use of the canned cooked wheat, if it's available, will save you a good amount of preparation time. Fresh ricotta cheese is best; however, the usual supermarket variety is fine to use, provided it is made from whole milk.

Pasta frolla, meaning "tender dough," is the classic pie crust for this and other Italian desserts. It differs from American pie crusts, which are much lighter and flakier. It's also easier to roll out, bakes up beautifully, and is bursting with flavor in its own right. Make the pie a day or two ahead and store in the refrigerator before bringing to room temperature to serve.

1. Prepare the pie crust: Combine the flour, sugar, baking powder, salt, lemon rind, and butter in a food processor and pulse until mixture resembles sand, but butter bits are still visible, 5 to 10 seconds. You may also do this step with a pastry blender or fork, if desired. Add the egg, egg yolk, and vanilla, and process (or stir in) for several seconds until the dough forms a ball.

2. Remove the dough from the processor, transfer to a lightly floured surface, and gently knead until smooth, about 30 seconds. (You may add either a touch more flour or a few drops of water if necessary to bring the dough together.) Divide dough into 2 balls, flatten into thick disks, wrap well in plastic, and refrigerate for 1 hour or up to 2 days.

3. Prepare the filling: If not using canned cooked wheat, prepare the wheat berries by cooking them in 1½ cups of water with a pinch of salt at a low simmer, until the berries are tender but somewhat firm to the bite, about 45 minutes, adding water to prevent sticking, if necessary. Drain and set aside to cool. In a large mixing bowl, combine the ricotta cheese and sugar, and beat with an electric mixer on medium speed until well-blended, 2 to 3 minutes. Beat in the eggs one at a time, add the vanilla, lemon rind, and cinnamon, and beat a further minute. Stir in the cooked wheat and blend well.

4. To assemble: Preheat the oven to 350 degrees. Butter a 9-inch, deep-dish pie pan. On a lightly floured surface, roll out one of the dough disks to form a circle slightly larger than the pie pan. Transferring it carefully, fit it into the pan, crimping the edges decoratively. Pour the mixture into the prepared pie crust. Roll out the remaining disk into a 9-inch square and cut into ten ¾-inch strips. Carefully lay the strips over the top of the filling to form a lattice or woven effect. Pinch the ends of the strips to the outer pie crust to join together.

5. Bake for 40 to 50 minutes until the top of the pie is puffed and lightly golden and the center is firm. Allow to cool completely before serving.

Serves 8

Once a year, generations gather together around an elegantly adorned table to celebrate one of the most important of all Jewish holidays – *Pesach*, or Passover. Steeped in tradition, the Seder meal with its time-honored rituals celebrates the deliverance of the Israelites from slavery in ancient Egypt. Special food and drink are critical components of this festive occasion, and often the task of hosting the first or second night can prove a daunting prospect when a great number of family members are invited and every little detail requires the utmost attention.

With this menu, however, you'll be cool and collected from the moment your first guest arrives until the final accolades are bestowed. Easy, do-ahead dishes like the Roasted Chicken Soup with Herbed Matzo Balls and the Slow-Cooker Brisket will have you serving with ease and confidence, while delectable takes on the expected usual fare like Holiday Haroseth and Golden Potato Casserole will have everyone reaching for extra helpings and asking you for the recipes. By the time you present your Chocolate Soufflé Torte, you may already be enlisted for next year's hosting duties!

Traditionally, four cups of wine are consumed during the service, representing the four divine promises of redemption. For families who do not or cannot drink alcohol, the usual substitute is a nonalcoholic "fruit of the vine" in the form of grape juice. Surprise everyone this year with the extra-special version included here, which is not only refreshingly delicious but elegantly suited to the occasion and the menu. And don't forget to pour Elijah's cup as well – he too will be pleasantly surprised!

Easy Passover Seder for Ten

MENU

Dinner for Ten

TO BEGIN:

Seder Plate with Holiday Haroseth

APPETIZERS:

Gefilte Fish with Salad Garnish

FIRST COURSE:

Roasted Chicken Soup with Herbed Matzo Balls

MAIN COURSE:

Slow-Cooker Brisket with Dried Fruit and Root Vegetables

Golden Potato Casserole

Steamed Asparagus

DESSERT

Chocolate Soufflé Torte with Raspberry Cream Drizzle

Assorted Macaroons

BEVERAGE PAIRINGS:

For Seder Service and Main Meal:
Wine-Free Kosher Toaster

Dessert: *Red Raspberry Tea with Honey*

Tips on Purchased Ingredients

Every **Seder plate**, in addition to haroseth, will include *matzo* (unleavened bread), *karpas* (green herbs, usually parsley), *zeroa* (a roasted shank bone), saltwater (for dipping the herbs), *maror* (freshly grated horseradish), and *betzah* (a roasted egg). All of these can be readied ahead of time. Most supermarket butchers will put out shank bones, free of charge, several days before the beginning of Passover, while fresh horseradish and parsley will be prominently displayed in the produce section. Purchase these when you see them to avoid unnecessary running around later.

Gefilte fish is the time-honored appetizer of choice, and unless Aunt Sophie has offered to make her own special recipe to bring along, your best bet is to purchase a good-quality canned or jarred version. It's usually made from ground carp, pike, or whitefish (although salmon versions are also popular), and is shaped like a *quenelle* (oval dumpling) and seasoned either sweet or savory. The usual gefilte fish accompaniment is red (mixed with red beet) or white (plain) *chrain*, a vinegar-horseradish condiment. It's a good idea to have a bottle of both on hand if you're unsure of people's preferences. Dress up the plate with romaine lettuce leaves, shredded carrots, and radishes with a drizzle of oil and vinegar.

The abundant supply of spring **asparagus** at this time of year makes it the perfect vegetable choice, simply prepared by steaming, boiling, or even microwaving. For thicker spears, trim well and use a vegetable peeler to remove the bottom-third outside skin, which can be unpleasantly chewy. You can cook the asparagus ahead and immediately refresh in ice water to stop the cooking, draining and setting aside until you are ready to serve your entrée. Reheat in a skillet with a little water or microwave for a minute or two in the serving dish.

Assorted macaroons are always a hit and come in a variety of flavors, including chocolate chip, almond, and even tropical fruit – all kosher for Passover. Purchase a variety of these for nibbling at the table, and focus your time and energy on your splendid Chocolate Soufflé Torte instead.

Red raspberry tea is a great complement for the intensely rich chocolate torte. Flavored kosher teas like this are easily found these days (see Resources) and make a terrific change of pace from black coffee. Pass around a honey jar with a wooden honey dipper for guests to sweeten their cup.

A word about kosher for Passover: Fortunately, the array of products now bearing this label of approval has grown tremendously over the years and added delightful variety to the traditional Seder meal. Consequently, it is relatively easy to adhere to custom while enjoying some more unusual versions of handed-down recipes and traditional foods. However, the rules of *kashrut* (the dietary laws of Judaism, such as not eating meat and dairy in the same sitting) are usually observed faithfully. Hence, *pareve*, or nondairy items, are generally used in place of ingredients like butter and cream, and the recipes that follow reflect this adherence. At other times of the year, feel free to substitute the real thing, measure for measure.

Ingredients:

¼ cup sweetened pomegranate juice

1 cup pitted dates, coarsely chopped

1 cup walnut pieces

1 large Granny Smith apple, peeled, cored, and coarsely chopped

¼ teaspoon each ground cinnamon and ground ginger

One pinch each ground cardamom, ground coriander, and cayenne pepper

Holiday Haroseth

This integral part of the Seder plate represents the mortar used by the Hebrew slaves when building the pyramids in Egypt. Deliciously sweet, it's usually made with apples, nuts, sweet wine, and sometimes honey, but variations abound depending on family origin and tradition. Because Jews traveled the world throughout the centuries, the recipe was adapted to local and seasonal ingredients.

Sometimes more than one variety is served at the table, and you'll find that ingredients include everything from dates and raisins to coconut, bananas, and chestnuts. More often than not, however, the inclusion of a high-sugar Passover wine binds these diverse elements together and sweetens the result. When usual alcohol-free versions are made, most cooks simply substitute grape juice for wine as they would at the table for drinking. In this recipe, we'll make use of pomegranate, the newest (although popular back in biblical times) darling of fruit juices. It is sometimes also combined with other juices such as blueberry, cherry, or tangerine (see Note). Any of these is fine to use here and adds another layer of wonderful flavor.

This version combines the best of Ashkenazi (European) and Yemenite (Middle Eastern) haroseth tradition, sure to please every guest at the table. It is customary to chop all ingredients by hand, but food processors have been known to step in on occasion. Make the haroseth up to 24 hours ahead, refrigerate, and bring to room temperature before serving. This recipe yields 2 cups (about 3 tablespoons per person) and can be easily doubled.

1. Heat the pomegranate juice in a small saucepan, add the dates, remove from the heat, and allow to soak for 10 minutes.

2. In a medium-size mixing bowl, combine the pomegranate-date mixture with the remaining ingredients and stir to combine. Chill, covered, in the refrigerator and bring to room temperature before serving.

Serves 10

Note: Pom Wonderful® pomegranate juice has been O/U (Union of Orthodox Rabbis) certified as kosher for Passover. You can visit www.kosherquest.org for a continually updated list of approved products.

Wine-Free Kosher Toaster

Raising the glass in celebration need not raise concern with this delicious, alcohol-free drink that combines unfermented fruit of the vine with refreshing citrus and sparkle. Not only perfect for the reading of the Haggadah (a narrative of the Exodus), this flavorful accompaniment for the boundless meal to follow will bring out the best in each dish, from soup to nuts!

Make ahead in decorative pitchers (one for each end of the table) and serve slightly chilled.

Two 64-ounce bottles
Concord grape juice

2 cups fresh-squeezed orange juice
(about 6 medium-size navel
or juicing oranges)

Juice of 2 limes

One 32-ounce bottle cherry-flavored
seltzer water

Combine all the ingredients, dividing between two 2-quart pitchers, and stir well. If making ahead, stir in the seltzer just before serving.

Serves 10

Roasted-Chicken Soup with Herbed Matzo Balls

Brown Chicken Broth:

6 to 7 pounds chicken backs, wings, necks, and bones

2 large onions, peeled and quartered

3 medium-size carrots, peeled and cut into chunks

2 large celery stalks, cut into chunks

1 parsnip, cut into chunks

4 garlic cloves, smashed

2 tablespoons tomato paste

Handful each, parsley and dill sprigs, including stems

2 bay leaves

1 tablespoon black peppercorns

Salt to taste

Dill sprigs to garnish (optional)

Homemade chicken soup served with matzo balls has become a true staple at the Seder table. A rich, flavorful broth is a must, while the matzo balls have a bit more leeway as to their texture and taste. There are heavy "sinkers" and light, airy "floaters," all depending upon the proportion of matzo meal and eggs used (as well as a few secret tips passed down through the generations). Matzo balls can be flavored with *schmaltz* (chicken fat), vegetable oil, herbs, or spices; they can even be stuffed.

For the soup, we'll be making the richest of broths, based on a brown chicken stock, whose secret lies in the caramelization of chicken bones and vegetables. Its flavor is superb and the outcome not unlike an elegant consommé. You can make this two days ahead and keep it refrigerated before bringing to a simmer to serve. The accompanying matzo balls are deliciously fragrant with fresh herbs that complement the rich, dark broth and are perfectly delicate, yet heartily satisfying. Make them the day they'll be served and simmer them in salted water, so as not to cloud the beautiful broth.

1. Preheat the oven to 450 degrees. In a large roasting pan, spread out the chicken pieces and roast them, stirring occasionally, until well-browned, 40 to 50 minutes. Transfer the browned chicken pieces to a large stockpot and set aside. Add the onion, carrots, celery, parsnip, and garlic cloves to the roasting pan, stir to coat, and return to the oven, roasting until the vegetables have caramelized, about 25 minutes. Stir in the tomato paste and roast a further 15 minutes. Transfer the vegetables to the stockpot with the chicken.

2. Add a little water to the hot roasting pan and scrape up the browned bits with a wooden spoon. Place over a burner, if necessary, to loosen all bits. Pour into the stockpot. Add the parsley, dill, bay leaves, and peppercorns to the pot, add enough water to cover (about 6 quarts), bring to a simmer over high heat, and skim any foam that appears. Reduce the heat to low and simmer gently, occasionally skimming any fat, until the liquid has reduced by half, 2 to 3 hours.

3. Strain the broth through a large colander into a clean pot, pressing on the solids to extract all the liquid. Allow to cool for 2 hours, then transfer, uncovered, to the refrigerator. Cover the pot when thoroughly chilled, or transfer to smaller containers. Makes about 3 quarts.

Herbed Matzo Balls

1. In a medium-size mixing bowl, beat together the eggs, fat, or oil, and soda or seltzer. In another medium-size bowl, whisk together the matzo meal, salt, pepper, and herbs. Add the matzo meal mixture to the egg mixture and combine with a fork. Cover the bowl with plastic wrap and refrigerate for 20 to 30 minutes.

2. Bring a large pot of salted water to a boil.

3. Using wet hands, shape the matzo mixture into twenty 1½-inch balls, and using a slotted spoon, carefully lower them into the simmering water. Cook, covered, at a low simmer until the matzo balls are tender and float to the surface, about 40 minutes.

4. To serve the soup: Skim any excess fat from the top of the chilled broth and strain through a fine sieve into a clean soup pot. Bring to a simmer over medium heat and add salt to taste. Ladle the hot broth into warmed soup bowls, add 2 matzo balls to each, and garnish with the dill sprigs, if using.

Serves 10

EASY DOES IT: A quick, brown broth also can be made with the help of a plain, store-bought rotisserie chicken. Cut into large pieces, reserving the meat for another purpose, and place the bones and skin in a large soup pot. Brown the vegetables in a skillet with a little vegetable oil and add them to the pot. Follow the rest of

the instructions for Brown Chicken Broth, but reduce the amount of water by half and add 1 quart of canned, low-sodium chicken broth. Simmer for 1 hour and strain.

Ingredients:

4 large eggs, slightly beaten

¼ cup melted chicken fat or vegetable oil

2 tablespoons club soda or plain seltzer

1 cup matzo meal

1 teaspoon salt (or to taste)

Freshly ground black pepper

1 tablespoon each finely chopped, fresh parsley, dill, and chives

Slow-Cooker Brisket with Dried Fruit and Root Vegetables

Ingredients:

One 6- to 7-pound beef brisket, cut in half

Salt and freshly ground pepper to taste

3 tablespoons vegetable oil

2 large onions, peeled and thinly sliced

3 garlic cloves, minced

3 tablespoons potato starch

1 teaspoon paprika

¼ teaspoon allspice

¼ cup red wine vinegar

½ cup apple juice

4 cups low-sodium beef broth

1½ cups water

One 16-ounce bag peeled baby carrots

4 medium-size sweet potatoes, peeled and cut into 2-inch pieces

1 medium-size celeriac (celery knob), peeled and cut into 1-inch pieces

1 cup dried apricots

½ cup each dried, pitted prunes and dried apple rings

Slow cookers were no doubt designed with briskets and pot roasts in mind as the outcome is always tender and delicious, not to mention stress-free. Why bother keeping watch over a Dutch oven when you can prep this recipe in no time, then sit back and let the wondrous slow cooker do all the work?

A 6-quart cooker is best here, given the amount of vegetables and fruit included; it also provides ample space for the cooking liquid, which will become the flavorful gravy that accompanies your brisket. Here we really have two dishes rolled into one – beef brisket and tzimmes (a vegetable and fruit stew), with all the ingredients enhancing each other, producing a delectable main course that's sure to create raves at the table! Make this a day ahead, refrigerate so the flavors can intensify, and reheat the next day on low in the slow cooker itself while preparing the other parts of your menu.

First-cut brisket, which is leaner, will require less fat-skimming later, but the more marbled second cut is also fine to use if you prefer. To comfortably accommodate all the ingredients and encourage even cooking, cut the brisket in half or purchase two smaller cuts. The potato starch will help to thicken the gravy in lieu of flour, as will the dried fruit as it begins to melt. You can vary the choices and amounts of the fruit and vegetables depending on the preference of your guests, but I particularly like this combination as it creates a varied layer of delectable flavor while suggesting bounty and richness.

1. Season the brisket pieces with salt and pepper. Heat the oil in a nonstick skillet over high heat until it is almost smoking. Brown the brisket on both sides and transfer to the slow cooker in a single layer. Add the onions to the skillet, sprinkle with salt and pepper, and cook, stirring often, over medium-high heat until softened, about 8 minutes. Add the garlic and cook a further minute. Sprinkle the potato starch, paprika, and allspice over the onion mixture and stir well to coat. Pour in the vinegar and apple juice and cook until the liquid is reduced by half. Transfer the skillet contents to the slow cooker.

2. Combine the beef broth and water in a medium saucepan and bring to a boil. Pour over the brisket and onions. Distribute the remaining ingredients in the liquid around the beef. Cover and cook on the low-heat setting for 8 to 10 hours until the brisket and vegetables are fork-tender. Cool and refrigerate overnight.

3. Remove the cooked brisket from the refrigerator and skim any excess fat from the surface. While the meat is still cold, slice it thinly across the grain. Return the brisket slices to the gravy with the vegetable/fruit mixture, and reheat all on the low setting of the slow cooker. To serve, arrange the brisket slices on a large, heated platter, and using a slotted spoon, place the vegetables and fruit around. Taste the gravy for seasoning and pour over all.

Serves 10

Golden Potato Casserole

Take a break from the customary potato kugel and serve up this delicious dish of layered Yukon Gold potatoes. Lightly seasoned and dairy-free, it's the perfect accompaniment for your sweet-and-savory brisket. Bake in two separate rectangular baking dishes, one for each end of the table, and serve by cutting into squares with a metal spatula.

Yukon Gold potatoes are extremely creamy in texture and buttery in taste. They're increasingly popular as an all-purpose potato, as well as for mashing and baking. Enjoy them here where they will crisp up beautifully on the bottom and top of the casserole, while retaining their signature smoothness in the middle. Once you taste this fabulous dish, I guarantee that you'll be whipping it up more often than once a year!

1. Preheat the oven to 400 degrees.

2. Brush the bottom and sides of two 9- by 13-inch glass or ceramic baking dishes with 2 tablespoons of the oil. Cover the bottom of each dish with a layer of potatoes, sprinkle with salt and pepper, and dot with 1 tablespoon of margarine. Repeat twice.

3. Pour 1 cup of the chicken broth over each casserole, cover with foil, and bake until the potatoes are just fork-tender, about 40 minutes. Remove the foil, lightly brush the top of each casserole with the remaining oil, and continue baking, uncovered, until the tops are golden, 20 to 30 minutes. Keep the casseroles warm until you're ready to serve.

Serves 10

Ingredients:

3 tablespoons vegetable oil

5 pounds Yukon Gold potatoes, peeled and cut into ¼-inch slices

6 tablespoons unsalted, pareve margarine

Salt and pepper to taste

2 cups low-sodium chicken broth

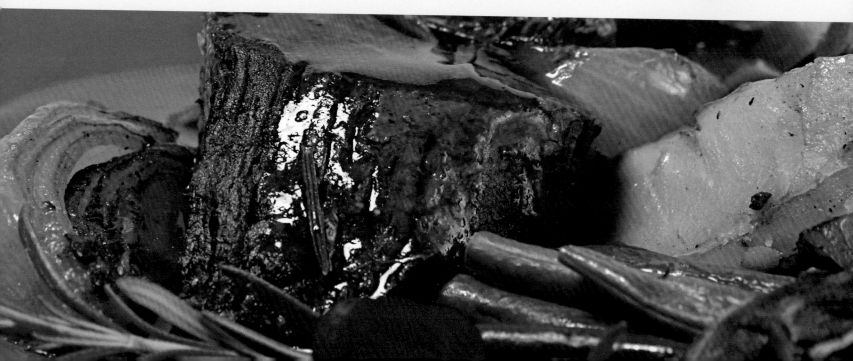

Chocolate Soufflé Torte with Raspberry Cream Drizzle

Ingredients

Chocolate Torte:

1 pound semisweet chocolate, chopped

1 cup (2 sticks) unsalted pareve margarine, plus 2 tablespoons melted to coat the pan

9 large eggs, separated

Pinch of salt

¼ cup granulated sugar, plus 1 tablespoon to dust the pan

Raspberry Cream:

1 cup seedless raspberry jam

½ cup raspberry syrup

1 tablespoon raspberry vinegar

⅔ cup nondairy creamer

To Garnish:

1 cup fresh raspberries

Confectioners' sugar

Be sure to tell your guests to save room for this amazing, delightfully rich dessert. Served warm with a cool drizzle of raspberry cream (nondairy), it's the perfect ending to your Seder meal. Unlike a true soufflé, which is served straight from the oven, poufed and airy, soufflé cakes and tortes are meant to fall and crack, creating a thick, chocolaty-rich center. You can serve this torte warm from the oven, or make it in the morning and gently reheat it in a warm oven or microwave before serving.

Raspberry sauces often contain liqueur in the form of cassis or framboise. Here, a subtle splash of raspberry vinegar will add piquancy and tang while the combination of raspberry jam and syrup will create the sweet consistency we are after. The raspberry cream can be made up to 2 days ahead. Be sure to use an unflavored, nondairy creamer – even a soy creamer works extremely well. Keep the sauce well-chilled in a jar or squeeze bottle, and shake it before drizzling. On other occasions when dairy is not an issue, you may substitute butter and heavy cream for the margarine and creamer in exact proportions.

1. Make the raspberry cream: In a medium-size saucepan, whisk together the raspberry jam, syrup, and vinegar and bring to a simmer over medium heat. Whisk until the jam has melted and the mixture has thinned. Remove from the heat, whisk in the creamer, and transfer to a jar or squeeze-bottle to chill.

2. Make the chocolate torte: Preheat the oven to 350 degrees. Brush the bottom and sides of a 9- or 10-inch springform pan with the 2 tablespoons of margarine. Line the bottom with a circle of parchment paper and dust the sides of the pan with the tablespoon of sugar, knocking out any excess.

3. In a double boiler over simmering water, melt the chocolate with the margarine and whisk until smooth. Remove from heat and cool to room temperature.

4. In a large mixing bowl, using an electric mixer, beat the egg yolks, salt, and ½ cup of the sugar on high speed until thick and pale, about 5 minutes. In another mixing bowl with clean beaters, beat the egg whites on medium-high speed until frothy. Gradually add the remaining ¼ cup of sugar and beat on high to soft peaks (when the beaters are turned upside down, the whites should stay in place).

5. Add the chocolate mixture to the egg yolk mixture and stir with a rubber spatula to combine. Add ⅓ of the egg white mixture and stir well. Gently fold in the remaining egg whites until just blended. Spoon the mixture into the prepared pan, and bake in the middle of the oven for 30 to 35 minutes, until the cake is puffy and the edges are firm, but the center is still slightly moist when a toothpick is inserted.

6. Cool on a wire rack for 20 minutes. Run a sharp knife around the edges of the pan and remove the sides. Transfer (using the parchment to slide off) to a round cake plate. If not serving immediately, cool the cake completely, then cover with plastic wrap and set aside. Reheat in a 250-degree oven, covered with foil, or microwave uncovered for 1 to 2 minutes. To serve: Cut into 10 wedges, place each on a dessert plate, and drizzle the chilled raspberry cream over. Garnish with a few fresh raspberries and a dusting of confectioners' sugar.

Serves 10

Religious Rites and the Role of Alcohol

Since biblical times, alcohol has been an integral part of rites, rituals, and sacred tradition. There are numerous references in both the Old and New Testaments to the medicinal and spiritual benefits of wine consumption in particular, wine being the most prevalent of fermented drinks during this period of history. Having "plenty" of wine was considered a blessing (Genesis 27:28), while St. Paul suggested taking "a little wine for the sake of your stomach and your frequent ailments" (1 Timothy 5:23). As was true during many periods of history, drinking wine (albeit a much more diluted version of today's wines) was an accepted daily practice and even sometimes a healthy alternative to drinking the water, which was often more susceptible to bacteria and disease. Times were most definitely different from our own, and consequently, the traditions that arose from this period reflected the attitudes and customs of that age. As a result, the Bible in no way discourages the drinking of alcohol, although it does condemn the drunkenness and excess that can result. Advice such as "wine is to be avoided if it stumbles a brother" (Romans 14:21) is an early indication that even without the benefit of modern science, the ancients were aware that while some people possessed the ability to drink in moderation, others crossed the line into impairment and addiction.

Today, we still witness the consumption of the Eucharist (communion wine) and the use of wine in the Passover service, but for many who do not drink, nonalcoholic versions of the "fruit of the vine" are considered acceptable substitutes for the real thing. Yet there are Catholic priests in recovery who still sip alcoholic wine during Mass and rabbis who imbibe during holiday rituals without consequence. With everything we know about the science of addiction, the effect of traces of alcohol on the brain, and the necessary avoidance of familiar visual cues, how can this be? It's a question that has perplexed many addiction science professionals but which may find its answer in the area of the brain often associated with drug and alcohol dependence – the anterior cingulated cortex, which governs the executive function. This part of the brain begins developing at an early age with the interaction between parent and child. Self-regulatory skills and discipline are a few of the ways the executive function manifests itself in our daily activity. It appears that when strong associations of this kind are developed at an early age, they are less likely to be dismissed even when addiction to drugs and alcohol takes hold. It has been argued that one of the reasons we find a remarkably low proportion of Jewish alcoholics is because the moderate drinking habits learned during religious rituals are so ingrained that the idea of getting drunk becomes something completely separate, which would need to be learned elsewhere and at a later age. Consequently, the normal environmental cues of wine, goblets, and toasting may hold much less power for Jewish alcoholics than for others, and the same may be true for those who have entered the priesthood at an early age.

A recent study at Columbia University, however, which addressed the low incidence of alcoholism among Jews, has suggested that it's not simply the religious learning at work here but a rare gene form that discourages excess alcohol consumption. Not unlike the well-publicized gene that affects Asian peoples, making them less likely to drink because of the unpleasant "flush" effect, a high prevalence of a similar gene, ADH2*2, was found in Jewish samples. These genes affect the initial metabolism of alcohol and can ultimately be protective against heavy drinking because of the negative physical effects. Subjects who had this gene demonstrated less-frequent drinking and fewer instances of alcohol dependence in their families. This genetic trait is often found in Ashkenazi and Sephardic Jews but not among Russians, which would explain, in part, the higher incidence of alcoholism in that group.

The way in which we process alcohol, our learned behavior, early exposure, and recent pattern of consumption are critical to understanding the reason why some people become alcohol-dependent and others do not. Once we choose recovery, however, these specifics become far less important than the actions and decisions we employ to protect and maintain sobriety. So unless you are a priest or a rabbi, sipping wine on any occasion, religious or otherwise, is obviously not a good idea. When rites and rituals present themselves, explain to family and friends the need to abstain and remain firm in your resolve by tapping into that executive function of your brain. Instead, partake of the uplifting effects of sacred traditions and family continuity as you celebrate the spring holidays without the need for alcohol.

Chapter 4

Outdoor Summer Holiday Parties

Granny's Peanut Butter Cream Pie

From the first day of summer through Labor Day weekend, we all head outdoors to celebrate the warm weather with great food in the company of friends and family. Grills are fired up and picnic tables set for gregarious get-togethers while we commemorate some of our most important national holidays. Typical parties prevail, with plenty of beer, hot dogs, and salads, without anticipation of anything different or special. Why not surprise everyone by hosting these two creative holiday spreads that feature extraordinary dishes, inspired drinks, and an atmosphere of innovative entertaining?

From a Texas-themed Fourth of July BBQ to a relaxed Indian-style picnic, you'll have the party everyone will be talking about. Surprise yourself as to how easy it all was to put together and wonder how you ever endured those boring outdoor parties of the past (no wonder everyone was drinking!). No chance of the humdrum here when you're serving some of the finest culinary creations you've ever made. Guests will be thrilled by your attention to detail and the way each delicious course is followed by another. There's no doubt your friends and family will be sorry when summer comes to a close – but they'll be waiting anxiously for next year's celebrations, to be sure!

For giant-sized fireworks on Independence Day, nothing beats an authentic Texas-style BBQ. While your neighbors are grilling the usual hot dogs and hamburgers, you'll be offering up a spicy array of traditional Texas fare to make them green with envy as the tantalizing aroma of "kicked-up" spareribs wafts over the fence. And they won't believe that all the exuberant "Yee haws!" they hear could be possible without even a drop of alcohol!

While you're grilling up the finger-licking good Spareribs with Sarsaparilla Barbecue Sauce, your guests will be dipping into the zesty, black-eyed-pea Texas Caviar while sipping away at a super-refreshing "Pink Champagne," Texas-style. The hoopla will truly begin, however, when you bring to the table your medley of traditional good old Texas BBQ dishes, including a Creamy Mac 'n' Cheese Salad and the real-deal Garlic Butter Texas Toast. By the time you're slicing Granny's Peanut Butter Cream Pie for dessert, your cowhands will be wondering whether the fireworks haven't already started. Eatin' sure never tasted so good!

A Fourth of July Texas BBQ

MENU

BBQ for Ten

APPETIZERS:

Texas Caviar with Corn Chips

Diced Pepper Jack Cheese

Honey-Roasted Peanuts

MAIN COURSE:

Grilled Spareribs with Sarsaparilla Barbecue Sauce

Creamy Mac 'n' Cheese Salad

Garlic-Butter Texas Toast

Corn on the Cob

Sliced Beefsteak Tomatoes

DESSERT:

Granny's Peanut Butter Cream Pie

Fruit Cobbler or Crumble

BEVERAGES:

To Start: Texas Pink Champagne

Throughout: *Iced Tea, Soda*

Tips on Purchased Ingredients

For cheese nibbles with a kick, nothing beats diced **Pepper Jack cheese**, a Monterey Jack laced with bits of jalapeño peppers. You may even find varieties of Jack cheese with bits of habanero chile (super hot!) or green chile and salsa. Any of these, cut into bite-size pieces, will be great for an appetizer platter. Be sure to include some other less "heated" varieties, like plain Jack or cheddar, for those who may prefer it. In fact, to go with your theme, you can even order Texas-shaped red, white, and blue wax-coated cheddar cheese cutouts online from Strykly Texas Cheese in Schulenburg, Texas (see Resources).

Honey-roasted peanuts by the handful will keep hungry folks at bay while you finish up the ribs and get everything on the table. The little bit of sweetness they offer will balance the spiciness of the Texas Caviar and Pepper Jack nicely.

When **corn on the cob** is in season, it's surely required eating at backyard barbecues, and frankly, who would argue? Tender and sweet, fresh corn needs very little cooking or doctoring. You can drop the husked cobs in a large pot of boiling water for a couple of minutes and serve them right away. Or wrap them in foil and reheat later on the grill if you have room. Everyone has a favorite method, and any one of them is fine here. Provide plenty of unsalted butter, and if you are feeling creative, brush the corn with some melted butter that's been mixed with fresh, chopped herbs before grilling – basil is particularly good.

Again, seasonality dictates, and large, fresh, sweetly ripe **beefsteak tomatoes** will definitely be a hit at the table. As with corn, when they're in peak season, little needs to be added beyond a sprinkling of coarse salt and a drizzle of olive oil. Remember never to refrigerate your tomatoes, which will cause them to lose their flavor and texture quickly.

While you're picking up the fresh corn and tomatoes at your local farmers' market, check out the baked goods that many farmers now offer as an economical use of a plentiful crop. These are usually incredibly tasty and not too expensive, so pick up a **fruit cobbler, crumble, or pie** to supplement your dessert course. And look for peaches, nectarines, plums, and all sorts of berries that will be available during the summer. They would make a dynamite fresh fruit salad if you're feeling inspired.

Texans love **iced tea** and will drink it by the gallon on a hot summer day. Buy or brew plenty and serve up pitchers on the table at mealtime. Ice-cold **soda** is also a good old standby and in fact, Texans love Dr. Pepper®! Keep cans and bottled water on ice for thirsty guests – it all will be appreciated, especially with a meal like this, full of spice and heat.

Ingredients:

Three 15-ounce cans black-eyed peas, drained and rinsed

One 4-ounce jar chopped pimientos, juice included

2 to 3 jalapeño peppers, seeded and minced

3 garlic cloves, peeled and minced

4 scallions, trimmed and thinly sliced

½ medium-size green bell pepper, cored, seeded, and finely chopped

1 medium-firm ripe tomato, seeded and chopped

¼ cup finely chopped, fresh parsley leaves

¼ teaspoon or more red cayenne pepper

⅓ cup light olive oil

½ cup apple cider vinegar

Salt and pepper to taste

Texas Caviar with Corn Chips

What to serve with Texas Pink Champagne? Why, Texas Caviar, of course! This famous dip made from black-eyed peas has many variations, but one thing is for certain: All Texans agree it must be made in advance and allowed to marinate so the flavor is at its best when served. Two or three days are probably enough – just keep it in a covered container in the refrigerator and give it an occasional stir. While this dish is usually quite spicy, the level of heat is up to you in the quantity of jalapeños you add as well as the cayenne pepper. Remember, however, that it will get hotter and hotter the longer it's allowed to sit.

You can replace one can of black-eyed peas with an equivalent amount of canned white hominy (delicious cooked corn kernels that have had the hull and husk removed), popularly used in Hispanic cuisine. I love hominy and am always looking for an excuse to use it in a recipe, but sometimes it is difficult to find so I am excluding it here. The usual "scoops" for your "caviar" are tortilla chips (or saltine crackers – a Texas favorite). But any type of large corn chip goes well, Fritos Scoops!® being my favorite.

1. In a large mixing bowl, combine all the ingredients and stir together with a rubber spatula. Transfer to a covered container and refrigerate, stirring occasionally, for 1 or 2 days and up to 1 week.

2. To serve, mound the "caviar" on a large, round serving platter and surround with the corn chips or crackers.

Serves 10

Garlic-Butter Texas Toast

1 cup (2 sticks) unsalted butter, softened

6 garlic cloves, peeled and minced

Salt and cayenne pepper to taste

2 loaves firm white bread, cut into 1-inch-thick slices

No Texas-style barbecue would be complete without Texas toast, the Lone Star State's answer to garlic bread. Huge slices of firm white bread, slathered with garlic butter and plopped on the grill, Texas toast is the perfect accompaniment for your Independence Day cookout.

Buy whole, unsliced loaves of bread, sometimes called Pullman loaves, or look for thick, presliced packages occasionally available in the bread aisle. Sourdough and Italian varieties of bread also work well, but to be authentic, stick with the real thing. These take mere minutes to grill, so they can be done just before you sit down to eat. You can also embellish them by sprinkling some shredded cheese on top for melting or adding chopped fresh or dried parsley flakes to the butter mixture.

In a small mixing bowl, stir together the butter, garlic, salt, and cayenne pepper. Spread a thin layer of the butter mixture on both sides of the bread slices and toast on the outer edge of a gas or charcoal grill until lightly golden, 1 to 2 minutes per side. Serve immediately.

Serves 10

Alcohol-Free Substitutes for Wine and Spirits

To simply leave out something from a recipe when we run across an unwanted ingredient, such as alcohol, can result in a drastic change in the outcome of a dish. Usually, that ingredient contributes something to the flavor, texture, and overall balance evident in the result and, as such, needs an appropriate substitute if we hope to re-create something as close to the original as possible.

When alcohol is called for in reasonably small amounts (½ cup or less for wines and spirits), the following list of substitutes will work fine (see also pages 177, Substituting for Liqueurs: Adding More Than Flavor). Use this list as a base for your own enhancements and preferences. For a recipe where alcohol is a primary ingredient and called for in a large amount, it's best to either forgo making the dish or create a "mock" version of the original by changing other ingredients and perhaps even the technique used in the recipe. For example, a dish like *coq au vin*, in which wine is required in a great amount, would need to be reworked from its initial marinating stage to the resulting sauce. The outcome will not be exact, but it can be very close. Basic trial and error is required in instances such as these but will be well worth the effort. Experiment with some of the new flavored vinegars, reduce fruit juices into concentrates, and add alcohol-free flavored syrups and extracts for even more variety. Before long, you'll gain a feel for what the right substitute should be.

When very small amounts of alcohol are called for in a recipe (what I like to refer to as "cameo roles"), the alcohol can sometimes be eliminated entirely, especially if its contribution is for no more than show. By increasing another liquid in the recipe by the same amount you are eliminating, you may be able to resolve the issue. But consider whether there's something unique the alcohol is adding before doing so, and think about how it could be replaced with another flavorful ingredient that's alcohol-free and safe to use.

Alcohol Ingredient	Substitute	Tips and Uses
White Wine (light and dry)	3 parts white grape juice 1 part white wine vinegar	poultry and general use
White Wine (dry and tart)	3 parts white grape juice 1 part lemon juice	shellfish and seafood
White Wine (slightly sweet)	3 parts apple juice 1 part apple cider vinegar	pork and veal
White Wine (sweet)	3 parts white cranberry juice 1 part white balsamic vinegar	desserts
Red Wine (light and dry)	3 parts red grape juice 1 part red wine vinegar	general use
Red Wine (full-bodied)	3 parts red grape juice 1 part balsamic vinegar	beef and game
Red Wine, Port (dark and sweet)	3 parts red grape juice 1 part black currant juice	desserts
Champagne (bubbly and tart)	3 parts sparkling grape juice 1 part lemon juice	light sauces

Alcohol Ingredient	Substitute	Tips and Uses
Brandy, Cognac	1 part apple cider 1 part balsamic vinegar	full-bodied sauces
Sherry (dry)	2 parts apple juice 1 part sherry vinegar	marinades
Sherry (sweet)	2 parts apple juice 1 part sherry vinegar 1 teaspoon sugar	desserts
Bourbon, Whiskey	3 parts apple juice 1 part balsamic vinegar dash alcohol-free vanilla extract	pan sauces
Rum	1 part brewed tea 1 part simple syrup*	sauces and moistening cakes
Beer	ginger beer or club soda splash of barley water	batters for frying
Dark Beer, Stout	root beer or birch beer splash of strong tea	braising

* Simple sugar consists of equal parts granulated sugar and water brought to a boil to dissolve the sugar.

Grilled Spareribs with Sarsaparilla Barbecue Sauce

Ingredients

Dry Rub:

1 cup granulated sugar

3 tablespoons sweet paprika

2½ tablespoons coarse salt

2 tablespoons ground black pepper

1½ tablespoons garlic powder

½ teaspoon cayenne pepper, or to taste

Spareribs:

3 or 4 racks pork spareribs, cut in half and trimmed of excess fat

3 cups hickory wood smoking chips, soaked in cold water for 30 minutes

Oil for the grill

Sarsaparilla Barbecue Sauce
(see recipe that follows)

You can be sure that the Fourth of July will find some type of ribs on the grill – baby back or beef, rubbed, or smoked; all cuts and methods are popular barbecue fare, but true Texas rib aficionados will be turning to the common pork sparerib for the most uncommonly delicious and flavorful result. Spareribs come from the lower portion of the ribs and are usually fattier, contributing to their flavor. A normal rack can weigh about 3 to 5 pounds (mostly bone) and in general, one pound per person is an adequate portion size. Three racks will serve 10 people nicely, but if your BBQ guests are big eaters, err on the side of more and throw in one extra. When racks are cut in half, they're called slabs. Slabs are easier to work with, so cut each rack in two and trim away any excess fat before beginning.

Dry rubs are a great way to enhance the flavor of all meats that end up on the grill so plan to rub the slabs a day ahead. Smoking is another way to enhance flavor, and many experienced grill masters swear by it. It can be an intricate and long process, however, so to get the best of both worlds, we'll be roasting the ribs first in the oven and then finishing them on the grill over some smoky wood chips. A last-minute baste with the delicious accompanying barbecue sauce will add a final layer of flavor.

Many basting and barbecue sauces contain alcohol in the form of beer or bourbon because their tenderizing properties contribute to a better result. Here, sarsaparilla soda, a popular beverage of the Old West, will perform the same function and add a subtle sweetness to the sauce. Birch beer or root beer also can be used. For the best flavor and finish, try to find a good-quality soda made from pure cane sugar rather than high-fructose corn syrup. The sauce can be made up to a week ahead and refrigerated until the Fourth of July.

1. In a small mixing bowl, whisk together the dry-rub ingredients. Massage the rub into the meat sides of the sparerib slabs, wrap well in plastic (2 slabs together is fine), and refrigerate overnight.

2. Preheat the oven to 275 degrees. Unwrap the slabs and place, slightly overlapping, in 2 large roasting pans. Bake uncovered, periodically pouring out the rendered fat, until the ribs are tender, 3 to 4 hours.

3. Preheat a charcoal or gas grill to medium low and place the soaked wood chips over the coals or in a smoker box. Lightly oil the grill grates and place the ribs in a single layer on the grill (work in batches if necessary) and cook, turning occasionally, 20 minutes. Baste the ribs with the barbecue sauce during the last 10 minutes of grilling. Transfer to a cutting board, slice down between the rib bones to make individual portions, and serve immediately with extra barbecue sauce for dipping.

Serves 10

Creamy Mac 'n' Cheese Salad

This cool and creamy macaroni salad, dotted with bits of delicious orange cheddar cheese, is the perfect complement to your smoked and spicy ribs. The secret to its creaminess is a double dose of mayonnaise and milk, one the night before and the other just before serving. Your guests will be reaching for seconds and thirds before the meal is through.

Finely diced cheddar cheese works best in this dish, and if you're able to find pre-diced or crumbled cheese (as opposed to shredded) in packages, it will save you time. If not, simply slice a cheddar chunk into ¼-inch-thick slices and crumble with your fingers. Half a pound of solid cheese will yield about 2 cups diced or crumbled. Mild, medium, or sharp cheddar is fine to use, whichever you prefer.

1. In a large mixing bowl, combine the cooked macaroni, onion, celery, relish, and pimiento and stir gently. In a small mixing bowl, whisk together 1 cup of the mayonnaise, all the sour cream, and ¼ cup of the milk. Add to the macaroni and stir well to coat. Season lightly with salt and pepper, and stir in the cheese. Cover with plastic wrap and refrigerate overnight.

2. Remove the macaroni salad from the refrigerator and stir to loosen (mixture will be somewhat dry). In a small mixing bowl, whisk together the remaining ½ cup mayonnaise and ¼ cup of milk, and add to the salad, stirring until creamy. Taste for the addition of salt and pepper, and serve immediately.

Serves 10

Ingredients:

1 pound elbow macaroni, cooked, drained, and rinsed under cold water to cool

1 small onion, finely chopped

1 medium-size celery stalk, peeled and finely chopped

½ cup sweet pickle relish

⅓ cup chopped pimiento

1½ cups mayonnaise

½ cup sour cream

½ cup milk

Salt and pepper to taste

1½ cups diced or crumbled orange cheddar cheese

Sarsaparilla Barbecue Sauce

1. Combine all the ingredients in a medium-size saucepan. Bring to a boil over medium heat, stirring occasionally. Reduce heat to medium low and allow mixture to simmer about 20 minutes, until thickened and reduced by half. Stir to prevent sticking.

2. Taste for seasoning, including sugar and lemon juice, adjust if necessary, and cool before storing in a covered container in the refrigerator. Use to baste spareribs and as a dipping sauce.

Serves 10

2 cups sarsaparilla soda

2 cups ketchup

½ medium-size onion, finely chopped

¼ cup apple cider vinegar

¼ cup fresh lemon juice

1 tablespoon Worcestershire sauce

1 tablespoon light molasses

1 tablespoon brown sugar

2 teaspoons chili powder

1 teaspoon each ground cumin, paprika, and garlic powder

½ teaspoon each ground ginger and coriander

Salt and pepper to taste

Dash cayenne pepper or more to taste

Granny's Peanut Butter Cream Pie

Ingredients:

1 cup creamy peanut butter

One 8-ounce package
cream cheese, softened

1 cup sugar

2 tablespoons
unsalted butter, melted

1 cup whipping cream

1 teaspoon alcohol-free vanilla
extract

One 9-inch prepared
graham cracker pie crust

1 jar hot fudge sauce

Here's a super finish to your Fourth of July Texas barbecue – and a dessert that will no doubt be requested in the future on a regular basis. Surprisingly light and fluffy, but full of creamy flavor, this no-bake peanut butter cream pie is so easy to prepare you may decide to make two, just in case.

Ordinary commercial creamy peanut butter is best for this recipe as the fresh-ground natural types have a tendency to separate. Pre-made graham cracker pie crusts make this a breeze to prepare, but you can make one from scratch if you prefer. You can also try using prepared chocolate cookie crusts, which would go equally well with the peanut butter flavor. Purchase a good-quality hot fudge sauce and just before serving, heat it in the microwave and drizzle over the top of the pie or over each individual slice. When you serve up this incredible finale, don't be surprised to hear a universal "Yum" and "Yes, please," no matter how full of ribs your guests may be!

1. In a medium-size bowl using an electric mixer, beat together the peanut butter, cream cheese, sugar, and butter on high speed until smooth and creamy, 2 to 3 minutes. In another medium-size mixing bowl with clean beaters, beat the cream and vanilla together to form stiff peaks. Stir ⅓ of the whipped cream into the peanut butter mixture to loosen it, then fold in the rest. Pour the mixture into the pie crust and spread evenly. Refrigerate overnight.

2. When ready to serve, heat the hot fudge sauce in the microwave according to jar directions and, using a fork, dip and drizzle the hot fudge over the top of the pie or over each slice of pie. Serve immediately.

Serves 10

Texas Pink Champagne

Start things off with this novel, refreshing drink that makes the most of the state fruit of Texas – the red grapefruit. Texas produces two of the world's finest varieties: the Ruby Sweet and the Rio Star, important crops since the early 1900s. These grapefruits are enjoyed in many recipes as well as on their own, and here they add a lovely pink hue to lemon-lime soda for a super thirst-quenching drink. Fresh-squeezed is of course the best for flavor, but feel free to purchase a carton of ruby red grapefruit juice to save time. In a pinch, you can substitute pink grapefruits or their juice, or even the red-colored blood orange for those who shouldn't mix grapefruit with certain medications. In any case, strain the grapefruit juice, fresh or refrigerated, to remove the pulp so the appearance of your "champagne" is less cloudy.

Make Texas Pink Champagne just before serving to maximize the fizz of the soda. Having everything well chilled will eliminate the need for ice in the glasses unless it's a really hot day. Champagne flutes are a bit too dainty for a Texas BBQ. Choose tumblers or collins glasses instead, or festive red, white, and blue plastic cups.

Stir together the grapefruit juice and soda, and serve ice-cold in tumblers or cups. Keep unused portions refrigerated.

Serves 10

8 cups (64 ounces)
ruby red grapefruit juice
(about a dozen whole
grapefruits juiced),
strained and chilled

Two 32-ounce bottles
lemon-lime soda, chilled

Why not enjoy the last day of official summer celebrations without the usual backyard and grill, and plan a picnic with pizzazz away from home? Load up everybody with the food and head out to a beautiful state park or a local picnic area to enjoy the final holiday of summer. And to make it a picnic to remember, try this Indian-inspired menu full of flavor and spice.

A Cool Cucumber Soup will start things off while guests munch on crispy pappadums and their fixings. And traditional picnic fare with a Punjabi twist will delight your guests as they soak up the last of the summer sun. From Bombay Fried Chicken to an extraordinarily delicious version of strawberry shortcake, your creativity will be applauded with every bite. And each dish is easy to transport and even easier to set up. Bring along a colorful Indian-patterned tablecloth for the table and some comfy pillows for lounging. No one will miss the alcohol as they sip the fabulously refreshing Pineapple Lemonade Spritzers you've concocted to cool the "heat" of Punjabi spices and curry. It's a picnic that everyone will remember and relish in the months to come, and a nearly "laborless" Labor Day celebration for you!

A Labor Day Punjabi Picnic

MENU

Picnic for Six

APPETIZERS:

Punjabi Snack Mix

Cool Cucumber Soup with Mint and Cumin

Pappadums with Relishes and Chutneys

MAIN COURSE:

Bombay Fried Chicken

Curried Rice Salad with Mango Raita

Indian-Spiced Ratatouille

Naan

DESSERT:

Cardamom Shortcakes with Strawberries in Honey Syrup

Nut Brittle and Coconut Clusters

BEVERAGES:

Appetizers and Main Course:

Pineapple Lemonade Spritzers

Dessert: *Assorted Iced Coffee Drinks*

Tips on Purchased Ingredients

Crunchy snack medleys like *Punjabi snack mix* are India's answer to Chex® Party Mix. Highly spiced and deliciously tangy, these mixes vary from region to region but generally contain nuts, crackers, and roasted legumes like lentils and peas. Many grocery stores carry a generic variety, but Indian specialty stores will have dozens of mixes to choose from, ranging in heat from mild to super hot.

Pappadums are delightfully crunchy, wafer-thin crisp breads made from lentil flour and come plain or flavored, usually with black pepper or garlic. They're served at many Indian restaurants before the meal, with an array of spicy and sweet condiments called relishes, pickles, and chutneys. Pappadums usually come in flat disks, which are then fried or microwaved to puff them up. Some specialty grocers sell ready-made pappadums or pappadum chips, which would save you some time. If frying, prepare them ahead and store in a zipper-locked bag to retain crispness. Bring a basket along to serve them in.

Indian **relishes** and **pickles** are distinctly tangy and are usually quite sour and/or spicy. Diners apply little dabs (very little!) on pieces of pappadums as a condiment. The most popular Indian pickles, usually found in the international section of your supermarket, are lime, chili, and garlic. **Chutneys**, which are essentially sweet but also can be spicy, help to counterbalance the intense sourness of the pickles. Most are mango-based, like Major Grey's Chutney, but many other fruits are also used to make chutneys. Pear, date, and even tomato are just some of the varieties available. If you're able to find an Indian grocer, you'll discover a diverse selection of relishes, pickles, and chutneys to choose from. You can also order many items online (see Resources). Select several and bring them to serve directly from the jar with small spoons. These require refrigeration only after they're opened.

Naan is probably the most well-known Indian bread, traditionally baked in Tandoori ovens. It's usually found fresh in the bread aisle. More unusual types of Indian breads include *paratha* (flaky flatbreads often stuffed with spiced potatoes), *chapatis*, and *rotis*. Although restaurants will serve them warm, they're just as delicious at room temperature. One or two varieties would be nice, wrapped in a large, colorful cloth napkin and placed on the picnic table to accompany your main course.

For continued munching after dessert, a variety of **nut brittles** such as cashew, almond, and of course peanut would be a nice touch. And for a bit of chocolate, offer some **toasted coconut clusters** to complement your iced coffees.

On a hot, end-of-summer day, a cup of steaming coffee is probably not what we're after to accompany our dessert, yet we may still have a hankering for the flavor. The solution is one of the many **assorted iced coffee drinks** now available in the beverage aisle of the supermarket. Starbucks and other companies make a nice variety, including iced coffee frappés and cappuccinos. Chill a selection in the cooler to offer when dessert time rolls around.

Pineapple Lemonade Spritzer

This zesty spritzer is the perfect refreshing cold drink to sip with your Punjabi menu. It's easy to prepare ahead and compact to travel with. Simply make the pineapple syrup the night before and keep it well chilled. Also, chill some bottles of club soda or sparkling water, and when you get to your destination, you can combine them with ice for a super-quick serve.

The proportion of soda to syrup is about 5:1, but guests can decide how sweet they'd like their spritzer to be and add as little or as much soda as they please.

Canned or fresh pineapple juice is fine to use, but freshly squeezed lemons will add a much better flavor than a bottled version, so take the time to do this. When choosing your lemons, they should be heavy for their size, firm, plump, and unblemished. A brief zap in the microwave (about 15 seconds) will maximize the juice yield before squeezing.

Ingredients:

6 cups pineapple juice

Juice of 6 large lemons

2 cups granulated sugar

1 cup honey

Two 2-liter bottles club soda
or sparkling water

1. In a medium-size saucepan, combine the pineapple and lemon juices, as well as the sugar and honey, and bring to a boil over medium heat, stirring occasionally. Cook for 1 minute, remove from the heat, and transfer to 1 or 2 heat-proof jars. Cool, then chill in the refrigerator several hours or overnight.

2. To make the spritzers, fill a 12- to 14-ounce tumbler with ice, add about ¼ cup of the syrup, and stir in the club soda to fill. Serve immediately.

Serves 6

Alcohol Abuse and Dependence in the Labor Market: Who's at Risk?

According to SAMHSA (Substance Abuse and Mental Health Services Administration), approximately 10 percent of America's workforce regularly abuses or is dependent on alcohol or drugs. Those who work in the construction and mining industries topped a recent list that examined alcoholism in America's workplace. But it appears that corporate employees may be just as much at risk. Drinking in high-pressure professional environments can also create potential for substance abuse and dependence. In fact, the American Bar Association has found that the legal profession carries the highest risk, with between 15 and 18 percent of attorneys admitting to abuse of alcohol or drugs.

Although absenteeism and poor job performance related to alcohol are estimated to cost as much as $148 billion annually, it does not appear that the alcohol-dependent are to blame. New research has discovered that it's the light to moderate drinkers who, primarily due to hangovers, miss work or are unable to carry out their duties when they

Cool Cucumber Soup with Mint and Cumin

On a hot day, a chilled and creamy soup can hit the spot, and this one will start your Indian-style picnic off beautifully. Sort of a cross between a yogurt *raita* and a *lassi* drink, the cucumbers combined with fresh mint and cumin provide a unique taste experience that's cooling to the palate as you munch on pappadums with spicy pickles and chutneys.

If you purchase the seedless, burpless English cucumbers, your little bit of labor will be even more reduced as they don't require peeling. Just wash them, cut off the ends, and you're ready to chop. If you use regular cucumbers, you'll need to remove their waxy skins and seeds. After you peel them, slice them in half lengthwise and use a teaspoon to scoop out the seedy middle section before you chop them and add them to the blender. If you prepare this dish the night before, the flavors will intensify and you may find that it doesn't require further seasoning, so hold off on making any heavy additions of salt and pepper until then. Some diced cucumber, stored in a little sandwich bag, can be kept in the cooler and spooned on top of everyone's soup as a garnish.

1. Working in 2 batches if necessary, purée all the ingredients in an electric blender until smooth. Transfer the mixture to a storage container, taste for seasoning, and chill for several hours or overnight.

2. To serve, stir well and pour into bowls or cups, garnishing with the diced cucumber.

Serves 6

Ingredients:

1½ medium-size English cucumbers or 2 to 3 waxy cucumbers, prepared as directed in recipe (to make about 4 cups roughly chopped)

3 scallions, trimmed and roughly chopped

2 cups plain low-fat yogurt

1 cup buttermilk

½ cup milk

¼ cup roughly chopped, fresh mint leaves

1 teaspoon ground cumin

Juice of half a lemon

Salt and pepper to taste

To garnish: 1 small Kirby, or pickling, cucumber, ends trimmed, and cut into small dice

---

do report to the job. Employees with hangovers pose a danger not only to themselves but also to their colleagues, even long after their blood-alcohol levels return to normal. This is because hangovers greatly diminish cognitive abilities, concentration, and technical skills; surprisingly, in many instances impairment during a hangover can be greater than if the employee were still inebriated.

Companies that offer an Employee Assistance Program (EAP) for help with abuse, addiction, and/or a family member's alcohol or drug problem have shown significant improvements in job-related performance, with a recent study in Ohio finding between an 88 and 97 percent reduction in absenteeism, problems with colleagues, mistakes, and injuries at work where EAPs are in effect. According to the U.S. Department of Labor, establishing similar programs throughout the American labor force can only result in a "win-win" situation for all. For more information on EAPs and Drug-Free Workplace Programs, visit http://dwp.samhsa.gov.

Bombay Fried Chicken

Ingredients:

2 cups buttermilk

3 tablespoons curry powder

1 teaspoon ground cumin

Salt and pepper to taste

6 chicken drumsticks on the bone with skin

6 chicken thighs on the bone with skin

4 split chicken breasts, cut into halves

For Dredging:

2 cups all-purpose flour

1 tablespoon paprika

2 teaspoons curry powder

1 teaspoon red cayenne pepper

Salt and pepper to taste

Canola oil for frying

This super-delicious fried chicken with an Indian kick will put all other Labor Day fried chicken dishes to shame. It's marinated in true Punjabi style, with buttermilk and spices, then coated and fried crispy and golden. Make sure there is plenty to go around. Plan to marinate your chicken pieces overnight, then fry them up the morning of the picnic for peak results.

When it comes to frying chicken of any variety, legs and thighs tend to do best, but you can certainly add a few breasts for those who prefer them. Use a cleaver or heavy chef's knife to cut the breasts in half so they're a manageable size for frying, and to avoid overcooking them, fry in a separate skillet to keep a watchful eye on them. Wings also fry well, but trim off the wing tips before pan-frying. Fry the chicken at least a couple of hours beforehand, and serve at room temperature.

1. In a large shallow pan or casserole, whisk together the buttermilk, curry powder, and cumin. Place the chicken pieces in the mixture, sprinkle with salt and pepper, and turn the pieces a few times to coat. Cover with foil and refrigerate overnight.

2. In a medium-size mixing bowl, whisk together the flour, paprika, curry powder, cayenne, salt, and pepper. Remove the chicken from the refrigerator, and one piece at a time, dredge in the flour, shake off the excess, and place on a wire rack. After all the pieces have been coated, dredge them again, shake off the excess, and let them rest on the rack until the oil is ready to fry.

3. In a large, heavy skillet (or 2 skillets), pour ½ inch canola oil. Heat the oil on medium high to about 375 degrees (or until the oil sizzles and browns a cube of bread added to the skillet). Carefully place the chicken pieces skin side down in the hot oil without crowding, reduce the heat to medium low, and cover the skillet. Cook until golden brown, 10 to 12 minutes. Remove the lid, turn the chicken pieces over with tongs, and continue to fry, uncovered, until completely browned and cooked through, about 5 minutes more for the white meat and 10 minutes more for the dark. Transfer to brown paper or paper towels and allow to cool to room temperature.

Pack in a container for picnicking or serve immediately.

Serves 6

Indian-Spiced Ratatouille

The classic French vegetable dish gets a Punjabi twist in this rendition of ratatouille. Fresh ginger, jalapeño, and Indian spices add a wonderful aroma and flavor that go perfectly with the rice salad and fried chicken. This dish is served cold like a salad, and the delicious Indian breads you've purchased are great for scooping up every delectable bit.

As in the making of traditional ratatouille, it's important to sauté and season each element so that the result is a continuous layer of deep flavor. And like many other dishes, it will continue to develop its flavor the longer it has to sit, so making it a day ahead, or more, is certainly encouraged. There should be no shortage of eggplant, zucchini, summer squash, and bell peppers this time of year, and this is a great way to use these farm-fresh vegetables we often find in such abundance during the late summer. As for the tomatoes, use fresh, if available (remove their peels after dipping them briefly in boiling water, then seed and chop them to make about 2 cups). If you come across white eggplant, definitely use it. It has a terrific taste, is less bitter than its purple counterpart, and tends to have fewer seeds than other varieties. Although its skin is a bit thinner and in many recipes does not require peeling, I still prefer to remove the skin for a dish like this. Lavender-colored eggplant is very similar and can be used as well.

1. Heat the oil in a large skillet over medium-high heat and add the onions and bell peppers. Sprinkle with salt and pepper and cook, stirring often, until the vegetables are softened and nearly tender, about 5 minutes. Add 1/3 of the garlic, ginger root, and jalapeño, stir to combine, and cook a further minute. Transfer contents of skillet to a large, heavy pot and set aside.

2. Add a touch more oil to the skillet and cook the zucchini and yellow squash in the same manner, transferring when done to the pot with the onions and peppers. Again, add more oil to the pan, and cook the eggplant (add oil as necessary) in the same way until nearly fork-tender, finishing with the remaining garlic, ginger root, and jalapeño. Combine with the other vegetables in the large pot.

3. Add the chopped tomatoes, tomato sauce, all the spices, and sugar to the vegetable pot, stir well to combine, and cook over medium heat, stirring often, until all the vegetables are fork-tender and nearly all the liquid has evaporated. Taste for seasoning, stir in the lemon juice, cilantro, and mint leaves, and remove from the heat. Cool and store in a covered container in the refrigerator. Bring to room temperature before serving.

Serves 6

Ingredients:

3 tablespoons olive oil, plus more for sautéing all the vegetables

2 medium-size onions, chopped

1 medium-size green bell pepper, cored, seeded, and cut into 3/4-inch dice

1 medium-size red or orange bell pepper, cored, seeded, and cut into 3/4-inch dice

Salt and pepper to taste

5 garlic cloves, minced

One 1-inch piece fresh ginger root, peeled and minced

1 jalapeño pepper, trimmed, seeded, and minced

1 1/2 pounds eggplant (preferably white), trimmed, peeled, and cut into 3/4-inch dice

2 medium-size zucchini, cut into 1/2-inch-thick half-moons

1 medium-size yellow summer squash, cut into 1/2-inch-thick half-moons

One 15-ounce can diced tomatoes, including juice (or 2 cups fresh – see recipe introduction)

1 cup tomato sauce

2 teaspoons turmeric

1 teaspoon ground cumin

1/4 teaspoon each ground coriander and cardamom

Pinch of sugar

1 tablespoon fresh lemon juice

2 tablespoons finely chopped fresh cilantro leaves

1 tablespoon finely chopped fresh mint leaves

Curried Rice Salad with Mango Raita

Rice salads are usually upstaged by traditional macaroni or potato salads during the summer because they often lack flavor and interest. One of the best ways to create a lively rice salad is to make use of intense spices such as those used in Indian cooking. Curry goes hand in hand with rice, and in a salad – embellished with a little onion, bell pepper, and other delightful ingredients – they are super partners. You'll be looking for an excuse to whip this up in the future. Although basmati rice is certainly the rice of choice for curry dishes served hot, in this instance, a long-grain variety works best to provide substance and absorb the layers of flavor. Be sure it has cooled well before dressing.

Raita is the traditional yogurt sauce accompaniment for Indian food and is most often made with cucumbers and spices. But fruit raitas are also very popular in this type of cuisine because they add a simple sweetness that complements the spicy heat of many recipes. Purchase mangoes that are nicely ripe yet still firm to the touch for the best dicing results. Cut down on each side of the large, flat seed, crosshatch the flesh of each half with a sharp paring knife to create a small dice pattern, then turn the mango half inside out. From there, you can easily cut the little cubes away from the skin directly into the bowl.

Travel with the separate components of this dish tucked inside the cooler and put together the platter when you arrive. A bag of pre-shredded lettuce will make things easy. The raita can be served straight from its container or transferred to a decorative bowl. Don't forget the serving spoons.

Ingredients

Rice Salad:

2 cups raw long-grain rice, cooked according to package directions (about 7 cups cooked)

3 tablespoons canola oil

1 large onion, cut into small dice

Salt and pepper to taste

8 ounces white mushrooms, wiped clean, stems trimmed, and thinly sliced

1/2 large red bell pepper, cut into small dice

1 cup frozen petit peas, thawed

3/4 cup seedless raisins

1/2 cup slivered almonds

1 cup low-sodium chicken broth

1/4 cup mango chutney

Juice of 1 lemon

1 1/2 tablespoons curry powder

Olive oil for drizzling

To Serve:

4 cups shredded lettuce

Mango raita
(see recipe on next page)

1. Once the rice is cooked, fluff with a fork and immediately spread out on 2 large, rimmed baking sheets. Refrigerate uncovered on the sheets until very cold.

2. Heat the oil in a large skillet, add the onion and a sprinkle of salt and pepper, and cook over medium-high heat, stirring often, until the onions are soft and translucent, about 5 minutes. Reduce the heat, if necessary, to prevent browning. Add the mushrooms and continue to cook, stirring occasionally, until they have softened but not browned. Stir in the bell pepper, peas, raisins, and almonds, and cook for 1 minute. Remove from the heat.

3. In a small mixing bowl, whisk together the chicken broth, chutney, lemon juice, and curry powder, and pour this over the vegetable mixture in the skillet. Stir to coat and allow to come to room temperature.

4. Transfer the chilled rice to a large mixing bowl. Add the cooled skillet mixture and gently fold in. Season with salt and pepper, cover, and refrigerate several hours or overnight, tossing occasionally. Before serving, gently stir in a drizzle of olive oil and taste for additional seasoning.

5. To present: Arrange the shredded lettuce around the edge of a large, round platter and mound the rice salad in the middle. Serve with the mango raita on the side.

Serves 6

Mango Raita

In a medium-size mixing bowl, stir together all the ingredients until well combined. Cover and refrigerate until ready to serve. Can be prepared a day ahead.

Serves 6

Ingredients:

2 cups plain low-fat yogurt, drained of excess liquid

2 large mangoes, cut into small dice (see recipe introduction)

Juice of half a lemon

1 teaspoon granulated sugar

2 tablespoons each finely chopped fresh mint and cilantro leaves

Cardamom Shortcakes with Strawberries in Honey Syrup

Ingredients

Shortcakes:

1½ cups all-purpose flour

½ cup cake flour (not self-rising)

2 tablespoons granulated sugar

1 tablespoon baking powder

1 teaspoon ground cardamom

½ teaspoon baking soda

½ teaspoon salt

6 tablespoons (¾ stick) unsalted butter, diced and slightly softened

1 cup buttermilk

Strawberries:

2 pounds fresh strawberries, washed, hulled, and sliced

2 tablespoons granulated sugar

1 cup honey

½ cup water

Pinch ground cardamom

2 teaspoons rosewater

To Serve:

Sweetened whipped cream

Here's the perfect end-of-summer dessert for your Punjabi picnic – an exotic take on the common strawberry shortcake. Tender, flaky buttermilk biscuits with a hint of cardamom are deliciously doused in a honey and rosewater syrup with fresh, sweet strawberries. Some fresh whipped cream that you've surreptitiously tucked away in the cooler will top this off with delicious style.

Shortcake- or biscuit-making is really an easy thing to do. Minimal working of the dough is important to maintain a light and flaky texture, and a 2-inch biscuit cutter dipped in flour will allow for easy uniformity. You can make the shortcakes the night before and, when they are cooled, store them in a zipper-locked bag to retain freshness. Remember to bring a small serrated knife to slice them at the picnic.

Fresh strawberries will naturally make a sweet syrup of their own when sprinkled with a bit of sugar and allowed to macerate. Sometimes, to provide more flavor and liquid, this marinating process includes a liqueur or other alcoholic beverage. Here, we'll be adding honey and the wonderfully fragrant rosewater for another boost of delicious taste instead. Prepare the strawberries earlier in the day and allow them to develop their syrup and flavor in the refrigerator for a couple of hours. If you would rather not whip fresh cream for the topping, a can of sweetened whipped cream can easily be added to your cooler instead.

1. Make the biscuits: Preheat the oven to 375 degrees. In a large mixing bowl, whisk together both flours, sugar, baking powder, cardamom, baking soda, and salt. Add the diced butter and, using a pastry blender or your fingertips, gently work the butter into the dry ingredients until the mixture resembles sand and small peas. Add the buttermilk. Using a wooden spoon, stir quickly to combine, without overmixing. Bring the dough together with your hands (add a little flour if necessary) and transfer to a floured work surface.

2. Pat the dough out into a circle that is 1 inch thick. Using a 2-inch biscuit cutter, cut out individual shortcakes from the circle. Transfer them to a nonstick or lightly greased baking pan about 1½ inches apart. Gather any leftover dough together and use to make additional biscuits. Bake 15 to 20 minutes, until the bottoms are golden and a toothpick inserted in the center comes out clean. Transfer to a wire rack to cool.

3. Prepare the strawberries: Place the sliced strawberries in a large bowl and sprinkle with the 2 tablespoons of sugar. Toss gently and refrigerate.

4. In a small saucepan, stir together the honey, water, and cardamom. Over medium-high heat, bring to a boil, stirring occasionally. Boil for 1 minute, remove from the heat, and stir in the rosewater. Allow the syrup to cool completely. Pour the cooled syrup over the strawberry mixture, toss gently, cover, and refrigerate.

5. To serve, slice the shortcakes in half horizontally and place them opened up in individual serving bowls. Spoon the strawberry mixture with some of the syrup over the shortcake halves, add a dollop of whipped cream, and serve immediately. Or stack the shortcake halves, alternating the strawberry mixture and whipped cream.

Serves 6

Chapter 5

Creamed White Root Vegetables

Welcoming the Harvest

We can feel it in the air – that crisp nip that hints at the winter soon to come. Fall is suddenly upon us, and with it, two of our most cherished holidays: Halloween and Thanksgiving. It's a great season to gather together in the warmth of the place we call home and serve up comforting food as we enjoy each other's company and celebrate the beginning of a bountiful harvest. What better time to play host than when some of the most delicious foods and drinks are plentiful? From fresh apple ciders to super sweet potatoes, they all come into their own at this time of year and lure us into the kitchen for some extra-special cooking and celebrating.

If you've never planned a Halloween party for your inner child, now is the time. Make the most of what the season has to offer and host an amazing Spanish-themed tapas party with everything from wickedly spicy Vampiro Sangritas drinks to the traditional Pan de Muerto, or Bread of the Dead. Then take on, without trepidation, the annual Thanksgiving feast, with a menu guaranteed to please everyone, from the smallest pilgrim to the most seasoned relative, and all without a drop of alcohol in the pan or on the table. And they said it couldn't be done. Try these two deliciously innovative menus and prove the naysayers wrong. They'll be more than thankful that you did!

It's been said that Halloween is a holiday for kids, but I have known many adults who look forward to this time of year with the playfulness and excitement of a child. Eerily decorated houses, carved jack-o'-lanterns, and fanciful costumes delight as many grownups as children when late October rolls around, so why not indulge your inner child and plan a special celebration just for you and your friends? Whether you're hosting a murder-mystery evening or planning a costume party, borrow your theme and food ideas from Hispanic tradition, known for its fabulous fiestas! In fact, in Mexico, along with Halloween night, the two days following (All Saints' Day and All Souls' Day) are observed collectively as "Días de los Muertos" (Days of the Dead), marked by three days of grand festivities and, of course, grand eating.

One of the great eating traditions of Spain is the tapas, an array of "little bites" ranging from delicious platters of authentic cheeses and olives to spicy nibbles of chorizo-flavored potatoes and empanadas. Tapas easily become a meal before the evening is through. It will be a devilish delight for the senses when you host this super celebration, which is accompanied by a diverse selection of drinks, from the alcohol-free Vampiro Sangritas to creamy hot cocoa with a dash of cinnamon. Your guests are guaranteed to have a "bloody" good time while reveling the night away among the ghouls and goblins.

An All Hallows' Eve Tapas Party

MENU

Party for Twelve

COLD TAPAS:

Deviled Mussels in the Shell

Serrano Ham and Melon

Manchego Cheese, Membrillo, and Black Bread

Marcona Almonds and Manzanilla Olives

HOT TAPAS:

Empanadas or Croquetas

Albondigas (Meatballs in Garlic Tomato Sauce)

Red Rioja Potatoes with Chorizo

Pimientos Rellenos de Verduras

DESSERT:

Pan de Muerto (Bread of the Dead)

with Mexican Chocolate Butter

Caramels and Chocolate Bark

BEVERAGE PAIRINGS:

To Start: Vampiro Sangritas

Throughout: *Apple-Cranberry Cider, Flavored Seltzers*

Dessert: *Hot Cocoa with Whipped Cream and Cinnamon*

Tips on Purchased Ingredients

Jamón Serrano (Serrano ham) is a Spanish mountain-cured ham and a close cousin to Italian prosciutto, although usually a bit drier, less salty, and more intensely flavored. It is often served on tapas platters with *melon*, just as prosciutto is on antipasto plates, but the Spanish like to jazz up the presentation a bit before serving. Choose a sweet, ripe cantaloupe, honeydew, or other type of muskmelon, and make balls with a medium-size melon baller. One large melon and no more than ½ pound of Serrano ham will be sufficient as part of the tapas table. Mix the melon balls in a bowl with a drizzle of olive oil and sherry vinegar, and a pinch of salt and pepper, and allow to marinate for a couple of hours. Transfer them to a platter and drape the ham over. Chopped chives sprinkled on top make a nice finish.

Manchego is Spain's most popular cheese, and it's quickly becoming an American favorite as well. Named for the Manchego sheep (of La Mancha), from whose milk it was originally made, it's a rich and flavorful semifirm cheese, great for snacking, and goes with both sweet and savory dishes. It is most often served with a bit of *membrillo* (quince paste), which is usually found wherever Manchego is sold, although quince preserves are also fine to use. It's a delicious combination and can be served with bread or crackers. For this occasion, thinly sliced *black bread* makes a nice display. Precut the cheese into thin slices and either top them with a slice of the membrillo or, if you find quince preserves, serve it in the middle of the platter with a small spoon. About one pound of cheese should be enough for 12 people.

Marcona almonds are native to Spain alone and wonderfully sweet and delicate in flavor. A bit expensive, but certainly worth it, these oven-roasted nuts usually come dusted in sea salt or dried herbs. No tapas evening would be complete without a bowl of them on hand. *Manzanilla olives*, which hail from the Seville region of Spain, are picked young while still green. They often come stuffed with a variety of fillings, from pimientos to anchovies. Pick a variety to present on the tapas table, but avoid those spiked with tequila or vermouth.

Empanadas, Spanish-style turnovers stuffed with meat, chicken, or cheese, are popular snack foods that can often be found in your supermarket's frozen international food section, ready for frying. If you can find the miniature ones called empanaditas, they'll be perfect, as will *croquetas*, small croquettes usually made of chicken or ham and ready for reheating. Both types make a nice addition to the other hot tapas items you are preparing.

Apple-cranberry cider is just one of the combination ciders available and is particularly popular at this time of year. Another delicious blend, apple-pomegranate, will go well with your tapas menu, and you can serve either one heated or chilled. For those who prefer less sweetness, offer *flavored seltzers* like orange or lemon-lime with ice and a fruit-slice garnish.

On a cool autumn night, nothing hits the spot like a mug of *hot cocoa*. Make a batch up in a cocoa latte machine or thermo pitcher, or provide individual packets and hot water for guests to help themselves. A dollop of fresh whipped cream and a sprinkle of ground cinnamon will make it more festive and complement your Pan de Muerto with Mexican Chocolate Butter. Cinnamon-stick stirrers are a nice added touch.

The celebrations of the Days of the Dead always include candy and, in Mexico, little sugary skulls called *calaveritas* are seen everywhere. If you're able to find any of these traditional sweets, definitely add them to your table. Also, *caramels* are always popular, as is *chocolate bark* with plenty of nuts. Make up a few dishes of specialty chocolates and candy to enhance your dessert table display and provide some sweet nibbles for those who enjoy them.

Deviled Mussels in the Shell

Shellfish are always found on a tapas menu, and this cold appetizer with a devilish kick will impress your guests with its delicious simplicity. Definitely make these the night before so the vinaigrette has time to flavor the mussels. Pimentón, which is smoked Spanish paprika, and an ingredient you'll see included in some of the other tapas recipes in this menu, is highly flavorful and a far cry from the usual bland paprikas we find in the supermarket. It comes in *dulce* (sweet and mild), *agridulce* (bittersweet, medium hot), and *picante* (spicy), and is available in Spanish-ethnic groceries and online (see Resources). Unless you really like a lot of heat, go for the sweet or slightly hot bittersweet versions. Some supermarkets carry ordinary Spanish paprika in their international foods section, and in a pinch, though it's probably not quite as flavorful, you could use it without hesitation.

Mussels enjoy the sand, and you'll need to scrub them well under cold running water to remove it along with the "beard" that protrudes from the shell opening. Discard any mussels that have open shells before cooking. Plan to cook your mussels within 24 hours of their purchase. As part of a tapas selection, one 2-pound bag should be enough, but double the amount if you feel it necessary.

1. In a large pot with a lid, steam the mussels in a little water until they open, 4 to 5 minutes. Using a slotted spoon, transfer the mussels and shells to a bowl and let cool until easily handled. Discard any unopened mussels. Remove the meat from the shells and place in a medium-size bowl. Reserve half the shells, rinse under cold water, and set aside in another bowl, lined with paper towels, in the refrigerator.

2. Make the vinaigrette: In a small mixing bowl, whisk together all the ingredients until well combined. Pour over the mussels and toss to coat. Cover with plastic wrap and chill in the refrigerator until ready to serve (up to 12 hours ahead). Remove from the refrigerator 20 minutes before setting up the serving platter.

3. To serve, arrange the shredded lettuce in a circle around the edge of a large round or oval platter. Place the empty mussel shells in a single layer in the middle. Spoon the mussels and their vinaigrette into and over the shells. Sprinkle with parsley and serve immediately.

Serves 12

Ingredients:

One 2-pound bag live mussels, scrubbed and debearded

Vinaigrette:

¼ cup extra virgin olive oil

2 tablespoons sherry vinegar

3 scallions,
trimmed and minced

1 garlic clove,
peeled and minced

½ small red bell pepper, cored, trimmed, and finely chopped

Dash of hot sauce

Large pinch of pimentón
(smoked Spanish paprika)

Salt and pepper to taste

To Serve:

2 cups shredded lettuce
(optional)

2 tablespoons finely chopped
fresh parsley leaves

Pimientos Rellenos de Verduras

These Spanish-style peppers stuffed with vegetable *paella* will nicely round out your hot tapas selections. In honor of Halloween, you could use a combination of orange bell peppers and the unusual black bell peppers we sometimes see this time of year. Cut them in half from top to bottom and leave the stem intact for presentation. You can either grill them out on the barbecue or roast them in the oven before stuffing.

For ease of preparation, we'll use a box of Spanish yellow rice and enhance it a bit with some flavorful sautéed vegetables to stuff the peppers. Topped with melted cheese, these peppers will disappear quickly when you bring them to the table. You can cook the peppers and stuff them a day ahead, then top with cheese just before baking. *Mahon* is Spain's second-most-beloved cheese after *Manchego* and is gaining popularity in the U.S. as well. Its flavor and texture are similar to Gouda or Edam, either of which could be substituted below if Mahon proves elusive. Finally, a little dollop of sour cream on each pepper and a sprinkling of chopped cilantro are a terrific finish for these delectable delights.

Ingredients:

6 medium-size red or orange bell peppers, halved and cored, stem intact

Canola oil for grilling or roasting

Salt and pepper to taste

Two 8-ounce boxes yellow rice, such as Goya®, cooked according to package directions

2 tablespoons olive oil

½ medium-size red onion, chopped

1 small zucchini, cut into ¼-inch dice

1 cup frozen artichoke hearts, thawed and roughly chopped

⅔ cup frozen green peas, thawed

½ cup small pimiento-stuffed olives, roughly chopped

Pinch of pimentón (smoked Spanish paprika)

2 cups shredded Spanish Mahon cheese (see recipe introduction)

1 cup sour cream

1 tablespoon finely chopped cilantro leaves

1. Lightly coat the bell pepper halves with oil, season with salt and pepper, and cook on a medium-high, preheated grill, turning over a few times until softened, but still firm enough to hold their shape. Alternatively, roast the pepper halves in a 375-degree oven on a foil-lined baking sheet, turning once, 12 to 15 minutes. Transfer with tongs to a clean parchment-lined baking sheet and set aside.

2. Transfer the cooked yellow rice to a large mixing bowl and fluff with a fork. Allow to cool completely.

3. Heat the olive oil in a medium-size skillet, add the onion, sprinkle with salt and pepper, and sauté over medium heat until soft and just beginning to brown, about 5 minutes. Add the zucchini and continue to cook, stirring often, until tender, 3 to 5 minutes. Stir in the artichokes, peas, and olives, and gently combine. Add the pimentón, stir to distribute, and cook a further minute. Transfer the contents of the skillet into the rice bowl and using a rubber spatula, gently fold the vegetables in. Mound spoonfuls of the rice and vegetable mixture into the pepper halves, and press down the stuffing with your hand cupped. Cover the entire baking sheet with plastic wrap and keep refrigerated until ready to bake.

4. Preheat the oven to 400 degrees. Sprinkle some of the cheese on top of each stuffed pepper and bake uncovered until the rice is heated through and the cheese has melted, 15 to 20 minutes. Remove from the oven and transfer with tongs to a large serving platter. Place a small dollop of sour cream on top of each pepper, sprinkle with the cilantro, and serve immediately.

Serves 12

Vampiro Sangritas

Ingredients:

One 46-ounce bottle Spicy Hot V8® juice

3 cups orange juice

½ cup freshly squeezed lime juice

1 tablespoon Worcestershire sauce

1 tablespoon granulated sugar

2 teaspoons chili powder

1 teaspoon celery salt

1 teaspoon hot sauce (such as Tabasco® sauce), or more or less to taste

To Coat the Glass Rims:

½ cup light corn syrup

5 or 6 drops red food coloring

Sangritas, not to be confused with *sangria*, are actually "chaser" drinks often served with shots of tequila. On its own, a sangrita is a spicy concoction reminiscent of a Bloody Mary with a tangy citrus finish. Traditionally, a sangrita that has tequila already in it instead of on the side is called a *Vampiro*, or Vampire. Here, however, the ghoulish quality of this alcohol-free version will be seen in its presentation – glass rims dripping with mock "blood" made from corn syrup and red food coloring.

Start with Spicy Hot V8® juice and add the desired amount of "heat" from there. Usually sangritas are extremely spicy, but you may prefer a somewhat less potent version by limiting the amount of hot sauce you add. Taste as you go, and remember that if you make these ahead of time, they'll naturally become spicier as the flavors meld together. Martini, wine, or small juice glasses are great for serving. Sangritas go extremely well with the cold tapas selections, after which your guests will probably switch to cider or seltzer, so this recipe makes enough for one drink per person. However, you can double the amounts if you like and keep some extras in the refrigerator for any particularly thirsty vampires who drop by!

1. In a large pitcher, whisk together all the ingredients except the hot sauce. Taste for spiciness and add the hot sauce to taste. Chill at least 2 hours.

2. In a small bowl, stir together the corn syrup and food coloring. Dip the rim of each glass in the bowl, twist to coat, and turn upright on a tray, allowing the liquid to drip down. Allow to set briefly before pouring the sangrita into each glass and serving.

Serves 12

Ingredients:

1 pound lean ground beef

½ pound ground veal

½ pound ground pork

1 cup dry, unflavored bread crumbs

1 large egg

6 garlic cloves, peeled and minced

2 tablespoons finely chopped,
fresh parsley leaves

1 teaspoon pimentón
(smoked Spanish paprika)

½ teaspoon each ground
cumin and coriander

¼ teaspoon ground nutmeg

Pinch red cayenne pepper

Salt and freshly ground black pepper to taste

2 tablespoons olive oil

1 medium-size onion, finely chopped

¼ cup white wine substitute
(3 tablespoons white grape juice and
1 tablespoon white wine vinegar)

Two 28-ounce cans whole Italian plum
tomatoes, including juice, gently crushed

1 teaspoon dried oregano

Albondigas (Meatballs in Garlic Tomato Sauce)

These little meatballs are popular Spanish appetizers and are sometimes part of a traditional hearty soup. Usually made from a combination of meats, including pork, they can also be made of beef only, or even ground turkey. You can buy a meatloaf mix that contains beef, veal, and pork, or buy each separately. The combination of spices is what gives albondigas their unique taste, while the delicious garlic and tomato sauce that accompanies them is full of robust flavor. Making these ahead of time and storing them in the sauce will result in even more flavor, so plan on cooking them at least a day before the party.

Some types of canned whole Italian plum tomatoes are better than others. Look for *San Marzano* on the label, which refers to the region in which they are grown – even the Spanish seek them out. They have better flavor, color, and texture than others, and when used in a sauce such as this with very few other ingredients, the quality is noticeable. Use your fingers to break them apart a bit in the can before adding them to the saucepan. The white wine substitute used here is appropriate for many dishes that traditionally call for small amounts of a light, dry white wine (see page 73).

1. In a large mixing bowl, combine the beef, veal, pork, bread crumbs, egg, half the garlic, parsley, pimentón, cumin, nutmeg, cayenne, salt, and pepper, and mix together until well combined. Form into approximately 36 walnut-size meatballs and place on a baking sheet.

2. Heat the olive oil in a large, heavy skillet over medium-high heat and fry the meatballs in batches until they are evenly browned. Transfer to a parchment-lined baking sheet and set aside.

3. Pour out all but 2 tablespoons of the accumulated grease in the skillet, add the onion, sprinkle with salt, and fry over medium heat, stirring often, until soft and lightly browned, about 8 minutes. Add the remaining garlic and cook a further minute. Add the wine substitute and, using a wooden spoon, scrape up any browned bits in the pan as the liquid cooks. After 2 minutes, stir in the tomatoes, their juices, and the oregano, increase the heat to high, and bring to a boil. Place the browned meatballs in the sauce and simmer covered, over low heat, stirring occasionally, until the meatballs are tender and the sauce has thickened, about 25 minutes.

4. Taste the sauce for additional salt, transfer with the meatballs to a storage container to cool, and refrigerate until ready to use. Reheat the meatballs gently in the sauce in a covered pot or skillet until heated through. Transfer all to a large, warmed platter, and serve immediately.

Serves 12

Red Rioja Potatoes with Chorizo

The Spanish love their potatoes almost as much as they love their rice, but as is the case with many other dishes, potatoes must be full of flavor and pizzazz. Here, the famous spicy chorizo sausage provides the kick and, when used with pimentón, it creates the ruby red Rioja color. The choice of potato is less important than the chorizo, but russet baking potatoes absorb the intense flavors better than most. As for the chorizo, you may only find the dried sausage, in which case, dice it and use according to the instructions that follow. If you're lucky enough to find fresh chorizo in your search, remove the casings and then crumble the meat for frying. There is some debate as to which chorizo, Mexican or Spanish, is better. Both are made from pork, but the Spanish version is smoked, which often adds more flavor. You be the judge.

Try not to make these too far ahead – earlier in the day is fine, but once they're refrigerated, the reheating process takes much longer and may turn your beautiful potatoes into mush. The best way to avoid this is to transfer the cooked potatoes to a roasting pan, cover with foil, and leave them at room temperature (a couple of hours is fine, but not overnight). When getting ready to serve, heat them covered in a hot oven, shaking the pan occasionally until just heated through.

1. Heat the oil in a large, heavy-bottomed pot or Dutch oven over medium-high heat, add the potatoes, sprinkle with salt and pepper and fry, stirring often, until lightly browned. Transfer the potatoes with a slotted spoon to a large bowl and set aside. Add the onion to the pot and cook over medium heat, stirring occasionally until softened, about 6 minutes. Stir in the garlic and pimentón and cook a further minute.

2. Add the fresh, crumbled chorizo, if using, and cook with the onions, stirring often until lightly browned, about 5 minutes. If using dried chorizo, stir in and cook for 2 minutes. Add the rosemary, the browned potatoes, and just enough water to cover, and bring to a boil. Reduce the heat to low and simmer, covered, until the potatoes are fork-tender and nearly all the liquid is evaporated, about 15 minutes.

3. Taste for the addition of salt and pepper, remove the rosemary sprigs, transfer to a warm platter, and serve immediately, or place in a roasting pan, set aside, and reheat in a 375-degree oven for about 20 minutes before serving.

Serves 12

Ingredients:

⅓ cup olive oil

5 pounds russet potatoes, peeled and roughly cut into 1-inch chunks

Salt and pepper to taste

1 large onion, thinly sliced

2 garlic cloves, peeled and minced

1½ tablespoons pimentón (smoked Spanish paprika)

1 pound fresh chorizo sausage, casings removed and crumbled, or 9 ounces dry-cured chorizo, cut into ¼-inch dice

2 small sprigs fresh rosemary

Pan de Muerto (Bread of the Dead) with Mexican Chocolate Butter

Ingredients:

½ cup warm water

1 package active dry yeast

¾ cup plus 1 tablespoon granulated sugar

5 large eggs, slightly beaten

½ cup (1 stick) unsalted butter, melted

2 teaspoons whole anise seeds

2 tablespoons orange juice

2 teaspoons grated orange rind

1 teaspoon salt

4½ to 5 cups all-purpose flour

Glaze:

½ cup granulated sugar

⅓ cup orange juice

1 tablespoon grated orange rind

No "Days of the Dead" party would be complete without this bread, which is traditionally placed on the graveside altars of departed loved ones in Mexico. Slightly sweet like many European breads, Pan de Muerto is particularly delicious served up with a nontraditional Mexican chocolate butter spread. I also like to offer whipped, unsalted butter and orange marmalade, which complement the bread and go well with the hot cocoa.

This is one of the easier types of yeast breads to make as it doesn't require extensive kneading. Still, the rising process is important, so plan on being near the kitchen for several hours from start to finish. Some of the dough is used to shape into "bones," which are placed on top of the round loaf before baking. These don't need to be perfect in shape or design – a rough resemblance to bones is enough. The glaze that is applied can be as decorative or simple as you wish. Some put colored candies or sprinkle sugar on top for added festiveness. Bake the loaves a day ahead and keep them fresh in paper bags. The butter, which needs to set, should be made at least the night before.

1. In a large mixing bowl, whisk together the water, yeast, and 1 tablespoon of sugar. Set the bowl aside in a warm place until the mixture is frothy and you're certain the yeast is active, about 15 minutes.

2. Beat in the eggs, butter, anise seeds, orange juice, and rind until well combined. Add the remaining ¾ cup sugar and the salt, and beat until smooth. Add the flour 1 cup at a time, beating well until the dough begins to pull away from the sides of the bowl. (You may need to add more or less flour, depending on humidity in the air.)

3. Place the dough on a floured board and knead for 3 minutes. Transfer to a lightly oiled bowl, cover with plastic wrap or a towel, and allow to rise in a warm place until doubled in volume, 1½ to 2 hours.

4. Punch down the dough and transfer to a floured board. Divide into two pieces, one twice as large as the other. Shape the large piece into a flat, round loaf and place on a parchment-lined baking sheet. Form the remaining dough into several "bone" shapes: 4- or 5-inch-long logs, with each end pinched and shaped into a knob. Lightly brush the large, round loaf with water and attach the "bones" on top in a circle. Cover again with plastic wrap or a towel, and allow to rise for 1 hour in a warm place.

5. Preheat the oven to 350 degrees. Bake the bread until it is brown and the bottom sounds hollow when tapped, 35 to 45 minutes. Transfer to a rack to cool.

6. Make the glaze: Combine the ingredients in a small saucepan and bring to a boil, stirring constantly. Boil for 1 minute and remove from the heat. Use a pastry brush to evenly glaze the still slightly warm bread. Cool completely and store the bread in a paper bag until ready to serve.

7. Make the chocolate butter: In a medium-size saucepan, combine the cocoa, water, and sugar, whisk together, and bring to a simmer. Cook, stirring often, over medium heat until the sugar has completely dissolved. Remove from the heat and whisk in the butter pieces a few at a time. When the butter is well incorporated, whisk in the vanilla and cinnamon. Pour into a large ramekin or decorative bowl and chill in the refrigerator until set. Serve with slices of the Pan de Muertos.

Serves 12

Chocolate Butter:

¾ cup unsweetened cocoa powder

½ cup water

1 cup granulated sugar

½ cup (1 stick) unsalted butter, cut into pieces

1 teaspoon alcohol-free vanilla extract

¼ teaspoon ground cinnamon

Alcohol Ingredients in Disguise

Some products we run across in the supermarket announce their alcohol ingredients "loud and clear." There's no mistaking that vodka sauce, cabernet sauce, or even Jack Daniels'® BBQ sauce are made with alcoholic beverages. But what about those that are less obvious and perhaps even unexpected? We know that baking extracts can contain a good amount of alcohol by volume (see page 43), but what about other products that contain those same extracts we're looking to avoid? Flavored syrups used in coffees and desserts are often heavily doused with extracts and as such contain just as much alcohol as if we were using the real thing. We may also find heavy use of extracts in fancy chocolates, creamers, ice cream, and even cigars, which have been known to be "laced" with alcohol flavors. If total abstention is necessary, or the taste or smell of the ingredient is a trigger for those in recovery, these products must be avoided. In addition, many condiments and bottled sauces unexpectedly contain alcohol as an ingredient. You may know that Dijon mustard always has white wine added, but did you know that teriyaki sauce may have it as well? It pays to read labels carefully.

On the other hand, we can certainly become overzealous in our detective work, since not all fermented products go through alcohol-specific fermentation. Foods like miso, yogurt, and even pickles are fermented, but the byproduct given off is not ethyl alcohol: It can be lactic acid in the case of dairy products or acetic acid in the case of vinegars. None of these particular products contains alcohol and they are quite safe to use. However, since alcohol itself is an excellent preservative, lesser-quality products that are fermented by other means may sometimes introduce alcohol to speed up fermentation or increase the shelf life. Reading the label will show whether alcohol has been added and in what percent by volume.

Finally, there are the "pretenders" – those products with deceptive names that simply do not have anything to do with alcohol. Chocolate liquor, the term used for the pure essence of cocoa bean, is often seen listed on cookie, cake, and candy labels – a complete misnomer and the cause of much confusion. Sugar alcohols are another of these – substitutes used for sugar in many low-carb and diabetic products are unfortunately named "alcohols" because part of their chemical structure resembles alcohol, but not one drop is present. And Bourbon vanilla, named for the islands and not the whiskey, can be doubly confusing for those looking to buy vanilla products such as whole beans, powder, or paste, which do not contain alcohol as do their extract counterparts.

Before we know it, autumn leaves and chilly evenings are upon us, and Thanksgiving Day is right around the corner. Discussions among family members abound as to who will take on hosting duties this season and which traditional dishes should appear on the table. With this terrific menu and the accompanying tips to guide you, don't be afraid to volunteer this year. Thanksgiving dinner will never be more delicious than this one, in your capable hands. From perfectly matched alcohol-free drinks with each course to the tenderest turkey imaginable, this meal will have your guests purring with pleasure up through the last bite of your Pumpkin Spice Cheesecake with Dulce de Leche Sauce.

So much of this menu can be done in make-ahead stages that you'll never feel stressed or overwhelmed with the prospect of feeding a crowd. A delightful, alcohol-free Pilgrim's Punch and prepared munchies will keep everyone busy as you get ready to awe them with the main course. Set the table with entertaining touches, like names written on miniature pumpkins for place cards, and a centerpiece of fresh fruit surrounded by colorful fallen leaves. Little shimmering votives placed here and there instead of the typical candlesticks will add a more intimate touch.

The best way to serve a seated group of this size – and avoid the danger of glasses toppling when serving dishes are passed during the meal – is to pass everything once and then use your cleared-off buffet top or sideboard to accommodate the turkey and side dishes. Guests can easily go for seconds and thirds without disrupting others, while warming plates and covered dishes will help keep everything hot. When it's all over, the family will be impressed by how perfect every last detail really was, and they will no doubt be "thankful" to you for the best Thanksgiving yet!

A Bountiful Thanksgiving Dinner

MENU
Dinner for Ten

HORS D'OEUVRES:
Pepitas with Mixed Nuts
Crudités Plate with Two Dips

MAIN COURSE:
Apple Cider-Brined Turkey with Herb Gravy
Sausage, Apple, and Sourdough Stuffing
Perfect Candied Sweet Potatoes
Shaved Brussels Sprouts with Lemon Butter
Creamed White Root Vegetables
Cranberry Sauce

DESSERT:
Pumpkin Spice Cheesecake
with Dulce de Leche Sauce

BEVERAGE PAIRINGS:
Hors d'Oeuvres: Pilgrim's Punch
Main Course: *Sparkling Apple Cider*
Dessert: *Cinnamon Coffee*

Tips on Purchased Ingredients

Pepitas, or pumpkin seeds, make a nice addition to the usual array of mixed nuts. Buy them lightly salted, raw or toasted, and combine with a large can or two of "no peanut" nuts. People have a tendency to eat handful after handful of peanuts, risking spoiling their appetites for the main event, while nibbling single nuts is more likely when an interesting variety is offered.

Raw vegetables, or *crudités*, are a classic standby and these days can even be purchased pre-cut for dipping. Make your life as easy as possible by buying bags of baby carrots, sugar snap peas (which are entirely edible), cauliflower and broccoli florets, and cut celery sticks. Arrange two platters with a couple of purchased dips such as the universally liked French onion or ranch, and add a more unusual one such as New England clam or horseradish to add interest. The beauty of these simple hors d'oeuvres is that you'll be free to focus on the turkey and side dishes, you won't have a set of first-course dishes to clear from the table, your guests will be less likely to overindulge, and most important, everyone will be out of the kitchen and out of your hair as you maneuver toward the final countdown.

Some people wouldn't dream of Thanksgiving turkey without *cranberry sauce*, while others won't go near it, but it is a must at the table. Gourmet home cooks who spend the time making their own sauce are probably also adding a good dose of booze in some form or other for the sake of "festivity." Stick to the usual whole berry or jellied cranberry sauce from a can and serve it in pretty dishes, one at each end of the table.

To complement the cider-brining of the turkey and the flavor of the stuffing, *sparkling cider* is the ideal beverage choice for your main course. There is a variety of alcohol-free bottled sparklers these days, including grape, raspberry, and even loganberry. All are fine choices here – just try to find brands with minimal sugar, so the taste is not overpoweringly sweet, but rather crisp and refreshing.

Surprise everyone with a deliciously brewed *Cinnamon Coffee* to harmonize nicely with the Pumpkin Spice Cheesecake. Flavored coffees are plentifully available, even in bean form, so splurge in this area and serve in an attractive urn or pot. Offer half-and-half, regular milk, and a bowl of cinnamon sugar to add a bit of extra kick, in addition to regular sugar or cubes.

Pilgrim's Punch

Get out the old punch bowl and whip up this refreshing aperitif to keep the "pilgrims" at bay while you put the finishing touches on your turkey and fixings. Cranberry juice or cocktail makes no difference; however, if sugar is an issue, feel free to substitute a light, reduced-sugar version. If you can't find tangerine juice and don't want to take the time to squeeze from fresh, regular orange juice will do just fine.

Follow the directions below for making a simple ice mold to keep your punch well chilled. Serve with a ladle into punch bowl glasses or short "Old-Fashioned" tumblers.

Combine the cranberry, tangerine, and lime juices in a punch bowl and stir well. Place the tangerine slices and ice mold in the bowl and serve immediately.

Serves 10

To make an ice mold: For punches that will not be sitting for long periods, such as this one, it's fine to use only water as the liquid in your ice mold; otherwise, you'll run the risk of diluting the punch as the ice melts. (For longer-sitting punches, use a liquid that's an ingredient of the punch itself, such as juice or soda.) A round, doughnut-shaped mold like those used for gelatin desserts is ideal, though you can certainly improvise by using anything from muffin tins (for several small ice molds) to decorative bundt or cake molds (filling only halfway.) First, pour water about 1 inch deep, allow to partially freeze, then top with bits of fruit included in the punch flavor; here, a combination of whole cranberries and lime slices would make a nice presentation. Allow to freeze completely, then add another inch or two of water, and freeze again. To remove from the mold, run warm water over the bottom. Invert and float in the punch bowl.

Ingredients:

One 64-ounce bottle cranberry juice or cocktail, chilled

1 quart tangerine juice (about 16 tangerines juiced), chilled

½ cup fresh-squeezed lime juice (about 6 medium limes), chilled

2 tangerines, unpeeled and sliced into ¼-inch rounds

Ice mold (see instructions at right)

Ingredients:

6 to 8 medium-size sweet potatoes

6 tablespoons unsalted butter

⅔ cup dark corn syrup

⅓ cup firmly packed dark brown sugar

Salt and pepper to taste

½ bag miniature or regular-size marshmallows

Perfect Candied Sweet Potatoes

This no-fail recipe will have you volunteering every year to make this traditional Thanksgiving side dish. The secret lies in baking the sweet potatoes ahead (even the day before), which develops a lovely caramelization as well as cutting back on baking time. Be sure to remove the skin while the potatoes are still warm so that the pulp doesn't stick to it. You can make these in two separate, medium-size casseroles, one for each end of the table, which will also help when maneuvering space for them in the oven.

Marshmallows are, of course, the usual final touch, so don't forget them, especially if there will be kids (of all ages!) at the table.

Shaved Brussels Sprouts with Lemon Butter

Depart from the usual boiled Brussels sprouts and offer this crisp and delightful side dish instead. Once the ingredients are ready to go, it takes only minutes to prepare and can be done as the turkey rests. The lemon juice and zest add a terrific tang that every chef will tell you helps reduce the heaviness of fat-laden ingredients on the palate, ingredients in abundant supply on all Thanksgiving dinner plates! Your guests will be amazed and impressed with how well this simple side dish complements the rest of the meal.

You can trim and slice the sprouts a day ahead and store them in a plastic bag in the refrigerator, leaving a somewhat labor-intensive task off your Thanksgiving Day "to do" list. When preparing the lemon rind, use a

microplane grater or cover a standard grater with strong plastic wrap and grate right over it – the zest sticks to the plastic and can then be scraped off quickly, leaving the grater virtually clean as a whistle!

1. Place the halved and cored sprouts flat side down on a cutting board and slice thinly (⅛ to ¼ inch wide). Use your fingertips to separate the "shavings."

2. Melt the butter with the olive oil in a large, nonstick skillet, add the sprouts, sprinkle with salt and pepper, and cook, tossing often, until just wilted but still bright green in color, about 5 minutes. Add the lemon juice and grated rind and stir to coat. Serve immediately.

Serves 10

Ingredients:

2 pounds Brussels sprouts, trimmed, halved, and cored

4 tablespoons unsalted butter

2 tablespoons olive oil

Salt and pepper to taste

1 tablespoon fresh lemon juice

1 teaspoon grated lemon rind

---

1. Preheat the oven to 400 degrees. Place the sweet potatoes on an aluminum foil-lined baking sheet and bake until fork-tender, turning once, about 40 minutes. Some of the skin may blacken, and liquid may begin to ooze from the pulp, which is a good sign of caramelization. Remove the potatoes from the oven and allow to cool until easy to handle. Using a sharp paring knife, carefully remove the skin, cut the potatoes into quarters, and place flat side down in one large or two medium-sized buttered casserole dishes. At this point, you may cover the dishes with foil and refrigerate overnight.

2. Preheat the oven to 350 degrees. In a medium-size saucepan over medium heat, melt together the butter, corn syrup, and brown sugar, stirring well to combine. Simmer until the sugar has dissolved, 1 to 2 minutes.

3. Sprinkle the layered sweet potatoes with salt and pepper and pour the syrup mixture over them evenly. Bake, basting occasionally, until nicely glazed and bubbly, about 50 minutes. Sprinkle the marshmallows over and bake a further 5 to 10 minutes, until the top is golden.

Serves 10

EASY DOES IT: If a good number of your guests don't care for sweet potatoes or if oven space is an issue, you can use a frozen or canned variety. Heat it on top of the stove or in the microwave, transfer to a baking dish, and bake briefly with the marshmallows in the oven while the turkey is resting.

Ingredients

Brine:

½ gallon apple cider

¾ cup kosher salt

⅔ cup granulated sugar

1 tablespoon black peppercorns

1 tablespoon whole allspice berries

One 1-inch piece ginger root, unpeeled and roughly chopped

¼ teaspoon whole cloves

3 bay leaves

1 fresh sage sprig, roughly chopped

One 12- to 14-pound fresh or frozen (thawed) turkey

6 cups ice

Roasting:

½ cup (1 stick) unsalted butter

¼ cup canola oil

1 onion, peeled and quartered

2 large garlic cloves, smashed

1 Red Delicious apple, quartered

2 sprigs each fresh sage, thyme, and parsley

Salt and pepper to taste

Gravy:

Reserved turkey drippings

¼ cup all-purpose flour

2 to 3 cups turkey or chicken stock

Salt and pepper to taste

Apple Cider-Brined Turkey with Herb Gravy

If you've never tried brining a turkey, now is the time! This amazingly delicious recipe just might persuade you to make it an annual tradition. Brining, which is simply a technique used to tenderize and add flavor, consists of a water and salt solution, usually with an added sweetener of some kind, as well as spices and herbs. You'll need a large stockpot and turkey-sized plastic oven bags, and be sure to make room in your refrigerator for the stockpot to sit overnight.

Apple cider is the secret to both sweetness and tenderness, as it imparts a lovely, subtle flavor while its natural acidity helps break down the protein, resulting in the juiciest of meat. You need not turn the turkey over during the brining – allow the breast meat to gain the full benefit of the process. I've always found the dark meat to be flavorful enough in its own right.

You can make a quick turkey stock by simmering the neck and giblets (but not the liver) in a medium-size pot of water on the back of the stove for about two hours. Strain and reserve for your gravy-making. Alternatively, in place of the homemade broth, you can use a purchased low-sodium chicken or turkey broth diluted with half a can of water. Because of the heavy salting in the brine and in the roasting, be careful not to add too much salt to your gravy before tasting, especially when using canned broth.

As always, allow your turkey to rest for 20 to 30 minutes while you prepare the gravy. A fat-separating measuring cup and a gravy whisk will make this step a breeze.

1. Make the brining liquid by combining all the ingredients, except for the turkey and ice, in a large saucepan. Bring to a boil and cook, stirring occasionally, until the salt and sugar have dissolved, 5 to 10 minutes. Allow to cool completely.

2. Double-bag two turkey-sized plastic oven bags and place in a large stockpot. Place the turkey inside the bags, breast side down, and add the cider mixture and ice. Close with twist-ties and refrigerate in the stockpot for at least 12 hours or up to 24 hours.

3. In a small saucepan, melt together the butter and oil, and set aside. Preheat the oven to 500 degrees.

4. Remove the turkey from the brine, rinse well under cold water, and pat dry with paper towels. Place on a rack in a large roasting pan and arrange the onion, garlic, apple, and herbs around. Salt and pepper the inside and outside of the turkey, lift the wing tips up and over the back, and tie the legs together loosely with string. Brush the entire bird with the butter and oil mixture. Pour about ¼ cup water into the roasting pan and bake the turkey for 30 minutes, brushing after 15 minutes with more of the butter and oil.

5. Reduce the oven temperature to 350 degrees. Brush again with the remaining butter and oil, and roast about 1¼ to 1½ hours more, periodically basting with the accumulated pan juices, until an instant-read thermometer inserted in the meaty part of the thigh registers 165 degrees. Cover the breast loosely with foil, if necessary, to avoid overbrowning. Transfer the cooked turkey to a large platter and pour the pan drippings through a strainer into a fat separator, pressing on the vegetables to squeeze out their juices. Add a little water to the roasting pan and using a wooden spoon, scrape up any browned bits that have accumulated and add to the drippings.

6. To make the gravy, place 4 tablespoons of the fat from the top of the separator in a large skillet. Add the flour and over medium-high heat, whisk together until bubbly. Pour in the turkey drippings from the separator spout (avoiding any remaining fat on top) and whisk until smooth. Begin adding the turkey or chicken stock while continuing to whisk, until the desired consistency is reached. Taste for the addition of salt and pepper, and pour into a gravy boat or warmer. Serve immediately.

Serves 10

Sausage, Apple, and Sourdough Stuffing

Technically a dressing, since it's baked outside the turkey, this "stuffing" is a perfect match for the Apple Cider Brined Turkey. Surprisingly, the best type of sourdough bread to use here is the pre-sliced packaged variety found in the bread aisle of your supermarket. Keep the crusts on (discard the end slices) and with a serrated knife, cut four slices at a time into ½-inch cubes.

I will sometimes substitute fennel for the celery here to complement the sausage and bring another layer of flavor to the final result, so feel free to do the same if you are a fennel fan. Your choice of apple is not particularly important as long as it is the type that remains somewhat firm when cooked. Cortland, Rome Beauty, Granny Smith, and even Yellow Delicious are good choices. To save time, you can cube and toast the bread the day before and store it overnight in a plastic bag.

1. Preheat the oven to 400 degrees. Spread the cubed bread on two large, rimmed baking sheets and bake in the oven until just golden on the edges, stirring occasionally, about 10 minutes. Transfer to a large mixing bowl.

2. In a large skillet, fry the sausage over medium-high heat, breaking it up with a fork until cooked through, about 10 minutes. Transfer with a slotted spoon to the bowl with the bread cubes. Melt the butter in the same skillet, add the onions and celery (or fennel), sprinkle with salt and pepper, and sauté for 8 to 10 minutes until softened, stirring often. Add the apples and herbs, and continue to cook for 5 minutes. Transfer to the large mixing bowl with the sausage and bread. Add the eggs, apple juice, and chicken broth to the stuffing mixture, and stir well to combine.

3. Preheat the oven to 350 degrees. Loosely arrange the stuffing mixture in a buttered 9-inch by 13-inch baking dish, cover with nonstick or buttered foil, and bake for 30 minutes. Remove the foil and bake a further 15 minutes until the top is just crisp and slightly golden.

Serves 10

Ingredients:

One 24-ounce loaf of sliced sourdough bread, cut into ½-inch cubes

1½ pounds sweet Italian sausage, casings removed

6 tablespoons unsalted butter

2 medium-size onions, peeled and chopped

2 cups chopped celery stalks or fennel bulbs

Salt and pepper to taste

3 medium-size apples, peeled, cored, and cut into ½-inch dice

1½ tablespoons finely chopped fresh sage leaves

2 teaspoons each dried rubbed sage, dried thyme, and dried marjoram

2 large eggs, slightly beaten

½ cup apple juice

1 cup low-sodium chicken broth

Creamed White Root Vegetables

I've been making a version of this type of dish in place of mashed potatoes on Thanksgiving for quite some time, and it's always been received with relish and compliments. The deliciously fragrant celery root is often underused as most home cooks are baffled as to how one gets past the knobby exterior. It must be ruthlessly cut away with a sharp knife, even at the risk of taking some of the white interior with it, until it has the appearance of a peeled turnip. It can then be sliced or diced like a potato and used in a similar fashion.

You can make this dish a day ahead and reheat in a stainless steel saucepan on top of the stove over low heat, stirring occasionally to prevent sticking. If the sauce has become too thick, add a little milk to thin it out.

Ingredients:

1½ pounds celery root, well-trimmed and peeled, cut into ½-inch dice

1 pound parsnips, peeled and cut into ½-inch dice

1 pound redskin potatoes, peeled and cut into ½-inch dice

4 tablespoons unsalted butter

½ cup low-sodium chicken broth

1 cup heavy cream

Salt and pepper to taste

Dash of nutmeg

1 teaspoon finely chopped, fresh parsley leaves

1. Bring a pot of water to a boil, add a pinch of salt, and cook the diced celery root and parsnips until just fork-tender, about 6 minutes. Strain, run briefly under cold water, and set aside on paper towels to dry. In another pot, place the diced potatoes, cover with cold water, add a pinch of salt, and simmer over medium heat until barely fork-tender, about 8 minutes. Strain, rinse, and dry as above.

2. In a medium-size saucepan, combine the butter, broth, heavy cream, salt, pepper, and nutmeg. Bring to a simmer, whisking often, and cook until the sauce is somewhat thickened and coats the back of a spoon, 10 to 15 minutes. Be careful not to let the mixture boil over – keep at a very low heat.

3. Stir in the cooked celery root, parsnips, and potatoes, and cook over medium-low heat until the vegetables are heated through. Taste for seasoning and transfer to a heated serving bowl. Sprinkle with the chopped parsley and serve immediately.

Serves 10

Pumpkin Spice Cheesecake with Dulce de Leche Sauce

Ingredients

Crust:

1½ cups graham cracker crumbs (about 20 crackers)

2 tablespoons granulated sugar

4 tablespoons unsalted butter, melted

½ teaspoon ground cinnamon

Pinch of salt

Filling:

Four 8-ounce packages cream cheese, at room temperature

1½ cups granulated sugar

3 large eggs

1 cup heavy cream

One 15-ounce can pure pumpkin

1 teaspoon alcohol-free vanilla extract

1 teaspoon ground cinnamon

½ teaspoon ground ginger

¼ teaspoon each ground nutmeg and ground allspice

⅛ teaspoon ground cloves

Dulce de Leche Sauce:

2 cups whipping cream

2 cups firmly packed dark brown sugar

1 cup sweetened condensed milk

Only at Thanksgiving can we follow a rich meal with an even richer dessert! Rapidly becoming a seasonal favorite, pumpkin-flavored cheesecake runs a close second to traditional pumpkin pie in the popularity contest for dessert choices. There are numerous variations made with nuts, gingersnaps, and quite often, bourbon, so be aware if you are offered a slice prepared by someone else. This completely sober rendition uses a classic cheesecake crust made from graham crackers with a hint of cinnamon, and the creamy, aromatically spiced filling is easy to prepare. Bake the cheesecake ahead to allow at least an overnight chill in the refrigerator for best serving results.

Dulce de leche, meaning "sweet from milk," is quickly becoming a popular dessert element in American baking. It is essentially a Hispanic type of caramel sauce. Purists will insist on methods that range from boiling unopened cans of sweetened condensed milk to simmering goat's milk and sugar in a saucepan for hours until it reaches its characteristic golden hue and taste. Here, however, a quick combination of simple ingredients will turn out a deliciously warm dulce de leche sauce to drizzle over the cool and creamy cheesecake. You may also make this a day ahead and then warm it on top of the stove over medium-low heat until pourable.

1. Preheat the oven to 350 degrees. Wrap a double layer of heavy-duty foil around the outside of a 9- or 10-inch buttered springform pan.

2. To make the crust, combine all the ingredients in a small mixing bowl, and using a fork, stir until well combined. Press evenly onto only the bottom of the prepared pan. Bake for 8 minutes, remove from oven, and allow to cool.

3. In a large mixing bowl, using an electric mixer, beat together the cream cheese and sugar until light and fluffy. Beat in the eggs, one at a time, until well-combined. Add the remaining ingredients and beat until just blended. Pour the filling into the prepared crust, place the springform pan in a large roasting pan, and add enough hot water to come halfway up the sides of the pan, creating a water bath. HINT: Place the roasting pan on the oven rack first, before adding the cheesecake and water, to avoid spillage.

4. Bake the cheesecake until the outer edges are puffy and the center is just set, about 1½ hours. Transfer to a rack to cool. Using a sharp knife, cut around the edges to loosen the cake, but do not remove from the pan. Cover and refrigerate overnight.

5. To make the sauce, in a medium-size saucepan, whisk together the cream and brown sugar, and cook over medium heat until the sugar has dissolved. Allow to boil, stirring often with a wooden spoon, until the mixture has reduced slightly, about 5 minutes. Stir in the sweetened condensed milk and allow to cool somewhat before serving. If preparing ahead, transfer to a covered container and refrigerate.

6. To serve the cheesecake, remove the foil wrapping, run a sharp knife again around the edge of the springform pan to be sure it's not sticking, and remove the sides of the pan. Transfer, with the pan bottom, to a cake plate, and cut the cheesecake into wedges (unflavored dental floss will make a super-clean cut!), then spoon the warmed sauce over each serving.

Serves 10

Tips on Pairing Alcohol-Free Beverages with Food

Pairing food with wine has been popular for centuries, and more recently, beers, cocktails, and other alcoholic beverages have been matched to different types of food flavors and fare as well. Restaurant owners and chefs have long provided customers with an array of alcoholic beverage choices to complement their menus and now, happily, they're realizing the need to accommodate the growing number of nondrinkers who frequent their establishments. Whatever the customer's personal reason may be for abstaining (sobriety, pregnancy, medical concerns, or simply a need for staying sharp and alert), restaurateurs are meeting their needs with creativity and aplomb. Chefs like Charlie Trotter in Chicago and Nils Noren of Aquavit in New York see the sense and sophistication in offering alcohol-free beverages as part of a tasting menu – beverages beyond the usual soft drinks and carbonated waters. In fact, it's become a welcome challenge to open up a whole range of creative culinary ideas as a way to get chefs and home cooks alike to start thinking outside the "bottle."

In general, many of the tried-and-true rules of wine-pairing can be applied to any beverage chosen to accompany a certain dish. This is certainly a very good place to start. Qualities like astringency, aroma, texture, and intensity of flavor are all appropriate considerations when you're deciding what to pour. For example, the acidity and tannic bitterness of an iced tea simply flavored with fruit makes a great accompaniment for anything particularly rich or fatty, as they help to "cut" the fat as a dry red wine would do. Anything too sweet would end up damping the appetite as well as leaving a cloying feeling on the tongue. Sweet beverages, on the other hand, can certainly be combined with acidic ones such as vinegars or unsweetened juices to counteract this possibility and create the desired taste sensation. Think about the effect on the palate that your menu will have and then build on any number of base ingredients like tea, flavored sodas, fruit juices, or even water. You can also draw from the beverages of a specific cuisine when you want to match a drink to say, Indian or Greek food, and enhance and play upon that base.

Sometimes, however, it can be as simple as pairing an unassuming cola with pizza. In logical terms, the sugar and carbonation make great partners for the acidity of the tomato sauce and the richness of the cheese. When there are myriad prepared nonalcoholic beverages that would suit your menu without fuss, certainly make use of them and don't go overboard trying to invent new ones. Which leads to the only real "rule" of alcohol-free beverage pairing with food: Don't get carried away! Especially during an evening of continuous eating and potential food-drink pairing, offer at most one unusual concoction and let the rest of your beverage offerings be simple and familiar. An endless stream of unknown and exotic drink combinations will not only detract from the success of your initial creative libation; it will leave most folks asking, in the end, whether they could just have a plain old glass of water!

Chapter 6

The Christmas Season

Red Mahogany Glazed Ham

No other time of year can compare when it comes to the fast pace of celebrating and entertaining. Invitations to parties and get-togethers stream in while we tirelessly attempt to put all the finishing touches on our own family's seasonal gathering. And no other time of year finds us surrounded by such an abundance of alcohol and foods that contain it. From eggnog to hot toddies, alcohol is everywhere and often considered synonymous with "fun." It's a tough time for the newly sober and an equally difficult time for those who must be careful not to ingest even small amounts. But, as the following three menus reveal, holiday entertaining during the Christmas season, for those who abstain, is anything but sober! Whether you're hosting a traditional family Christmas dinner or a Hanukkah celebration with friends, making merry has never been easier or tastier.

Creating a relaxed atmosphere of joy and caring is every host's goal, and these menus will show you how to add thoughtful and special touches to every aspect of the party. Innovative alcohol-free drinks show your guests that you've given thought and attention to their needs, while creative takes on time-honored traditions will show your consideration and sensitivity to every detail. No one has to know what a snap it really was, however, so don't let on. Just bask in the compliments and take your bows gracefully! Then sit back and enjoy the wonderful atmosphere – and food! – you've created.

The night before Christmas brings family and friends together to officially begin the holiday celebrations. At last, the presents are wrapped, the tree and house are decorated with glistening splendor, and it's time to relax and make merry with those closest to us. Traditions and festivities may vary, depending upon our family heritage and background, but one thing is certain: If you are the Christmas Eve host, your work is definitely cut out for you, from making sure there is enough ice for cold drinks to passing out the dessert napkins. It seems there's no end to the list of details you need to think about, not to mention the menu. How do you do it all and still offer deliciously prepared food and a medley of "spirited" yet sober-safe drinks?

For a Christmas Eve gathering, the following menu is designed to please all ages, offering your guests both a bit of tradition and some innovative selections to relish and applaud. Loosely based on the Mediterranean practice of serving fish and pasta (usually seven different types of fish, for the purists at heart), the meal includes a medley of simple buffet-style seafood hors d'oeuvres that will please even the traditionalists and a make-ahead baked pasta dish that will satisfy everyone's need for indulgence. Finally, a deceptively easy-to-prepare, spectacularly presented dessert will end the meal with true holiday flair. No need for hot toddies here to make family and guests feel warm and comforted! When you bring out the White Hot Chocolate with Candy Cane Swizzle Sticks, your guests will "ooh" and "aah" until the end of the night, as you relax and enjoy your own fabulous efforts, smiling to yourself at what a "piece of cake" it was to pull off.

A Christmas Eve Gathering

MENU

Buffet for Eight

A MEDLEY OF HORS D'OEUVRES FROM THE SEA:

*Shrimp Cocktail
with Red and Green Dipping Sauces*

Eleanor's Clams Oreganata

Crispy Fried Calamari and Baby Scallops
with Creamy Aïoli

MAIN COURSE:

Baked Rigatoni Norma
with Eggplant and Ricotta Cheese

Assorted Greens with Olive Oil and Vinegar

Whole Wheat Baguette Garlic Bread

DESSERT:

Candy Cane Ice Cream Profiteroles
with Hot Fudge Sauce

BEVERAGE PAIRINGS:

Hors d'Oeuvres and Main Course:
Flavored Sodas and Sparklers

Dessert: White Hot Chocolate with
Candy Cane Swizzle Sticks

Tips on Purchased Ingredients

Ready-made **shrimp cocktail** platters are seen in every grocer's fish department at holiday time, but you can easily prepare your own from frozen, cooked tail-on shrimp for half the cost. Choose jumbo (11 to 15 shrimp per pound) or extra-large (16 to 20), and count on your guests devouring as many as four or five each – maybe more! Two pounds is not an extravagant amount, particularly if everyone is a big shrimp fan. Defrost under cold, running water, pat dry, and arrange decoratively on a round platter. You can do this early in the day, cover the platter tightly with plastic wrap, and keep it well-refrigerated until serving time. Your **red and green sauces** are simply a traditional commercial cocktail sauce and the increasingly popular wasabi-based sauce typically found in the condiment section of your supermarket. Put them side by side in small

bowls in the center of your platter for a seasonally colorful presentation.

Make use of packaged **assorted greens** for your salad, combining two or three different variety packs in a sparkly glass or crystal bowl. Nearby cruets of **oil and vinegar** will allow your guests to dress their own salad. A nice touch on the table would be a salt cellar and pepper mill for those who'll want to season their salads.

Seafood is best paired with citrus or slightly acidic beverages that have a little effervescence, so in choosing your **sodas and sparklers**, look for flavors like white grape, lemon-lime, and grapefruit. Celery soda, if you can find it, is a terrific match with a twist of lemon. Since it may be a long evening, be sure to have plenty of spring water and ice on hand as well as a few different types of fruit juices for children or adults who prefer it. And have the coffeepot and teakettle set up and ready to go just in case someone wants a hot drink – there's always someone who does!

Eleanor's Clams Oreganata

I have my mother's cousin to thank for this classic Christmas Eve hors d'oeuvre, which she still whips up every holiday, along with many other classic Italian dishes, at the age of 87! As always, there are some slight variations on this dish, depending upon your family heritage, but a few details always remain the same. Fresh bread crumbs are a must, as they add lightness and crispness to the result. (Make crumbs in the food processor – one average slice of white bread yields ¼ cup.) Fresh garlic is also a staple, as is a high-quality extra virgin olive oil. Some cooks add chopped bell pepper, tomatoes, and even more clams, but this simple and delicious recipe is the quintessential one and definitely the best I've tasted. Some cooks will moisten the crumb topping with white wine, so be sure to ask when dining out.

Since clamshells tend to wobble on the baking sheet, it helps to anchor them in a ½-inch-deep layer of coarse salt spread on the pan. However, I like to make use of aluminum foil, which is a lot less messy and super-easy to dispose of. Take a long sheet of foil, begin at one end, and roll into a loose, snakelike rope. Arrange it on the baking sheet, curving around to make rows, and set the clamshells on top.

As part of a medley of appetizers, usually three clams per person is sufficient, but if you make an extra one or two per guest, I guarantee that these will be eaten. The amount of crumb topping below will accommodate more than 3 dozen clams – if you find you have extra crumbs, don't pile on the topping just to use it up. Remember that the clams are the star of the show and need only a small enhancement.

Ingredients:

2 to 3 dozen littleneck or small cherrystone clams, scrubbed

Crumb Topping:

1 cup fresh bread crumbs

2 garlic cloves, minced

1 teaspoon finely chopped, fresh parsley leaves

1 teaspoon dried oregano

2 tablespoons extra virgin olive oil

Salt and pepper to taste

1. Shuck the clams over a small bowl, reserving the liquid. Once you've loosened each clam from its shell, place it in another small bowl. Discard half the shells.

2. Preheat the oven to 450 degrees. Arrange coiled aluminum foil or coarse salt (see above) on a large rimmed baking sheet and nestle the reserved shells on top. Put one clam in each shell.

3. Place the crumb ingredients in a small mixing bowl and stir with a fork to combine. Add a little of the clam juice to moisten further. The mixture should still be crumblike, not pasty. Top each clam with 1 to 1½ teaspoons of the crumb mixture and press down gently. (At this point, if you need to, you may cover and refrigerate the pan for up to 2 hours.)

4. Bake in the middle of the oven until the clams are heated through and the topping is golden, about 10 minutes. Transfer to a platter and serve immediately.

Serves 8

EASY DOES IT: Ask your fishmonger to shuck the clams for you, reserving the shells, liquid, and clams in plastic bags or small containers. You can keep these, if well chilled in the refrigerator (put them on ice), for a day before preparing them for baking.

Crispy Fried Calamari and Baby Scallops with Creamy Aïoli

Fried *calamari* (squid) is always a popular hot seafood appetizer and is surprisingly easy to prepare at home with the aid of a deep-fryer or a pot of oil, set up with a basket and thermometer. And adding little bay scallops to the mix will definitely delight your guests. Similar to an Italian *fritto misto* (mixed fry) in its light crispness, this recipe uses a combination of cornstarch and flour to coat the fish – which somewhat replicates the type of flour used in Italy.

Cleaning squid can be quite a task for the unfamiliar, so look for cleaned tubes and tentacles in your frozen food section (usually in a block), or see whether your grocer's fish department has some previously frozen squid thawed and on ice (if being used the same day). Bags of frozen baby scallops can also be purchased ahead of time and thawed under cold running water before preparing to fry. Be sure that the squid rings, tentacles, and scallops are dried well, however, before coating and frying.

Typically, a simple tomato sauce accompanies this dish, but here we'll be offering up something different: creamy aïoli, a delicious, garlicky dip made from mayonnaise and sour cream instead of the usual raw egg yolk and oil. Serve the aïoli in two small bowls (so there's no waiting for dipping!) and pile up the calamari and scallops on a large, heated platter, surrounded by lemon wedges and parsley sprigs. Cocktail forks or sturdy toothpicks are the perfect utensils to provide and will help make cleanup a snap.

Ingredients
Creamy Aïoli:

1½ cups mayonnaise

½ cup sour cream

2 tablespoons fresh-squeezed lemon juice

2 garlic cloves, minced

1½ tablespoons capers, chopped

Pinch of sugar

Calamari and Scallops:

6 to 8 cups olive oil

1 cup all-purpose flour

1 cup cornstarch

1½ pounds squid, cleaned, sacs cut into ¼-inch rings, tentacles left whole

1 pound bay scallops

Salt and pepper to taste

Lemon wedges for serving

Parsley sprigs for garnish

1. Make the aïoli: In a medium-size mixing bowl, whisk together the ingredients until well combined. Cover and refrigerate until ready to serve. Can be made a day ahead.

2. In a deep-fryer or large, deep saucepan set on the stove, heat the oil over medium-high heat until it reaches 375 degrees. Meanwhile, whisk together the flour and cornstarch in a medium-size bowl. Pat dry the squid pieces and scallops with paper towels.

3. Working in small batches, toss the fish in the flour mixture, shake off any excess, and fry in the oil until golden and crisp, about 1½ minutes. Using a fry basket or slotted spoon, transfer the fish to paper towels or brown paper to drain, and season lightly with salt and pepper. Continue the frying process, being sure to bring the oil temperature back to 375 degrees each time. Transfer to a warmed serving platter, surround with the lemon wedges, garnish with the parsley sprigs, and serve immediately with the aïoli.

Serves 8

Baked Rigatoni Norma with Eggplant and Ricotta Cheese

Ingredients:

¼ cup olive oil

2 medium-size eggplant (about 2 pounds), ends trimmed, peeled, and cut into ¾-inch cubes

Salt and pepper to taste

4 cups (about one-and-a-half 24-ounce jars) prepared spicy spaghetti sauce

1½ pounds rigatoni pasta, cooked *al dente*, drained and rinsed under cold water

1 pound whole-milk ricotta cheese

Handful of fresh basil leaves, roughly chopped

2 cups shredded whole-milk mozzarella cheese

This rich and satisfying main-course pasta dish will bring rave reviews – just like Bellini's opera *Norma*, after which it was named. You can set it up earlier in the day and bake it while enjoying your hors d'oeuvres. Making use of a good-quality prepared sauce will facilitate the preparation and free you up to focus on the rest of your menu. A "Norma"-style pasta sauce is typically characterized by a good deal of "heat" in the form of red pepper flakes. If you'd like to have more control over the spiciness or dispense with it altogether, purchase a regular hearty spaghetti sauce and season (or not) accordingly.

There is much debate as to whether eggplant requires salting to remove bitterness and moisture. I've never found it particularly advantageous to do so, and with the current dietary concerns about excess salt consumption, it's a step that is easily skipped. As for the ricotta cheese, go for the full-fat, whole-milk version, as it holds up better during baking. Fresh ricotta, if available, is ideal, as is fresh mozzarella for the top.

1. Heat the oil in a large, nonstick skillet over medium-high heat. Add the eggplant, sprinkle with salt and pepper, and fry, stirring often until soft in the middle and golden on the outside edges, about 10 minutes. (If using regular spaghetti sauce that needs spicing up, add a dash of red pepper flakes now to the eggplant while frying.) Set aside.

Ingredients:

2 medium-size whole wheat Italian loaves or French baguettes

4 garlic cloves, peeled and roughly chopped

A good pinch of coarse salt

4 tablespoons unsalted butter, softened

½ teaspoon finely chopped, fresh parsley leaves (optional)

Whole Wheat Baguette Garlic Bread

Homemade garlic bread is a wonderful treat to serve your guests. I love making mine from whole wheat Italian or French bread, an increasingly popular supermarket bakery item. You'll want to buy the bread the day of your party for best results. Go for two medium-size loaves instead of an extra-long one that may prove more difficult to maneuver in the oven. You'll also be able to keep one warm while the other is being devoured!

Making a fresh garlic paste is quite easy to do with the aid of a large-bladed knife and a sprinkling of coarse salt. Use back-and-forth motions with the blade at a 45-degree angle on a sturdy cutting board, holding the top of the blade with one hand and the handle with the other. Scrape up and repeat until the garlic pieces form a spreadable paste.

You can prepare the loaves a few hours ahead of time and keep well-wrapped in foil. Heat them in the oven while the baked pasta is resting and serve, nestled in the foil, in loaf-shaped baskets.

2. Preheat the oven to 375 degrees. Cover the bottom of a 12- by 15-inch lasagna or roasting pan with 1 cup of the sauce.

3. Coat the cooked rigatoni with 1 cup of sauce. Spoon ⅓ of the pasta evenly into the pan, distribute half the eggplant and half the basil over it, and top with heaping tablespoons of ricotta, reserving half for the next layer. Top with ½ cup of sauce and repeat. Finish with the remaining ⅓ of the pasta and 1 cup of sauce, spread over evenly. Sprinkle with the shredded mozzarella. At this point you can cover and refrigerate until ready to bake.

4. Bake covered with foil (preferably nonstick) for 30 minutes. Remove the foil and bake a further 15 to 25 minutes until the pasta is heated through and the mozzarella has melted. Let rest for 10 minutes before serving.

Serves 8

1. Preheat the oven to 400 degrees.

2. Using a serrated knife, slice each loaf horizontally into two equal-sized halves. Toast in the oven, cut side up, until the edges begin to brown and the inside of the bread is no longer doughy to the touch, 5 to 10 minutes. Meanwhile, place the garlic on the center of a cutting board and sprinkle with the salt. Make a paste following the directions on the previous page.

3. Remove the loaves from the oven and butter each cut side evenly. Spread the garlic paste over the butter and sprinkle with the parsley (if using). Put the loaves back together and, using a serrated knife, cut 3-inch pieces down through the top and halfway through the bottom. Wrap well in foil and set aside until ready to bake.

4. To finish the loaves, preheat the oven to 350 degrees. Bake them in the foil until heated through, about 8 minutes, and serve immediately.

Serves 8

Candy Cane Ice Cream Profiteroles with Hot Fudge Sauce

Ingredients

Candy Cane Ice Cream:

2 pints vanilla ice cream, softened

1¼ cups crushed red and white candy canes (about 10 ounces)

Food coloring (optional)

Profiteroles:

¾ cup water

6 tablespoons unsalted butter, cut into pieces

1 teaspoon sugar

Pinch of salt

¾ cup all-purpose flour

3 large eggs

Hot Fudge Sauce:

¾ cup heavy cream

⅓ cup light corn syrup

10 ounces semisweet chocolate, chopped

Warn your guests to save room for this heavenly dessert! Cool, creamy peppermint ice cream combines with the decadence of hot fudge to make a spectacular Christmas Eve dessert that will be remembered well into the New Year. And it couldn't be easier.

The making of the profiteroles (puffs) is the only real effort required, and it can be done a day ahead, storing the puffs in an airtight container, or even a week ahead, freezing them in a plastic zip bag. Learning to make this classic dough, called *pâte à choux*, will greatly enhance your entertaining repertoire, as it can be adapted to make savory hors d'oeuvres (by eliminating the sugar), as well as to form receptacles for other sweet fillings such as whipped cream, pastry cream, and mousse. You'll need a pastry bag fitted with a ½-inch plain tip and parchment paper to line the baking sheets.

If you'd like, you can fill the puffs a few hours ahead and store them in the freezer before arranging them on a large, round platter for serving. Allow them to sit for 5 minutes to soften a little while you reheat the hot fudge sauce.

1. Place the ice cream in a large mixing bowl and stir in 1 cup of the crushed candy canes, reserving the remaining ¼ cup for garnish. Add food coloring, if you like, to make the ice cream pink. Cover it with plastic wrap and freeze until firm, 3 to 4 hours.

2. Make the profiteroles: Preheat the oven to 400 degrees. Line two baking sheets with parchment paper. In a medium-size saucepan, combine the water, butter, sugar, and salt, and bring to a boil over medium-high heat, stirring occasionally. When the butter has melted, add the flour all at once and stir with a wooden spoon until the dough comes away from the sides of the pan and forms a ball, 1 to 2 minutes. Transfer to a large mixing bowl and allow to cool for 5 minutes.

3. Using an electric mixer, beat in the eggs one at a time. Wait until each egg is well incorporated before adding the next. Spoon the dough into a pastry bag fitted with a ½-inch plain tip. Pipe 1½-inch-wide mounds of the dough onto the lined baking sheets, 2 to 3 inches apart, 8 mounds per sheet. Wet your fingertips with water and round out the tops. Bake the puffs for 20 minutes, reduce the oven temperature to 350 degrees, and continue to bake them until they are golden, about 10 minutes. Using a sharp paring knife, pierce the side of each puff (to allow steam to escape) and bake 5 more minutes. Transfer them to a wire rack and cool completely before filling, storing, or freezing.

EASY DOES IT: Around holiday time, it's possible to find ready-made candy cane or peppermint ice cream in your grocer's freezer, in which case you can skip step one – just remember to crush a few candy canes for garnish. Similarly, if you have a favorite commercial hot fudge sauce, feel free to substitute it for step four, heating according to label directions. Watch for alcohol-spiked fudge and chocolate sauces, however, when purchasing ready-made versions.

4. Make the hot fudge sauce. In a medium-size saucepan, bring the cream and corn syrup to a simmer. Remove from the heat, add the chocolate, and whisk until melted and smooth. Cool and refrigerate if making ahead.

5. To serve: Use a serrated knife to cut the puffs in half, crosswise. Place one scoop of ice cream in the bottom of each and cover with the top. Arrange in a circular mound on a large, round platter. Rewarm the fudge sauce over low heat until pourable. Drizzle the sauce over the profiteroles,

White Hot Chocolate with Candy Cane Swizzle Sticks

Ingredients

Swizzle Sticks:

2 to 4 ounces white chocolate, chopped

8 to 16 candy canes

Red and green candy sprinkles

White Hot Chocolate:

4 cups (1 quart) light cream

4 cups (1 quart) whole milk

12 ounces white chocolate, chopped

Sweetened whipped cream (optional)

The perfect ending to your holiday evening and a great complement to Candy Cane Ice Cream Profiteroles with Hot Fudge sauce, this creamy, soothing drink will impress your guests with its originality and produce more than a few "oohs" and "aahs" with every sip. White chocolate is not chocolate in the true sense, as it contains only cocoa butter but no chocolate liquor (a misnomer that refers merely to the essence of cocoa bean), but its distinctive flavor is savored by chocolate fans everywhere. Look for a good-quality variety such as Lindt® or Ghirardelli® and avoid imitations in the form of vanilla chips or white confection, which lack the essential cocoa butter.

Innovative candy cane swizzle sticks will definitely add to the presentation and are easy to make ahead. Dipped in melted white chocolate and coated in red or green sprinkles, they are fun and festive. Use a combination of red and white (peppermint) and green and white (spearmint) candy canes for a colorful display. Providing one of each for each guest is a delightful touch.

Serve the hot chocolate in one-cup mugs set on a saucer with a doily, and place the swizzle sticks alongside. A dollop of whipped cream topped with more sprinkles, although not necessary, will take this sweet ending over the top!

1. To make the swizzle sticks, melt the chocolate in a small bowl set over a pan of boiling water, stirring until smooth. Remove from the heat and let cool until lukewarm to the touch. Have ready a baking sheet lined with wax or parchment paper. Place the sprinkles in a small juice glass. Dip the candy canes, one at a time, halfway into the chocolate, allow any excess to drip off, then submerge in one of the glasses with the sprinkles. Place on the baking sheet to set. Store in a covered tin until ready to use.

2. Make the hot chocolate: Place the white chocolate in a large heat-proof mixing bowl. In a large saucepan, combine the cream and milk over medium heat and bring to "scalding" – just until bubbles appear around the edges. This will take 4 to 5 minutes. Pour the cream mixture over the chocolate and whisk them together until the chocolate has melted and the liquid is slightly foamy. Immediately ladle into the mugs, add a dollop of whipped cream if you like, top with more sprinkles, and serve with one or two swizzle sticks on the saucer.

Serves 8

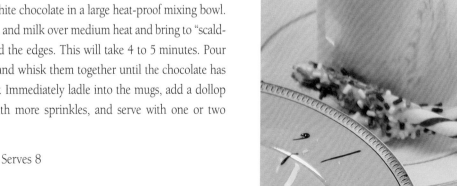

Avoiding a White-Knuckle Christmas: Advice for the Newly Sober

Now that the packages of red and green M&M's® have arrived in the super-market candy aisle, we can rest assured that the holiday season is truly upon us. Commercially, this time of year is the biggest for specialty foods and good-ies from fruitcake to candy canes, and more often than not "festive" food is syn-onymous with "booze-laden." Brandy-soaked cakes and plum puddings, mulled wine, and spiked chocolates are just a few of the places that alcohol will be lurking. A whirlwind of holiday office parties, cocktail get-togethers, and family reunions with rum eggnog will be a challenge to sobriety, especially for those who are newly sober. How do we avoid a Christmas of "white-knuckling" (a recovery euphemism meaning to stay sober out of sheer will power) when the odds are so heavily stacked against us?

Here are a few tips for the holidays that will help keep you and your abstinent loved ones safe and sober:

• First and foremost, if you are invited to a hol-iday party or gathering where booze is a big component and you know you'll feel uncomfort-able, simply don't go. There will be many more holidays (thanks to that coura-geous decision to get clean and sober) to enjoy in the future. Stay home with the kids and bake some Christmas cookies instead.

• Before you eat or drink anything at a party, make sure you know what's in it. Don't be afraid to ask: It's not impolite, it's imperative. If you're not sure or can't get a straight answer, then skip it and reach for something more familiar. Remember that small ingested amounts of alcohol, although incapable of mak-ing us drunk, can spark unwanted neurochemical recognition that, under stress-ful conditions, could contribute to craving.

• At seated dinners, turning over your wineglass is a signal to the waitress that you won't be imbibing. At parties with an open bar, get an alcohol-free drink as soon as you enter and hang onto it. If you're uncomfortable saying why you're not drinking, simply make a joke or explain that you are refraining for medical reasons (which is true). Personally, I think it's always best to be upfront – and there's no time better than the present to claim your new sobriety with pride and conviction. It says who you are, and in the end, the people who matter will respect you for it.

• Always eat before you go out to a function, even if food will be served. Empty stomachs have a way of convincing us that what we are really hungry for is a drink. The symptoms of craving and low blood sugar (due to not eating) are almost identical – nausea, irritability, sweating, and lightheadedness. Keep some healthy snacks in the car in case you need them and drink plenty of water to avoid dehy-dration, which can also create craving-like symptoms.

• Always have an escape plan. When holiday parties and get-togethers are being organized, especially among friends, there's a tendency to pile everyone together (the "more the merrier" attitude) more than on other occasions, so if things start to get a bit hairy, have a "Plan B" for get-ting home. Sometimes, however, a total escape is not necessary. A little respite in some fresh air can do wonders to clear our minds. Go outside, take a few deep breaths, walk around a bit, call someone on your cell phone, and tell your-self that "this too shall pass," because the truth is, it always does.

• When you've successfully survived a stressful evening, reward yourself! Whatever it is that comforts you, whether a hot bubble bath, watching your favorite movie for the umpteenth time, or devouring a bag of those red and green M&M's®, go for it. Most important, be gentle and kind to yourself. It's tough out there, but guess what? *You made it!*

At many American Christmas dinner tables, a beautifully glazed ham provides the centerpiece for one of the most delicious meals of the year. Steeped in warm, old-fashioned tradition, a hearty meal of everything from soup to nuts is a must for Midwestern celebrations, and this heartwarming menu definitely fits the bill.

Cups of warm apple cider served with the easy yet festive Liptauer Cheese Wreath with crackers will let your guests know you haven't missed a beat as they "wet their whistles" for the scrumptious meal ahead. A rich and creamy Potato, Leek, and Oyster Soup will greet them as they're seated and satisfy their taste buds as they anxiously await the main event – the gorgeous Red Mahogany Glazed Ham, safely prepared with a cherry juice, molasses, and cola glaze, and not a drop of bourbon! Mouth-watering side dishes accompany your masterpiece and round out the meal. And just when they think your efforts can't be topped, the luscious Christmas Eggnog Bread Pudding with an alcohol-free twist will delight one and all.

For the finale, a variety of specialty iced teas and holiday roast coffee will complement your menu to perfection. From beginning to end, it will be a merry Christmas dinner that will be savored and remembered in the hearts (and stomachs!) of your guests for years to come.

Christmas Dinner in the Heartland

MENU
Dinner for Six

APPETIZER:
Liptauer Cheese Wreath
Butter Crackers

FIRST COURSE:
Potato, Leek, and Oyster Soup

MAIN COURSE:
Red Mahogany-Glazed Ham
Baked Sweet Potatoes
Roasted Green Beans with Cipollini Onions
Holiday Waldorf Salad
Corn Muffins with Jalapeño Jelly

DESSERT:
Christmas Eggnog Bread Pudding
Ice Cream

BEVERAGE PAIRINGS:
Appetizer: *Hot Spiced Cider*
First and Main Courses: *Variety Iced Teas*
Dessert: *Holiday Roast Coffee*

Tips on Purchased Ingredients

Butter crackers are perfect for creamy cheese spreads. Choose from Ritz®, Townhouse®, or another buttery variety without the addition of flavorings such as garlic, herbs, or seeds, which would compete with the spread. If you'd like to serve a purchased cheese log or ball in addition to or in place of the Liptauer cheese wreath, be sure to choose one without the addition of alcohol, most commonly in the form of port.

Baked sweet potatoes make for an easy side dish and a nice departure from the usual candied yams or casserole. Choose medium-size potatoes, wrap them in foil, and bake alongside your ham during the final 45 minutes. Offer whipped butter and a shaker with cinnamon sugar for a delightfully sweet accompaniment.

Corn muffins go hand in hand with ham, and you can purchase them ahead and heat them up for the table. Mini-size muffins are fun, especially with kids at the table – allow at least two per person. Red or green *jalapeño jelly* (or both) adds a festive touch and a bit of "heat" for those who enjoy it.

Bread pudding would be unthinkable without *ice cream*, so choose from butter pecan, maple walnut, or good old plain vanilla, all of which would be tasty here. Although rum raisin would also go well, be aware that the taste could be a trigger for the newly sober.

Hot spiced cider is the perfect greeting for your guests as they come in out of the wintry cold. Ciders of all flavors and descriptions are easily found in the supermarket, so choose one that you think will appeal to everyone. For casual occasions, you can keep it warm in a large pot on top of the stove and ladle servings as needed. Otherwise, don't discount the convenience of your slow cooker, which is a great receptacle for hot drinks and can be set out in the dining or living room for easy access.

Serve pitchers of prepared *iced tea* at the table to accompany the main meal. Or let guests choose from a variety of bottled teas, from decaf to diet to unsweetened. You can cater to every need and whim this way. Be sure to have plenty of ice on hand. The astringency of tea is great for freshening the palate (just as wine would do) and is a great counterpart to rich, cream-laden dishes.

At Christmastime, we find many limited-edition flavored coffees drummed up by manufacturers to incorporate flavors of the season. Everything from pumpkin spice to eggnog is available, so choose a *holiday roast coffee* that will surprise and delight your guests. Serve with creamers of milk, half-and-half, and a bowl of raw sugar, such as turbinado, for a nice touch.

Liptauer Cheese Wreath

I've been making this wonderfully appetizing cheese spread in some shape or form for many years, and it's always a hit. A round, tube-shaped mold like those used for gelatin rings is perfect to decorate as a holiday wreath, but if you happen to have a Christmas tree mold, feel free to use it as an alternative presentation.

Liptauer is a traditional German and Austrian spread, popular in America's Midwest where there's a strong northern European influence. It's essentially the basis for cheese-and-pimiento-type spreads, also well-liked in the heartland. The key to this recipe is its three- to four-day "mellowing" in the refrigerator so be sure to make it in advance. A food processor will do all the work, made even easier when the ingredients are at room temperature. The amounts in the following recipe yield about three cups and can easily be doubled, if you like. Depending on the size of your mold, you may have extra Liptauer, in which case you can fill small ramekins or decorative bowls, cover tightly with plastic wrap, and refrigerate. When unexpected guests arrive during the holidays, you'll have a ready-made appetizer to serve!

Ingredients:

1 pound cream cheese, softened

⅓ pound sharp yellow cheddar cheese, diced

4 tablespoons (½ stick) unsalted butter, softened

2 tablespoons finely chopped onion

1½ teaspoons spicy brown mustard

¼ teaspoon sweet paprika

Fresh bay leaves and cranberries to garnish

1. Line a ring mold with pieces of plastic wrap draped over both sides.

2. Combine the cream cheese, cheddar, butter, onion, mustard, and paprika in the bowl of a food processor fitted with a sharp blade. Blend until completely smooth, occasionally stopping to scrape the sides. Using a rubber spatula, fill the ring mold, smooth the top, and use the draped plastic wrap to cover the surface. Press down firmly. Refrigerate for at least 3 days and up to 1 week.

3. To serve, undrape the plastic wrap from the surface and turn the mold over onto a large, round platter. Lift off the mold and remove the plastic. You can use a spreading knife to smooth out the surface. Decorate with the bay leaves and cranberries to make it resemble holly. Allow the Liptauer to soften at room temperature for 1 hour before serving with small spreaders and butter crackers.

Serves 6 to 8

Hold the Buzz! Tips for Dining Out at Holiday Time

Whether with family, friends, or co-workers, dinner get-togethers at restaurants for holiday celebrations rank high on the list of social events where we often find ourselves surrounded by plentiful drinking and alcohol-laden specialty foods. For those who cannot or choose not to imbibe, dining out can be a confusing endeavor at the best of times, but it's particularly precarious during the holidays, when restaurant selections and specials often contain more than the usual amount of alcoholic ingredients. Here are a few tips to help you wade through potential uncertainties:

Tip 1: Keep a close eye on your beverage glass. In a dimly lit restaurant with loud talking and laughter, it's easy to get distracted and pick up someone else's rum and coke instead of your Diet Pepsi. If you must, smell before you sip, or simply order a fresh drink. Ordering something visually different from typical alcoholic drinks might help too. Iced tea, served in a tall glass with a lemon wedge, long straw, and spoon, is pretty darn hard to mistake for just about anything else.

Tip 2: Good restaurant menus will give ample descriptions of what's in a dish, so usually you can tell whether wine, brandy, or another type of alcoholic ingredient is present. If you're not sure, don't be afraid to ask. Generally I encourage making a special request of the chef to substitute another ingredient for the alcohol in a dish, but now is probably not the time. During busy holiday seatings in a jam-packed restaurant, mistakes can be made and requests inadvertently ignored. Just this once, don't take the chance.

continued on page 130

Potato, Leek, and Oyster Soup

Here, the classic leek and potato soup combines with creamy oyster stew to become the perfect, soothingly rich start to your Christmas dinner. One of the great things about this recipe is its adaptability to likes and dislikes – since the potato-and-leek base is made first, kids and adults who shun oysters can be served this soup "oysterless." It can even be turned into a mock chowder by replacing the oysters with clams, but I much prefer the version below. Give it a try and don't be surprised if you win over some supposed non-oyster-eating folks with the first spoonful!

If shucking oysters is not your thing, solicit the help of your fishmonger, who can shuck them for you and retain the precious liquor (simply the name for the oyster juices – no alcohol involved). You can also sometimes find containers of pre-shucked oysters in their liquid, although they're not always the "cream of the crop." It's best to choose small ones, sometimes referred to as "cocktails," but "selects" are just as good. Ask the people behind the fish counter for their expert opinion and tell them what you're using the oysters for. They'll be more than happy to oblige.

Make the base a day or two ahead and reheat it over a very low flame, whisking to encourage a smooth consistency. Add the prepared oysters just before serving, ladle into warmed soup bowls, and don't forget to pass around the bowl of oyster crackers.

Ingredients:

4 tablespoons unsalted butter

2 medium-size leeks (white part only), ends trimmed, washed well, and chopped

Salt and pepper to taste

4 cups water

4 medium-size russet potatoes, peeled and diced

2 cups half-and-half

1½ cups shucked small oysters, liquor reserved (see recipe introduction)

Dash Tabasco® sauce

Oyster crackers

1. In a heavy-bottomed soup pot, melt the butter over medium heat, add the leeks, sprinkle with salt and pepper, and cook, stirring often, until the leeks are soft and translucent, about 10 minutes. Reduce heat to prevent browning, if necessary.

2. Add the water and potatoes, bring to a simmer, and allow to cook uncovered until the potatoes are fork-tender, 25 to 30 minutes. Stir in the half-and-half. Purée in batches in a blender until smooth. You may stop at this point, pour the soup into containers, and chill it until you're ready to use it. Otherwise, pour the soup into a clean saucepan, cover, and keep warm over very low heat.

3. To prepare the oysters, melt the remaining 2 tablespoons of butter in a nonstick skillet, add the oysters with ½ cup of their reserved liquid, and cook until just the edges of the oysters begin to curl, about 4 minutes. Transfer them to the saucepan containing the soup base, stir well, and allow to cook a further 5 minutes over low heat. Add the Tabasco® sauce, taste for the addition of salt, and serve immediately with oyster crackers.

Serves 6

Ingredients:

¾ cup sweet dried cherries

1 cup boiling water

⅔ cup mayonnaise

⅓ cup sour cream

Juice of half a lemon

1 tablespoon granulated sugar

4 Granny Smith apples, cored and cut into ½-inch dice

3 medium celery stalks, ends trimmed, peeled, and cut into ¼-inch slices

½ medium-size red bell pepper, cored, seeded, and diced

½ medium-size green bell pepper, cored, seeded, and diced

Salt and pepper to taste

Radicchio and romaine lettuce leaves

½ cup candied pecans

Holiday Waldorf Salad

Classic Waldorf salad may be on many a holiday menu, but this festive version will get raves for Christmases to come. Although you'll find some of the usual suspects, namely Granny Smith apples and celery, the addition of colorful, crunchy red and green bell peppers, as well as sweet dried cherries to complement your ham, will set this dish apart from the typically uninspired Waldorf salads everyone knows.

Candied nuts are easy to find around the holidays, and I've even seen praline pecans in the candy section year-round. However, feel free to use plain pecans if you prefer or substitute another type of glazed nut such as walnuts or almonds. For those with allergies to nuts who still like a bit of crunch, sprinkle some sunflower seeds on top before serving.

1. In a small bowl, soak the cherries in boiling water for 10 minutes. Drain and cut into halves.

2. In a large mixing bowl, whisk together the mayonnaise, sour cream, lemon juice, and sugar until they are well combined. Add the cherries, apples, celery, and bell peppers, and using a rubber spatula, stir together to coat. Season to taste with salt and pepper. Chill in the refrigerator for 1 hour.

3. To serve, arrange the radicchio and romaine lettuce leaves decoratively on a large platter, spoon the salad into a mound in the middle, and sprinkle the pecans over the top.

Serves 6

Red Mahogany-Glazed Ham

A Christmas ham is a heartland specialty and a glazed ham is a definite must! Types of glazes abound, but in general, a good one requires something sweet that will caramelize, creating a beautiful color and a delicious taste. Here, we'll be using an old Midwest standby – cola – along with a few other ingredients to create a richly colored exterior. Mahogany glazes often imply that scotch, bourbon, or some form of brandy has been added, but here, a touch of maraschino cherry juice will be the magic ingredient that puts the "red" in our mahogany.

Most supermarket hams are fully cooked, so it's really only a matter of glazing and heating through. Either bone-in (more flavorful) or boneless (easier to carve) is fine, although I prefer to have a bone left for soup-making. The usual serving estimate is between ½ and ¾ pound per person, but extra servings for unexpected guests, as well as leftovers, are always welcome, so it's best to opt for a good-sized ham. Studding the ham with cloves is optional, but the flavor it imparts is so wonderful that the task is well worth the trouble.

To retain moisture, I've discovered that placing the ham cut side down on a foil-covered roasting pan works wonders, as does tenting the ham with nonstick foil. Baste often for a nice glaze, and if it requires a bit more color by the time the ham is heated through, you can always turn the oven to broil for a few minutes at the end to burnish the ham into a fine red mahogany hue.

Ingredients:

One 9- to 10-pound fully cooked ham, preferably bone-in, shank, or butt end

Whole cloves

½ cup light molasses

⅓ cup maraschino cherry juice

¼ cup spicy brown mustard

One 12-ounce can cola

(not diet cola)

1. Preheat the oven to 350 degrees. Line a large roasting pan with foil.

2. Trim the ham, leaving about ¼ inch of fat, and with a sharp knife, score the fat layer diagonally to create a diamond pattern. Insert one whole clove into each diamond and transfer the ham, cut side down, to the roasting pan.

3. In a small mixing bowl, combine the molasses, cherry juice, and mustard, and stir until smooth. Using a pastry brush, coat the rind of the ham with the mixture. Pour the cola into the bottom of the pan, tent with nonstick foil, and bake untouched for 30 minutes. Begin basting with the pan liquid every 10 to 12 minutes, until the ham is nicely glazed and heated through, 1½ to 2 hours. Remove from the oven, transfer to a large platter, and allow to rest for 10 to 15 minutes before carving. Serve with the pan juices, if desired.

Serves 6 to 8

Roasted Green Beans with Cipollini Onions

One of the most delicious methods of preparing vegetables is roasting, and surprisingly, simple green beans gain a stellar presentation when prepared this way with buttery and sweet *cipollini* onions. These little Italian onion delicacies are found fresh more and more in local supermarkets, especially during the winter, so if you come across them, grab a couple of small bags. If they can't be found, substitute shallots.

If necessary, you can prepare these a few hours ahead and reheat them just before serving. Unlike most roasted vegetable dishes, we're not looking for crispness, but rather intensity of flavor, so making them ahead is actually a good idea. Reheat in the microwave or covered, in a low (250-degree) oven. Although the amount of green beans called for may seem like a lot, keep in mind that they'll shrink quite a bit. If you need to use two roasting pans or baking sheets to allow for adequate roasting space, by all means do so.

Ingredients:

½ pound cipollini onions, trimmed and peeled, root end left intact (larger onions halved)

4 tablespoons olive oil

Salt and pepper to taste

2 pounds green beans, stalk ends snipped and beans left whole

1 tablespoon balsamic vinegar

1. Preheat the oven to 400 degrees.

2. In a large roasting pan, toss the onions with 2 tablespoons of the olive oil and season with salt and pepper. Roast until lightly browned, stirring occasionally, about 15 minutes. Add the green beans and the remaining olive oil and toss with the onions. Continue roasting until the green beans are tender and somewhat shriveled, stirring to prevent overbrowning and sticking, 25 to 35 minutes.

3. Remove from the oven and immediately drizzle with vinegar. Stir gently to coat and taste for the addition of salt and pepper. Serve immediately or set aside, covered, to reheat later.

Serves 6

continued from page 126

Tip 3: For some reason, when they're dining out in groups at holiday time, people love to share what they have ordered with others. If someone sticks a forkful of food in your face, politely decline with "I couldn't eat another bite." Not only do you not know what's on the fork, but the other person would probably be hard-pressed to recite the ingredients as well. Better to be safe than sorry.

Tip 4: In spite of all our vigilance, we can't always prevent a mistake from happening, whether by sipping from someone's cocktail or biting into a brandy truffle. The taste and tingly feeling of alcohol in your mouth may linger and bother you, so sip or eat something with a strong flavor to counteract the effect. If alcohol is medically forbidden or personally unappealing and you accidentally ingest or drink something you suspect contains it, know that this very small amount will not hurt you. Chalk it up to a valuable learning experience and vow to be a bit more cautious in the future.

Tip 5: Relax, have a great time, and discover that holiday fun doesn't depend on alcohol. A clear head in the morning and a fond recollection of the night before will be proof enough! By the way, if at the end of the evening someone near you looks as if he or she may need a designated driver, be a seasonal "Good Samaritan" and offer your services. 'Tis the season, after all, to be both jolly and giving!

Christmas Eggnog Bread Pudding

Who can imagine Christmas without eggnog? Instead of serving it in the punch bowl (where expectations of alcohol reside), use it to make this amazingly decadent warm dessert. Bread pudding in its own right will often call for alcoholic ingredients, usually in the accompanying sauce, so beware when ordering out. But here, where the baking and serving are under your command, this recipe is not only sober-safe but "soberlicious"!

You can make the bread pudding in individual baking dishes or ramekins instead of spooning out portions from one large baking dish. If you make it earlier in the day and it requires a little reheating, cover the baking dish with foil and place it in a water bath (a large roasting pan with hot water) in a low-temperature oven to prevent the pudding from becoming dry. Individual ramekins can be quickly reheated in the microwave for a "just-baked" presentation.

1. Preheat the oven to 350 degrees. Lightly butter a 9- by 13-inch glass or ceramic baking dish, or individual ramekins.

2. Using a serrated bread knife, cut the crustless bread slices into ½-inch cubes. Transfer to a large mixing bowl and setaside.

3. In another large bowl, whisk together the eggs, eggnog, milk, sugar, and nutmeg until they're well combined. Pour the mixture over the bread cubes, stir gently with a rubber spatula, and let soak for 15 minutes until the bread has absorbed most of the liquid.

4. Transfer to the prepared baking dish, smooth out the surface, and bake until the top is lightly golden and puffed and a toothpick inserted in the center comes out clean, 30 to 40 minutes (about 20 minutes for smaller servings). Cool on a wire rack for 15 minutes and serve by spooning into individual bowls, topping with a scoop of ice cream.

Serves 6 to 8

Ingredients:

One 24-ounce loaf of sliced buttermilk or country-style bread, ends and crusts removed

4 large eggs

2 cups purchased eggnog

1 cup milk

⅓ cup granulated sugar

½ teaspoon ground nutmeg

½ gallon ice cream

Hanukkah, also known as the Festival of Lights, lasts eight days and nights, and is full of games, blessings, and of course, festive food. Celebrating the miracle of the Maccabees, who were able to burn a single day's supply of purified oil in the ancient temple of Jerusalem for eight full days, Hanukkah traditions embrace the remembrance of that oil in the lighting of the menorah, as well as by foods that are cooked with oil. Latkes, or potato pancakes, are the most popular of these foods and often the menu focus of a get-together such as this one.

An abundance of latkes, accompanied by a variety of toppings, is a great treat. Without meat on the menu (which would normally prohibit the use of dairy products), we can add ingredients like sour cream and cream cheese, which will contribute to the richness and lusciousness of the dishes served. Making latkes has never been easier when you use the base recipe given here and vary it three ways. And make-ahead instructions will ensure that you're not glued to the stove, but are part of your own celebrations. Serving latkes with a refreshingly crunchy Israeli Salad is the perfect way to go, while a terrific alternative to wine, Dry Concord Grape Fizz, will wash everything down in style. Save room for the incredibly moist Chocolate Walnut Carrot Cake, which will leave your guests more than satisfied and wondering how they managed to eat every last crumb!

A Hanukkah Latkes Party

MENU
Dinner for Ten

APPETIZER:

Hummus with
Flatbread and Celery Sticks

MAIN COURSE:

Latkes Three Ways:

Classic Potato Latkes
with Chunky Homemade Applesauce

Herbed Potato Latkes
with Dilled Sour Cream and Gravlax

Zucchini Potato Latkes with Eggplant Caviar

Israeli Salad with Watercress Garnish

DESSERT:

Chocolate Walnut Carrot Cake
Assorted Rugelach and Sufganiyot

BEVERAGE PAIRINGS:

Appetizer and Main Course: Dry Concord Grape Fizz
Dessert: *Chamomile Tea with Honey Sticks*

Tips on Purchased Ingredients

Hummus, made from chickpeas, can be found in a variety of flavors, from roasted garlic (perfect for garlic lovers) to chipotle pepper (for those who like a bit of heat). Choose three varieties that you think will please your guests and serve them in a trio of bowls surrounded by an assortment of deliciously crunchy **flatbreads**. The addition of **celery sticks** will provide some clean, crispy crunch to the appetizer tray as will carrot sticks. You can purchase pre-cut celery in the produce section, or simply buy a bag of celery hearts and cut them into 2- to 3-inch pieces.

Rugelach, a true Hanukkah tradition, is a pastry made from rich cream-cheese dough, spread with a filling such as apricot, raspberry, nuts, or even chocolate, then rolled into a crescent shape. A labor-intensive project, to say the least (especially when you're tackling latkes for 10), rugelach, happily, is found in supermarkets and bakeries during most of the year, so make use of these ready-made delicacies and serve them on a platter next to your Chocolate Walnut Carrot Cake masterpiece. Similarly, **sufganiyot**, or jelly doughnuts, are typical fare at the Hanukkah table and can be included as part of your dessert display. Generally deep-fried, these are another representation of the focus on precious oil, and some holiday tables wouldn't be considered complete without them.

After a meal laden with heavy ingredients like oil, the astringency of tea and stomach-calming characteristics of chamomile in particular make for the ideal final quaff. Bring out your prettiest tea cups and serve your **chamomile tea with honey sticks**, a wonderful added touch that can be found in gourmet food shops or ordered online.

Latkes Three Ways

Ingredients:

5 pounds russet or Idaho potatoes

1½ teaspoons baking powder

1 cup all-purpose flour

1 tablespoon kosher salt

Fresh ground pepper to taste

1 large onion, peeled and finely chopped

6 large eggs

Oil for frying (see recipe introduction)

1 tablespoon each finely chopped, fresh parsley leaves, chives, and dill sprigs

3 medium-size zucchini (about 1 pound), trimmed and shredded

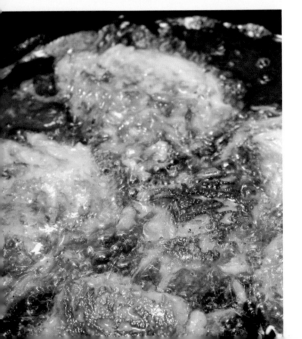

Although no one would argue that potato pancakes often taste best when straight from the pan, neither would anyone argue that you shouldn't be allowed to enjoy your own party, rather than be glued to the stove like a short-order fry cook! The simple solution is to make your latkes ahead of time and freeze them. They'll crisp up perfectly in a hot oven on the night of your party and keep you and your kitchen free from spattered grease.

The beauty of these latkes is that you get three delicious variations from one basic recipe. Pick an afternoon a few days (or even weeks) before the party and plan to fry them all up in batches. Electric frying pans are great for this task, but you can just as easily use the old-fashioned method of stovetop frying – and if you're up to it, keep two pans going at once and have plenty of paper towels on hand for draining. Before you know it, the biggest task of your latkes party will be done so that when the day arrives, you can focus on the small details as well as other parts of your menu.

A food processor for the potato-shredding will make life a lot easier, but if you prefer, you can grate them by hand. Russet or Idaho potatoes are the best choice due to their high-starch content, although Yukon Golds would also work well. Shred the potatoes as needed to prevent browning – have them ready to shred, however, by peeling them all and keeping them in a large pot of cold water. Make sure you have plenty of oil on hand to fry with – a neutral, high-smoke-point oil is best, such as canola, vegetable, or peanut. Some cooks like to add a bit of butter to the pan for flavor, but I find that if you do, you'll end up having to clean the pan more often between batches. Stick with straight oil and season your potato mixture well – the toppings will provide any additional flavor required. This recipe will make about 20 of each of the three kinds of latkes.

1. Peel the potatoes, remove any brown spots or blemishes, and transfer to a large pot of cold water, then set aside.

2. Line up three large mixing bowls. In the first bowl, whisk together ½ teaspoon baking powder, ⅓ cup flour, 1 teaspoon salt, and a grinding of pepper. Repeat with the other two bowls and set them aside.

To freeze the latkes: Place them in a single layer on a baking sheet in the freezer. After they've frozen solid, transfer the latkes to plastic zip-lock freezer bags and label accordingly.

To reheat the latkes: Place the defrosted latkes on a baking sheet in a single layer and bake in a 400-degree oven until crisp and heated through, about 7 minutes. Blot excess oil on a paper towel and serve with the appropriate toppings.

3. *To make Classic Potato Latkes:* Grate or shred 2 pounds of the potatoes, pour off half the accumulated liquid, and add the potatoes to the first bowl with ⅓ of the chopped onion and two of the eggs. Stir well to combine. Heat 3 to 4 tablespoons of oil in a large skillet. Work with two skillets if you feel comfortable with that. When the oil is hot (test by dropping a pinch of the potato mixture in the skillet – it should spatter and sizzle), drop heaping spoonfuls of the potato mixture into the oil and press each one down with a spatula. Fry until golden brown, 3 to 4 minutes per side. Transfer to paper towels to drain. Continue frying batches of the latkes, adding more oil as necessary, until the mixture in the first bowl has been used up.

4. *To make the Herbed Potato Latkes:* Follow the directions in step 3, adding the chopped herbs with the potatoes, onion, and eggs to the second bowl. If the oil in the skillet appears "dirty" or speckled with dark brown bits, pour out, wipe clean with a paper towel, and add fresh oil. Fry the latkes according to directions in step 3.

5. To make the Zucchini Potato Latkes: Follow the directions in step 3 using the remaining 1 pound of potatoes and the shredded zucchini. Combine with the onion and eggs in the third bowl and stir well. Fry the latkes according to directions in step 3.

Serves 10

The Toppings

These three toppings can be prepared ahead of time and kept refrigerated, but be sure to serve the applesauce and the eggplant caviar at room temperature for peak flavor. For both of these toppings, place them in a bowl in the center of a large platter and arrange the latkes around them. For the Herbed Potato Latkes, it's best to present them already topped (see following instructions). For those who like their sour cream "straight up" as an alternative topping for Classic Potato Latkes, set some aside from a one-pint container before making the dilled sour cream, and serve it along with the applesauce.

Gravlax is salmon that has been cured with salt, sugar, and dill, and is an attractive change from plain smoked salmon or lox. If you prefer, however, you can substitute one of the latter and simply garnish with a dill sprig.

Ingredients:

3 Golden Delicious and
3 Red Delicious apples (about 2 pounds total), peeled, cored, and cut into 1-inch chunks

1 cup apple cider

½ cup sugar

Juice of half a lemon

Chunky Homemade Applesauce

1. In a large saucepan, combine all the ingredients and bring to a simmer over medium-high heat. Reduce the heat to low and cook covered, stirring occasionally until the apples are tender, about 15 minutes. If excess liquid remains, cook a further 5 minutes, uncovered, until most of the liquid has evaporated. Remove from the heat and cool for 15 minutes.

2. Using a potato masher, roughly mash the apples until somewhat smooth, but still a little chunky. Transfer to a covered container and refrigerate until 2 hours before serving.

Ingredients:

1 cup sour cream

1½ teaspoons finely chopped, fresh dill sprigs

½ teaspoon fresh lemon juice

Pinch of sugar

Two 4-ounce packages of gravlax

Dill sprigs for garnish (optional)

Dilled Sour Cream with Gravlax

1. In a small mixing bowl, combine all the ingredients except the gravlax, stir well, cover with plastic wrap, and refrigerate until ready to serve.

2. When the Herbed Potato Pancakes are crisp and hot, place a small dollop of the dilled sour cream on top of each one and drape with a piece of the gravlax. Garnish with the dill sprigs, if using, and serve immediately on a platter in a single layer.

Eggplant Caviar

1. Heat the olive oil in a large, nonstick skillet over medium-high heat, add the eggplant, sprinkle with salt and pepper, and fry, stirring often until golden and tender, 12 to 15 minutes. Add more oil as necessary to prevent sticking. Transfer with a slotted spoon to a bowl lined with paper towels and set aside.

2. Add the onion to the skillet and cook, stirring until crispy tender, about 2 minutes. Add the garlic and cook a further minute. Return the eggplant to the skillet, add the tomato sauce, vinegar, sugar, and basil, and stir to combine well. Cook over medium heat, stirring frequently to allow the flavors to marry, about 3 minutes. Taste for the addition of salt and pepper, and transfer the mixture to a storage container to cool. Cover and refrigerate until 2 hours before serving.

Ingredients:

2 tablespoons olive oil

1 large eggplant, ends trimmed, peeled, and cut into ¼-inch dice

Salt and pepper to taste

½ cup finely chopped red onion

2 garlic cloves, peeled and minced

½ cup tomato sauce

Splash red wine vinegar

Pinch of sugar

1 tablespoon chopped, fresh basil leaves

Dry Concord Grape Fizz

Dry red wine is often the drink of choice when latkes are on the menu. Its tannic puckering and piquant quality can cut through the heavy, oil-laden ingredients of many Hanukkah dishes. In offering an alcohol-free alternative, we need to consider these qualities, and Dry Concord Grape Fizz, completely sober-safe, truly fits the bill.

Unsweetened Concord grape juice is the base, although know that "unsweetened" usually only implies that there is little or no added sugar. Certain brands are less sweet than others, and those would be the best choice in this instance. R.W. Knudsen's™ "Just Concord" is an excellent one, as are the old, reliable Kedem® grape juices. Schweppes makes a delightful dry grape ginger ale that's the perfect complement to Concord grape juice. Together, they mimic the all-important astringent quality we're after.

You can combine them yourself and serve in pitchers or a punch bowl, or simply put each bottle on the table for guests to combine themselves. If kids are in attendance, you may want to supply them with a bottle of the more-familiar sweet grape juice, which they will no doubt prefer. Have the juice and soda well chilled to eliminate the need for ice, and provide wine or juice glasses for serving.

Pour one bottle each of the grape juice and dry grape ginger ale into a 3-quart-capacity pitcher (or divide between two 1½- to 2-quart pitchers) and stir to combine. Keep remaining bottles chilled and replenish as necessary.

Serves 10

Ingredients:

Two 32-ounce bottles unsweetened Concord grape juice, chilled

Two 2-liter bottles dry grape ginger ale, chilled

Ingredients:

1 large cucumber, peeled, seeded, and cut into ¼-inch dice

2 medium-size ripe tomatoes, cored, seeded, and cut into ½-inch dice

1 medium-size red bell pepper, trimmed, seeded, and cut into ¼-inch dice

1 medium-size yellow or orange bell pepper, trimmed, seeded, and cut into ¼-inch dice

½ of a large jicama, peeled and cut into ¼-inch dice

1 bunch of scallions, ends trimmed and minced

½ cup finely chopped radishes

1 large kosher dill pickle (or half-sour pickle), ends trimmed and finely chopped

¼ cup olive oil

Juice of half a lemon, or to taste

1 tablespoon finely chopped, fresh parsley leaves

Salt and pepper to taste

3 to 4 cups watercress, tough stems removed

Israeli Salad with Watercress Garnish

This beautiful salad is popular in Israeli homes and restaurants, and is the perfect accompaniment to our abundance of latkes. Its crisp vegetables, as well as the acidic tang added by the lemon and pickle, help cut the heaviness and richness of the fried potato pancakes.

A fine dicing of the vegetables is key to the presentation and, although a bit more work, is well worth it when your guests bestow their compliments on the chef – you. It's best not to make this too far ahead; otherwise, the oil and lemon cause the vegetables to lose their crispiness. However, you can get a jump-start on the preparation by chopping all the vegetables and storing them in separate containers in the refrigerator. Simply combine everything and toss the salad when ready to serve.

Jicama is a wonderfully refreshing and rarely used Mexican root vegetable that people often describe as a cross between an apple and a potato. Once you enjoy it in this recipe, you'll want to add it to other salads as well.

1. Just before serving, combine the cucumber, tomato, red and yellow bell peppers, jicama, scallions, radishes, and pickle in a large mixing bowl. In a small mixing bowl, whisk together the olive oil and lemon juice and pour over the vegetables. Add the parsley, salt, and pepper, and toss well to coat. Taste for seasoning and additional lemon juice.

2. Mound the salad in the middle of a large, round platter and surround with the watercress. Serve immediately.

Serves 10

Stop "Wining!" Exceptional Alternatives to "Heart-Healthy" Wine

When wine is no longer on the menu, does it mean we're missing out on some important health benefits? Absolutely not! Researchers have pinpointed many of the specific phytonutrients (protective plant-based chemicals) present in red wine that appear to have the ability to ward off disease and preserve our cardiovascular health. Not surprisingly, there are numerous other food and drink sources that contain the same healthy nutrients and, in some cases, offer even greater amounts. Here are some exceptional alternatives that will contribute to a healthy heart and overall well-being:

Fruit Juices	Whole Fruit	Tea	Vegetables	Snacks
Cranberry	Apples	Black	Red Onions	Peanuts
Pomegranate	Blueberries	Green	Garlic	Dark Chocolate
Grape	Raspberries	White	Chile Peppers	Dried Cherries

Chocolate Walnut Carrot Cake

Initial reactions to this combination are always skeptical, but once they taste it, all guests become loyal fans! Once again, oil adds the richness we're after, as well as contributing to the Hanukkah tradition, while carrots provide undeniable moistness. Be sure you're using unsweetened baking cocoa and not the type for hot chocolate, which has sugar added. If nuts present allergy problems for guests, you can substitute raisins or miniature chocolate chips.

It is essential that the cake be well cooled, even chilled, before you attempt to frost it; otherwise, the cream cheese will quickly melt. Make this a day ahead and allow it to firm up in the refrigerator overnight to ensure perfect slicing.

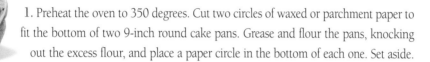

1. Preheat the oven to 350 degrees. Cut two circles of waxed or parchment paper to fit the bottom of two 9-inch round cake pans. Grease and flour the pans, knocking out the excess flour, and place a paper circle in the bottom of each one. Set aside.

2. In a medium-size mixing bowl, beat together the eggs, oil, and sugar with an electric mixer on medium speed until they're well combined. In another medium-size mixing bowl, whisk together the flour, cocoa powder, baking soda, salt, and cinnamon. On medium-low speed, beat half the flour mixture into the egg mixture, scraping the sides of the bowl. Add the remaining flour mixture and beat well to combine.

3. Stir in the carrots and walnuts, and pour the batter into the prepared pans. Bake until a toothpick inserted in the center comes out clean, about 35 minutes. Cool on a wire rack for 10 minutes; then invert each layer onto a plate and peel off the paper. Place in the refrigerator to chill.

4. Make the frosting by beating together the cream cheese, milk, and vanilla in a medium-size mixing bowl with an electric mixer on low speed. Gradually beat in the confectioners' sugar until completely smooth and spreadable.

5. Remove the cakes from the refrigerator, and transfer one layer to a round cake plate. Spread ⅓ of the frosting over the cake and place the second layer on top. Frost the sides and top of the entire cake with the remaining frosting. In a small bowl, mix together the chopped nuts and chocolate chips, and press handfuls of the mixture decoratively onto the sides. Refrigerate several hours or overnight before serving.

Serves 10

EASY DOES IT: Canned prepared frostings now include cream-cheese varieties so, in a pinch, you can use one of them instead of making your own frosting from scratch.

Ingredients
Cake:

4 large eggs

1½ cups canola or vegetable oil

1½ cups granulated sugar

1¾ cups all-purpose flour

½ cup unsweetened cocoa powder

2 teaspoons baking soda

½ teaspoon salt

½ teaspoon ground cinnamon

2 cups shredded, peeled carrots

⅓ cup chopped walnuts

Frosting:

Two 3-ounce packages cream cheese, softened

1 tablespoon milk

1 teaspoon alcohol-free vanilla extract

One 16-ounce box confectioners' sugar

⅔ cup finely chopped walnuts

⅓ cup miniature chocolate chips

Part Two

Special Occasions and Celebrations

Chapter 7

Happy Birthday!

*Petit Orange Chocolate
Birthday Gâteau*

Whether they're marked with a quiet dinner for two or a rousing surprise party for a crowd, birthdays always deserve a lively celebration. Although we may prefer to forget exactly how many years we've racked up, it's still nice to mark that memorable day we arrived on the scene. And it's even nicer to acknowledge someone else's special day with a gesture of appreciation and fun.

The most successful birthday celebrations tend to fall into two categories: special attention and pampering from a significant other with an intimate dinner out (or in), or a full-blown, "Let's party!" extravaganza with the gang. Both are memorable. And both are, more often than not, respectively accompanied by a bottle of fine wine or an open bar for nonstop drinking. For those who drink, the standard is set. But do we really need to be sipping a fine cabernet or downing shots of tequila to know it's birthday time? Let the following two menus prove that it's not the least bit necessary. These parties are so amazingly festive, no one will even notice that booze has taken a holiday. Your bistro dinner at home will be the envy of all, while the surprise party, pulled off without a hitch, will be talked about all year. And, as the host of each one, you'll be "surprised" yourself at how easy it all was to make happen. So take a deep breath, tie on that apron, and get cooking – we've got a birthday to celebrate!

Create your own intimate bistro dinner for two with this fabulous menu that offers all the best a real French bistro has to give, while staying surprisingly sober, safe, and alcohol-free. You may even fool yourself as to how authentic it all seems, from the first sip of Cranbernet Sauvignon to the last bite of Petit Orange Chocolate Birthday Gâteau! Celebrating a birthday has never been so inspired and easy at the same time. Simple appetizers followed by a semi-homemade Caesar Salad will set the stage, while a reworked version of the classic Filet Mignon au Poivre, without the brandy, is the highlight of your meal, served up with savory Bistro Garlic Fries. Your guest of honor won't believe you made the stunning little birthday cake yourself – a fitting tribute for a special night.

Set the scene by fixing up a cozy table for two with cloth napkins, candles, and a miniature vase holding a single fresh flower. Take your time between courses and relish every bite. Your time in the kitchen will be minimal thanks to the ease of preparation, which will give you the opportunity to pamper your birthday boy or girl through this special dining experience. As you sip your final cups of coffee, you'll both agree that you've just eaten at the best bistro around. Bon Appétit and Happy Birthday!

A Bistro Birthday for Two

MENU
Dinner for Two

APPETIZER:
Goat Cheese and Olive Tapenade Rounds

FIRST COURSE:
Caesar Salad for Two
French Baguette

MAIN COURSE:
Filet Mignon au Poivre
Bistro Garlic Fries

DESSERT:
Petit Orange Chocolate Birthday Gâteau

BEVERAGE PAIRINGS:
Appetizer and First Course:
Perrier with Lemon Twist
Main Course: Cranbernet Sauvignon
Dessert: *French Roast Coffee*

Tips on Purchased Ingredients

Caesar Salad, although not difficult to concoct, is one of those corners definitely worth cutting, given the good-quality dressings we're able to buy these days, which leave out the worry and fuss over raw eggs, anchovy bones, and the like when you make it yourself. Buy a bag of romaine hearts (already cleaned and ready to go), cut one or two of the hearts into 1-inch pieces, and toss them into a salad bowl. Look for either Girard's® or Cardini's® bottled Caesar dressings, which are among the best on the market. Don't use too much on the salad – less is definitely more when it comes to Caesar dressing. I like to top my Caesar salad with shaved *Grana Padano* cheese, a close relative of Parmesan that's gaining in popularity. It's available in wedges (to shave yourself on a grater or with a vegetable peeler) or in tubs of shaved pieces. Sprinkle on a few large garlic croutons to finish, and there you are – a simple, delicious salad that took minutes to prepare.

What bistro wouldn't offer crisp, crusted **baguettes**? Buy yours the day of the dinner from a bakery or store where you trust the quality and freshness. Some bakeries even make demi-baguettes (half-size), which are perfect for two. Serve the loaves on a little wooden cutting board with a serrated knife to add an authentic restaurant touch.

For a refreshing drink to start things off, simple, effervescent **Perrier®** bottled water is perfect for bistro dining. A large bottle to share, or individual bottles for each, should be well chilled. Serve with a small twist of lemon to help cleanse the palate and add a touch of flavor.

French Roast Coffee is, of course, the appropriate coffee to serve. It's the darkest of the dark roasts and has a strong, smoky aroma. Brewing the coffee in a French coffee press is the ideal way to go – Bodum® makes presses in several different sizes – but, it's not imperative that you use one. The French traditionally take their after-dinner coffee black (*café au lait* is for breakfast), but if your guest prefers milk and sugar, by all means provide it.

Goat Cheese and Olive Tapenade Rounds

These lovely little appetizers are super-easy to make and add a special touch to the table when served at the start of the meal. French chefs, at no extra charge, often provide a small bite such as this, called an *amuse-bouche*, which is meant to literally "delight the mouth" before the meal begins. It has also been called a kiss on the cheek from a chef who cares! Serve these appetizers on a small, chilled plate as you both sit down – no more than two or three per person, as they're only meant to "tease" the palate.

English cucumbers are ideal for this presentation. They're virtually seedless, and the skin, if left on, is light and easily digestible. If you have a channel garnishing knife, use it to remove several lengthwise pieces of the outside rind to give the sliced cucumber a decorative edge. The log of goat cheese, also known as *chèvre*, should be quite cold before you attempt to cut it into rounds – using dental floss (unflavored, of course!) will create a surprisingly perfect slice. Olive tapenade is a delicious French condiment made from olives, capers, and a variety of seasonings, and can be purchased in small jars in the pickle and olive section of your supermarket, and sometimes is available fresh and refrigerated in the cheese section. It's perfect with creamy goat cheese and also makes a fine topping for fish and vegetables.

Ingredients:

½ of an English seedless cucumber, unpeeled or channeled

One 4-ounce plain goat cheese log

1 jar olive tapenade

Fresh chervil or parsley leaves to garnish

Make these delightful bites up to an hour ahead and keep them well chilled before serving. You'll have leftover ingredients for making these another time, or using in other dishes.

Slice the widest part of the cucumber into several ¼-inch-thick rounds and pat dry with a paper towel. Arrange them on a small decorative plate. Using plain dental floss, slice down through the chilled goat cheese log to make an equal number of ¼-inch-thick rounds. Using your fingers and a small knife, carefully top each cucumber round with a round of goat cheese and gently spread 1 teaspoon of olive tapenade on each. Decorate with a chervil or parsley leaf and chill up to an hour before serving.

Serves 2

Bistro Garlic Fries

Ingredients:

2 medium-size Idaho or russet potatoes, peeled

1 tablespoon canola oil

Coarse salt to taste

1 tablespoon unsalted butter

1 garlic clove, minced

Pinch of paprika

These *pommes frites* are the perfect side for your beef filets. Crisped in the oven, then tossed with buttery sautéed garlic, they're uniquely delectable with a hint of richness. Use Idaho or russet potatoes, and if peeling and cutting ahead, keep them in a bowl of cold water to prevent browning. A heavy, nonstick baking sheet is ideal for oven-frying; otherwise, use double-thickness parchment paper to line an uncoated pan.

You don't need any special equipment to cut French fries, although there are such gadgets available if you enjoy using them. A large, sharp chef's knife will do the trick quite easily. Be careful when making the initial lengthwise cuts, however, as the potato may slip about on the cutting board. To remedy this, cut a small piece off one of the long ends, so the potato can be set flat on the board before making downward cuts.

Cranbernet Sauvignon

When you order a *steak au poivre* at the bistro, your waiter will no doubt recommend a glass of cabernet sauvignon, one of the most popular red wines worldwide. Its distinctive black-currant aroma with strong astringency pairs well with beef dishes prepared with sharp flavors such as black peppercorns and rich sauces that contain cream.

This completely alcohol-free copycat will astound you by its similarity and provides the perfect accompaniment to your main course. Be sure to purchase unsweetened cranberry juice, which is actually quite sour, not cranberry juice cocktail. R.W. Knudsen™ makes a "Just Cranberry" version that's ideal. Black currant juice, a popular everyday beverage abroad, is becoming increasingly available in supermarkets in America (as many are discovering its powerful antioxidant content) and can often be found in a pinch at many ethnic grocery stores. When choosing the balsamic vinegar for this recipe, don't go for the dark, rich varieties that are usually preferable in other recipes. We want a clean, clear hint of flavor – not syrupy intensity. Keep all the ingredients at room temperature for optimal flavor.

Sip your Cranbernet Sauvignon as you would a wine – one glass per person is sufficient to savor its ideal pairing with your meal. A word of warning, however: Because this looks, smells, and tastes so much like the real thing, if you're newly sober or find red wine to be a dangerous trigger for you, refrain from serving this until you're more comfortable with the idea. Good alternatives would be a cranberry-grape juice mix or plain iced tea.

Ingredients:

1 cup black currant juice

½ cup unsweetened cranberry juice

½ cup "no sugar added" red grape juice

½ cup plain seltzer

1½ tablespoons balsamic vinegar

Stir together all the ingredients in a glass pitcher. Allow to sit for 15 minutes at room temperature, then divide between two 10- or 12-ounce wineglasses. Serve immediately.

Serves 2

1. Preheat the oven to 425 degrees.

2. Cut potatoes lengthwise into ⅓-inch-thick slices, then again into ⅓-inch-wide strips. Keep the potatoes submerged in a bowl of cold water until ready to bake.

3. Pat dry the potatoes with paper towels, toss with the oil and a little salt, and spread in a single layer on the prepared baking sheet. Bake until the potatoes are golden brown, turning and rearranging them occasionally, about 40 minutes.

4. Meanwhile, in a small saucepan, melt the butter over medium-low heat, add the garlic, and cook, stirring often until just softened but not browned, about 1 minute. Set aside.

5. Transfer the potatoes to a bowl, toss with the cooked garlic and butter, and add more salt to taste if needed. Divide between two dinner plates and serve immediately.

Filet Mignon au Poivre

This classic dish of steak with a peppercorn crust and a creamy, brandy-doused sauce gets a total "sober" makeover in the delicious rendition below. To replace the small amount of alcohol in this dish, we'll be using a reduction of apple cider, an innovative idea for which I have to thank Leda, an excellent cook and avid fan of *The Sober Kitchen*. It provides the perfect consistency and sweet yet acidic quality we need, and when coupled with a splash of oak-scented balsamic vinegar, the resulting look and taste will be hard to match! If you like, try using a flavored vinegar such as fig or date in place of the balsamic. Unusual flavored vinegars are increasingly popular with restaurant chefs and are available at many specialty food stores.

Peppercorns come in all colors and flavors these days and any type you choose is fine to use here. I'm particularly fond of the Tellicherry peppercorn, which hails from India and can be found in ethnic food stores. Its aroma is incomparable and adds a hint of the exotic to any dish. Two 6- to 8-ounce filet mignon steaks will be more than generous, portionwise, though you can certainly go smaller or bigger depending on your appetite. And a strip steak, rib-eye, or sirloin can be substituted if you prefer.

Preparation of the steaks takes mere minutes, particularly if you are cooking to rare or medium rare, so be sure your fries are ready to go and the plates are heated. Garnish with some fresh parsley sprigs for a classic bistro presentation.

1. In a small saucepan over medium-high heat, simmer the apple cider until it has reduced by half. Transfer to a measuring cup, stir in the vinegar, and set aside.

2. Using a mortar and pestle or the back of a heavy skillet, crush the peppercorns to a coarse consistency. Press the peppercorns into both sides of the steaks and season well with salt. In a cast-iron skillet or heavy-bottomed frying pan, heat the oil over a high flame to slightly smoking. Add the steaks, press down firmly, reduce the heat to medium, and cook, turning once to desired doneness – about 6 minutes for rare, 8 minutes for medium. Transfer to heated serving plates and set aside to rest.

3. Add the chopped shallot to the skillet and cook, stirring constantly over medium heat until lightly browned, 1 to 2 minutes. Pour in the cider-vinegar mixture and using a wooden spoon, scrape up any browned bits on the bottom of the pan. Cook for 1 minute, then add the cream and butter. Raise the heat to medium high, and bring the sauce to a boil, whisking constantly until the sauce is able to coat the back of a spoon, about 2 minutes. Pour the sauce evenly over the steaks, garnish with the parsley sprigs, and serve immediately.

Serves 2

Ingredients:

½ cup apple cider

1 tablespoon balsamic vinegar

1 heaping tablespoon black peppercorns (or a mixture of black, green, and pink)

Two 6- to 8-ounce beef filets mignon, trimmed

Coarse salt to taste

1 tablespoon olive oil

½ shallot, peeled and finely chopped

¼ cup heavy cream

1 teaspoon butter

Fresh parsley sprigs to garnish

Celebrating Sobriety Birthdays

Most people in recovery can tell you the exact day they became "clean and sober." Support groups such as Alcoholics Anonymous, Life Ring, and Women for Sobriety make a point of marking these important days with "sober" parties, the giving out of year "chips," or simply a well-deserved "congratulations" recognizing the tremendous effort it took to get there. Whether it be the 1st or the 30th, these annual "birthdays," also called "anniversaries," should be acknowledged and celebrated with pride. So if you or someone you know has a "sobriety birthday" coming up, plan to mark it with at least a little pomp and circumstance. Here are a few ideas for celebrating in style:

• Start the day off right by inviting a few close friends over for breakfast or brunch. Serve omelets, pancakes, French toast, or anything else that suits your fancy. Or leave the cooking to someone else, and have everyone meet at your favorite diner for a delicious morning meal and pots of coffee.

• Plan a get-together for a game at a bowling alley, golf course, or baseball field, then invite everyone back home afterward for cake and some sparkling fruit drinks to toast the honoree.

• Take the family out to dinner, go off your diet, and order everything from appetizers to desserts. Tell the waitstaff that there's a birthday to celebrate, and they'll be sure to light a candle and even sing a round of "Happy Birthday."

• Invite some sober buddies over and rent a movie like *28 Days* or *Lost Weekend* to remind yourself why you quit in the first place and how far you've come! Serve popcorn, nachos, and plenty of chocolate, and enjoy the camaraderie of your faithful friends.

• Don't spend the day alone. Attend a meeting, call up a friend for coffee, or plan to visit a sober residence where you can offer hope and congratulations to others. Be grateful for the support you've received along the way and give yourself a great big pat on the back – you deserve it!

Ingredients

Cake:

10 tablespoons (1¼ sticks) unsalted butter, at room temperature

1½ cups granulated sugar

4 large eggs

3 tablespoons frozen orange juice concentrate, thawed

1 teaspoon grated orange peel

1 teaspoon alcohol-free vanilla extract

2½ cups plain cake flour (not self-rising)

2 teaspoons baking powder

½ teaspoon salt

1 cup whole milk

Filling:

2 ounces semisweet chocolate, roughly chopped

¼ cup heavy cream

1 large egg white

Ganache:

1 cup heavy cream

8 ounces bittersweet chocolate, chopped

2 drops orange oil

Candied or edible flowers to garnish (optional)

Petit Orange Chocolate Birthday Gâteau

Chocolate and orange are a classic combination in baking – their flavors complement each other deliciously. Usually, the orange flavoring is in the form of liqueur, whether Cointreau or Grand Marnier, but here, we'll go directly to the source for an intense orange experience. Orange juice concentrate and orange zest will provide the flavor for the cake, while orange oil will enhance our deep chocolate ganache coating. Citrus oils, like orange and lemon, are wonderful to use since they do not contain any alcohol as do extracts. And they are more concentrated than alcohol-containing extracts. One or two drops are usually all that's needed.

You can prepare the cake part ahead of time and even freeze it, well-wrapped in plastic. The filling and ganache can also be prepared ahead, and the entire gâteau can be assembled the night before so it has a chance to set in the refrigerator. Let it sit, however, at room temperature for about 30 minutes before serving to soften up the chocolate a bit. Use a sharp knife dipped in hot water to make perfect slices. If you'd like to decorate the finished cake, some supermarkets and all baking supply stores carry small candied flowers and leaves that you can use in the corners or on the edges. Edible flowers are also a nice touch. And don't forget to write "Happy Birthday!"

1. Make the cake: Preheat the oven to 350 degrees. Butter and flour a 9- by 13-inch baking pan, knocking out the excess flour. Line with a rectangular piece of waxed or parchment paper cut to fit the bottom of the pan. Set aside.

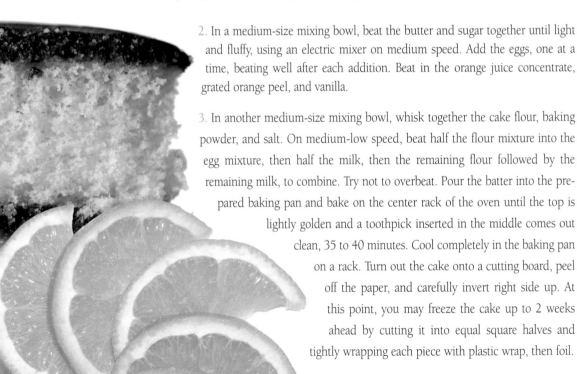

2. In a medium-size mixing bowl, beat the butter and sugar together until light and fluffy, using an electric mixer on medium speed. Add the eggs, one at a time, beating well after each addition. Beat in the orange juice concentrate, grated orange peel, and vanilla.

3. In another medium-size mixing bowl, whisk together the cake flour, baking powder, and salt. On medium-low speed, beat half the flour mixture into the egg mixture, then half the milk, then the remaining flour followed by the remaining milk, to combine. Try not to overbeat. Pour the batter into the prepared baking pan and bake on the center rack of the oven until the top is lightly golden and a toothpick inserted in the middle comes out clean, 35 to 40 minutes. Cool completely in the baking pan on a rack. Turn out the cake onto a cutting board, peel off the paper, and carefully invert right side up. At this point, you may freeze the cake up to 2 weeks ahead by cutting it into equal square halves and tightly wrapping each piece with plastic wrap, then foil.

4. Make the filling: In the top of a double boiler, melt the chocolate. Transfer to a small mixing bowl and allow to cool for 10 to 15 minutes, stirring occasionally. In another small bowl, using an electric mixer, whip the cream to soft peaks. Wash the beaters, dry them well, and in a third bowl, beat the egg white until stiff. All at once, add the melted chocolate and whipped cream to the egg white and vigorously whisk until completely blended, about 1 minute. Cover and refrigerate for 1 to 2 hours until somewhat set.

5. Make the ganache: In a small saucepan over medium-high heat, bring the cream to just a boil. Remove from the heat, add the chocolate and orange oil, and whisk until the chocolate is melted. Transfer to a small bowl and chill uncovered until cool and spreadable, about 30 minutes. If the ganache becomes too cold to spread, simply leave it out until it has softened a bit, then stir.

6. To assemble the gâteau: Using a serrated bread knife, even out the top of the cake to make it flat by cutting off slivers. Cut about 1 inch off each edge of the cake, then cut it into two square pieces of equal size. Transfer one piece to a cake plate. Spread the filling evenly over the cake layer and top it with the remaining layer. Using half the ganache, coat the sides and top of the gâteau with a thin layer, then chill for 20 minutes. Spread the remaining ganache evenly over the top and sides and decorate with the flowers, if using. Keep chilled until 30 minutes before serving.

Serves 2 to 4

If the idea of throwing a surprise party gives you the frights, think again: With this Mexican-themed menu and helpful tips, you'll be breezing through the preparations in no time. From setting up an alcohol-free bar featuring a super Margarita "mocktail" to serving the birthday cake, you'll be the most impressive host around, and your fiesta the most talked-about event of the year! Make-ahead appetizers, including the outstanding Colossal Five-Layer Dip, will start your guests off as they await the festivities and the arrival of the birthday honoree. A terrific main course of easy Baked Chicken Tortilla Rollups, served with Mexican-Style Rice and a colorful salad, will allow you to be part of the mingling, while a bakery sheet cake will save oodles of time and effort. All you'll need to do is remember the candles.

The biggest feat of any surprise party is, of course, keeping it a surprise from the birthday boy or girl. Weeks of surreptitious phone calling, shopping, and hiding of party accessories is the easy part. Having thrown many a surprise party in the past, I can say from experience that the most important thing in maintaining an element of surprise is actually the most obvious: Be sure your guests park their cars away from your house! It takes only one recognized vehicle to let the guest of honor know that something's afoot. If you can manage that, the rest is a walk in the park, as they say. And definitely enlist the help of a friend or two to set up the bar and buffet table and any other tasks you may need to perform. By the time you're ready to dim the lights and yell "Surprise!" you'll be confident that everything is in perfect order for a splendid bash.

It's a Surprise Party!

MENU

Party for Sixteen

APPETIZERS:

Spicy Chili Nuts

Colossal Five-Layer Dip

White and Blue Corn Tortilla Chips

MAIN COURSE:

Baked Chicken Tortilla Rollups
with Enchilada Sauce

Mexican-Style Rice

Bibb, Baby Spinach, and Mango Salad

Poppy-Seed Dressing

DESSERT:

Birthday Sheet Cake

BEVERAGES:

An Open, Alcohol-Free Bar

Featuring

Frozen Margaritas in the Buff

Tips on Purchased Ingredients

You'll need at least two large bags of *tortilla chips*, depending on the amount of nibbling that will go on before the guest of honor arrives. Be sure to choose chips that are sturdy enough to handle the five-layer dip, such as Tostitos Gold® or a scoop variety. Some blue corn tortilla chips thrown in for good measure would add variety and interest. If there may be a particularly long wait before you're able to serve the main course, you can supplement your appetizers with a store-bought vegetable dip platter or a tray of olives and cheese.

Save time and effort by purchasing two bottles of *poppy-seed dressing* for your salad – Briana's® is my favorite variety. Allow guests to dress their own salad by serving the dressing in a bowl with a small ladle alongside the salad.

For large numbers of people, it's always best to order a bakery *birthday sheet cake*, preferably one that doesn't require refrigeration unless you can spare the space. A ¼-sheet cake will be more than sufficient for 16 people. If you're buying from an Italian or other ethnic bakery, make sure it's not "punching" the cake with rum or another type of alcohol. "Punching" means that the dry sponge cake has been moistened with a liquid (usually alcohol-based) by dabbing it with a pastry brush before adding the filling and icing. Similarly, some premade bakery cake fillings are flavored with brandy or liqueur, so be specific about your requirements when ordering. The bakery should gladly oblige.

Setting up a party bar with alcohol has a pretty well-tested set of guidelines, but when it comes to an *open, alcohol-free bar*, you'll need to go through some trial and error and know a little bit about the tastes of your guests. Remember that simply offering sodas and water is nothing special for nondrinkers. You need to get creative and at the same time provide very basic beverages that are refreshing and light, especially when spicy food is being served. It might be helpful to solicit the assistance of one of your guests to "play" bartender – someone who knows a thing or two about concocting great-tasting refreshments. I know at least one or two folks who are really adept at this and enjoy being given something to do, so ask around and find a suitable volunteer. In general, it's a nice touch to prepare at least one special "mocktail" as, in this case, a take on Margaritas, given the Mexican theme of the party.

Chances are each person will try one or two of these drinks, then switch to something more familiar and thirst-quenching, so no more than the equivalent of two mocktails per person will be necessary. Here are some basic guidelines for purchasing and setting up other beverages and related items:

• Estimate three drinks per person per 2 hours (including water and coffee)

• Buy most beverages in single-serve cans or bottles. Larger sizes are less expensive, but if they're not consumed once they're open, they'll go to waste.

• Include popular beverages like Coke®, Ginger Ale, and 7-Up®, as well as a few diet and caffeine-free versions. Also include tonic water, club soda, and two or three different juices.

• Have small- and medium-size bottles of water available in abundance and out in plain view, so that people can help themselves.

• Encourage garnishing by cutting up and serving lemon and lime wedges, orange slices, and maraschino cherries.

• Have plenty of ice on hand and put someone in charge of replenishing the ice bucket.

• Provide plenty of glasses (plastic is fine) as well as swizzle sticks and cocktail napkins.

• Keep a trash can for recycling behind the bar area, and have a can for garbage in full view.

• Include drink enhancers like grenadine and Rose's lime juice for adventurous mixers – both are alcohol-free. The popular Angostura® bitters, however, contains a good amount of alcohol.

• Keep paper towels and sponges near the bar to quickly wipe up any spills.

• Finally, don't wait for dessert to brew the coffee. Nondrinkers will often enjoy a cup of java way before most people who drink alcohol. Rent and set up two urns: one with real coffee, the other with hot water for making instant decaf and tea. Don't forget the sugar and cream!

Spicy Chili Nuts

These irresistible party nuts will have your guests happily nibbling away as they sip their mocktails. You can make them up to four days ahead and store in an airtight container. The amount of "heat" you add is entirely up to you, so adjust the cayenne pepper according to taste.

Dry-roasted peanuts work best here, as the result is far less oily. Raw or roasted cashews, whichever you find available, work equally well. If you use a salted variety of peanuts or cashews instead of lightly salted or unsalted, you may not need to add salt to taste at the end. Wait until the nuts have cooled to decide.

Ingredients:

1 tablespoon chili powder

1 tablespoon ground cumin

1 tablespoon granulated sugar

2 teaspoons curry powder

1 teaspoon garlic powder

½ teaspoon paprika

¼ teaspoon cayenne pepper or more to taste

2 tablespoons peanut or canola oil

3½ cups dry-roasted peanuts, lightly salted or unsalted

1½ cups cashews, lightly salted or unsalted

Coarse salt to taste

1. Preheat the oven to 300 degrees.

2. In a small mixing bowl, whisk together all the spices except the salt. In a large skillet, heat the oil over medium heat. Add the spices and stir constantly with a wooden spoon until fragrant, about 1 minute. Add the peanuts and cashews, increase the heat to medium high, and stir until the nuts are well coated, about 2 minutes.

3. Transfer the nuts to a large baking sheet (or two medium-size baking sheets) and bake, stirring occasionally, until lightly golden and nearly dry, about 15 minutes. Remove from the oven, season with salt to taste (if needed), and stir well. Allow to cool completely on paper towels, then store in an airtight container until ready to serve.

Serves 16

Bibb, Baby Spinach, and Mango Salad

Ingredients:

Two 6-ounce packages baby spinach leaves

2 medium-size heads Bibb lettuce, washed, dried, and torn into bite-size pieces

1 medium-size red onion, peeled, halved, and sliced thinly

4 medium-size ripe mangoes, chilled

1 to 2 bottles purchased poppy-seed dressing

A refreshing side salad is just the thing to balance out the richness and spice of the main course. Delicate Bibb lettuce, sometimes called butterhead, combined with dark green, somewhat assertive baby spinach, makes for both a visual and tasty delight. Cool, refreshing mango slices and red onion slivers tie it all together. Serve on a large platter, rather than in a salad bowl, so guests can see the attractive presentation, and don't forget the poppy-seed dressing you bought; you can serve it in a small bowl on the side.

Mangoes can be a bit baffling to many, since the large, flat seed inside may be hard to visualize when cutting around it. You will want to slice down along the widest sides after peeling, leaving the seed in the middle. Some of the fruit may adhere to the seed, which is fine, but try to trim some strips along the edges, where a good amount of fruit can still be found. Look for mangoes that are soft to the touch, but not bruised or mushy. You can slice both the mangoes and the onions ahead of time and keep them in a plastic storage container until you're ready to compose the salad.

1. Toss together the spinach and Bibb lettuce leaves and spread out on a large platter. Scatter the sliced red onion over the greens.

2. Prepare the mangoes: Peel the skin off with a vegetable peeler and cut down on each side of the flat seed to make two rounded pieces. Place the flat side down on a cutting board and cut into ⅓-inch-thick slices. Cut any visible fruit from the sides of the seed. Arrange the mango slices and pieces decoratively around the edge of the platter and over the top. Serve with the dressing on the side.

Serves 16

Colossal Five-Layer Dip

The key to this amazing five-layer dip is the homemade guacamole, so plan ahead to ensure that your avocados are perfectly ripe. This showstopper of an appetizer is best presented in a large, wide, and shallow dish like those used to serve pasta for a crowd. A trifle dish will also work and has the added advantage of showing off the ingredients. If you can't locate the right dish, feel free to make this up into two shallow bowls.

Try to purchase a fresh salsa (from the refrigerated section of your grocer) instead of a bottled one – fresh will provide much better flavor. Be sure to drain excess water from fresh salsa before layering. You can make this earlier in the day or even the night before without worrying that the guacamole will turn brown. Because it contains a good amount of lime juice and is covered with the sour cream, oxidation will be prevented.

In the bottom of a large, shallow serving dish, evenly spread the refried beans with a wooden spoon. Sprinkle 2 cups of the cheese on top of the beans and spread the salsa over. Using a rubber spatula, carefully spread the guacamole over the salsa, then cover completely with the sour cream all the way to the edges to seal. Sprinkle the remaining cheese and sliced olives on top and serve immediately, or cover and refrigerate until ready.

Ingredients:

Two 16-ounce cans refried beans

3 cups shredded sharp
cheddar cheese

2 cups chunky salsa

3 cups homemade guacamole
(see recipe that follows)

2 cups sour cream

Two 2.25-ounce cans
sliced black olives

Homemade Guacamole

In a medium-size bowl, combine all the ingredients and, using a handheld electric mixer or a potato masher, blend together until almost completely smooth (little bits of avocado are fine). Use immediately to make the five-layer dip, or cover the surface with a paper towel moistened with lime juice and refrigerate until ready to use.

Serves 16

3 to 4 medium-size ripe avocados,
peeled, seeded, and roughly chopped

Juice of 1 lime

3 heaping tablespoons prepared salsa

2 tablespoons sour cream

Dash of Tabasco® sauce

Baked Chicken Tortilla Rollups with Enchilada Sauce

Ingredients:

4 tablespoons canola oil

16 boneless and skinless chicken breasts

1 tablespoon chili powder

2 teaspoons ground cumin

Salt and pepper to taste

2 cups sour cream

½ cup prepared salsa

Two 10-ounce cans
mild enchilada sauce

Thirty-two 8-inch flour tortillas

2 cups shredded Monterey Jack cheese

One bunch scallions,
trimmed and chopped

This dish is always a big hit at parties, especially with the host, as it's easy to prepare ahead and a snap to serve. Look for 8-inch flour tortillas, the perfect size for rolling up and fitting into the casseroles. You'll be making four rows of four snugly touching rollups, each containing approximately half a chicken breast. One casserole on each end of the buffet table will make for easy self-service. Count on two rollups per person, although lighter eaters will do fine with just one.

I usually make these topped with a mild enchilada sauce instead of medium or hot, to give guests a break from the array of spicy dishes, but if you think your guests would prefer more "heat," go for it! In fact, jalapeño Jack cheese would be a great, spicy alternative to the milder Monterey Jack suggested in this recipe, so feel free to "kick up" the spice, if you like. Have your scallions chopped and ready for garnish, and serve with a metal spatula and a large spoon. And have a bowl of plain sour cream nearby for people to dollop on their rollups and rice.

1. Heat 2 tablespoons of the oil in a large skillet over medium-high heat. Rub the chicken breasts on both sides with the chili powder and cumin, and season well with salt and pepper. When the oil is hot, add half the chicken breasts to the skillet and cook, lightly browning over medium heat until no longer pink, about 6 minutes per side. An internal-read thermometer should reach 165 degrees. Transfer the breasts to a plate and add the remaining oil to the skillet. Cook the rest of the chicken, transfer to a second plate, and set aside.

2. Preheat the oven to 350 degrees. Cut the chicken into bite-size pieces and place in a large mixing bowl. Stir in the sour cream and salsa to coat. Cover the bottom of two 9- by 13-inch baking dishes with a little enchilada sauce.

3. Make the rollups: Place a tortilla on a cutting board and mound some of the chicken mixture in the middle. Fold the sides in about 1 inch. Fold the bottom up a third and then a third over itself, and place seam side down in the baking dish. Repeat with the remaining tortillas and filling to make four rows of four rollups in each baking dish. Pour the remaining enchilada sauce over the top. You can prepare ahead up to this point, cover the baking dishes with foil, and keep refrigerated.

4. When ready to bake, remove the foil, sprinkle the cheese over evenly, and bake until the rollups are heated through and the cheese has melted, about 20 minutes. Remove from the oven, sprinkle with the chopped scallions, and serve immediately.

Serves 16

Ingredients:

3 tablespoons olive oil

3 cups uncooked, long-grain white rice

1 medium-size onion, peeled and chopped

1 medium-size green bell pepper, seeded and chopped

2 garlic cloves, minced

1 tablespoon chili powder

2 teaspoons paprika

1 teaspoon ground cumin

One 15-ounce can diced tomatoes, undrained

6 cups low-sodium chicken or vegetable broth, heated

Two 8-ounce cans tomato sauce

Salt and pepper to taste

2 tablespoons unsalted butter, softened (optional)

2 tablespoons finely chopped fresh cilantro leaves

Mexican-Style Rice

A delicious rice dish is always a safe bet for large groups as it is satisfying, filling, and an excellent choice for any vegetarian guests. Making any type of rice ahead of time is generally not recommended, so plan on fixing this just before party time. It can rest on top of the stove while your rollups are baking, however, so time things accordingly.

Long-grain rice is the best variety for this type of dish – 3 cups uncooked will make more than enough to go around. If you don't have a large, oven-proof pot with a lid, or a Dutch oven, you can use a medium or large roasting pan and cover it tightly with foil. Go easy on the salt in this dish, as canned tomatoes and sauce generally have a good amount of sodium added, and even the low-salt stock, once concentrated, can be quite salty. If in doubt, taste and season before serving. Although it's quite "un-Mexican" to do so, I like to stir in a pat or two of softened butter at the end for richness. This is an old French-chef trick and one that will make your rice truly glisten when presented!

1. Preheat the oven to 350 degrees.

2. Heat the oil in a large skillet, add the rice, and fry gently over medium-high heat, stirring often until the grains of rice begin to brown, about 3 minutes. Add the onion and bell pepper, sprinkle with a little salt and pepper, and cook, stirring frequently, until the vegetables are crisp-tender, about 5 minutes.

3. Add the garlic, chili powder, paprika, and cumin, stir to combine, and cook a further minute. Pour in the diced tomatoes with their juices, stir well, and immediately transfer the mixture to an oven-proof pot, Dutch oven, or roasting pan. Stir in the hot broth and the tomato sauce, cover, and bake in the oven until the liquid is absorbed and the rice is tender, 30 to 40 minutes. (You can add a touch more liquid in the form of stock or water during the cooking process if the rice is not yet tender.) Remove from the oven and keep covered. Just before serving, add the softened butter, if using, fluff the rice with a fork, then spoon onto a heated serving platter. Sprinkle with chopped cilantro.

Serves 16

Frozen Margaritas in the Buff

What better drink to serve at a Mexican-themed surprise party than the ever-popular frozen Margarita? Here, she'll be appropriately served in her "birthday suit," without a bit of alcohol to disguise her sweet yet refreshingly tart personality. This is a great party recipe because you can get these Margaritas started earlier in the day and finish them up just before serving. Make sure you have room in your freezer for three 1-gallon pitchers – Tupperware is your best bet, as it can withstand the extreme freezer temperature and is lighter to lift when it comes time to pour. You'll also need a blender and a good amount of crushed ice.

For serving, you can purchase plastic Margarita or wineglasses from your local party shop, or rent glass ones. Figure two 8-ounce-capacity glasses per person. For rimming the glasses with salt, run a lime wedge around the rim, then invert onto a plate of coarse salt. You can set these up ahead too and line them up on a serving tray. Have ready your lime slices for garnish and any other decorative additions, such as different-colored swizzle sticks, straws, or umbrellas that will help guests find their own drinks with ease. Start with two pitchers and if you see that they're beginning to run low, pull out the third from the freezer for another batch. Just remember, it will need at least 30 minutes to thaw before adding the club soda.

Ingredients:

Three 12-ounce cans frozen lemonade concentrate, thawed and undiluted

Three 12-ounce cans frozen limeade concentrate, thawed and undiluted

3 cups confectioners' sugar

18 cups crushed ice

Three 1-liter bottles orange-flavored club soda

Lime wedges and coarse salt for rimming

Lime slices for garnish

All About Mocktails: Copycat Drinks for Sober Celebrations

There was a time when nondrinkers had very few choices when it came to specialty drinks. Shirley Temples and Virgin Marys were the typical options – otherwise a club soda or cola was the usual request for kids and abstemious adults alike. But times have certainly changed! Bartender extraordinaire Tony Abou-Ganim of Las Vegas recently designed a special "mocktail" for Paris Hilton's birthday party, and alcohol-free pomegranate spritzers were served on an episode of *Queer Eye for the Straight Guy*. With more and more folks abstaining from the hard stuff, hosts need to offer mocktails as well as soft drinks when they entertain if they hope to throw a memorable party for their alcohol-shunning guests.

What makes a great mocktail? Simply leaving out the alcohol is not the answer. Cocktail mixers without a little something added can end up overwhelmingly sour or sweet. As in cooking, when we substitute for alcohol, we need to take into account the role it's playing and the overall taste it's contributing. For instance, for the Frozen Margaritas in the Buff, orange-flavored club soda fulfills two functions: It helps to replace the orange flavor of alcohol-containing Triple Sec, and at the same time, dilutes the sweet and sour taste of the limeade and lemon, which would be overpowering on its own. When concocting your mocktails, the best way to determine success is through testing and tasting. Once you find your ideal ingredients and

1. Work in three batches, one for each pitcher. Place one can each of the lemonade and limeade concentrate, 1 cup of sugar, and 6 cups of crushed ice in a blender and purée until smooth. Pour into a pitcher, cover, and freeze. Repeat twice more with the remaining ingredients and pitchers.

2. When the mixture has become firm (several hours later), remove the pitchers from the freezer and allow to thaw slightly for 30 minutes. Whisk one bottle of club soda into each pitcher until the Margarita is slushy. Pour immediately into the prepared glasses and serve.

Serves 16

measurements, write them down and keep on hand for future party hosting. You can also find many alcohol-free versions of famous cocktails on the Internet, as well as in several bar guides.

Sometimes, cleverly naming your mocktail can be the deciding factor in its success. People love to sip drinks that are witty conversation starters. Mocktails that poke fun at their namesakes, like UnFuzzy Navel, I'll Fake Manhattan, or Blameless Bloody Bull, are always laughingly welcomed by nondrinkers and drinkers alike! Serve them up in special festive glasses to make your guests feel equally special and festive. Creativity and presentation will go a long way toward a winning mocktail.

For people who are newly sober, even if they never ordered a classic cocktail in their lives, the whole idea of sipping imitation cocktails might feel more than a bit discomforting. The association can be far too dangerous a prospect while they're in the throes of early recovery. For them, even looking at someone else drinking a mocktail could spark some neurochemical recognition and induce a craving for the real thing, so it's important to know your guests and try to help them feel as unthreatened as possible. After a good period of abstinence, these types of triggers inevitably subside. And all of a sudden, your friends will be concocting the comically named refreshments. "Hey, anyone up for Safe Sex on the Beach?"

Chapter 8

Congratulations!

Southern Sweet Tea and Ginger Mint Julep

When it comes to patting ourselves on the back, we probably don't bestow such congratulations as often as we should. But just about any accomplishment deserves to be recognized. Whether you want to celebrate a new home, a new job, or simply a job well done, you'll find all you need in these two menus to create a party to remember.

If moving into your dream home has finally become a reality, invite your neighbors, old and new, for an open-house affair that has all the charm of Southern hospitality, no matter where in the country you may live. An afternoon open house is a great way to make everyone feel welcome and is the perfect venue for alcohol-free entertaining. If a big job has just been landed, pull out all the stops in opulent Greek fashion and invite your friends for a truly memorable evening of lavish eating and extravagant fun by focusing on a meal that would make the most sumptuous restaurants jealous. No matter what your achievement, you deserve to be celebrated. And with the following entertaining ideas, you'll be by far the most fêted host that anyone has ever raised a glass to!

The tradition of housewarming parties is a very old one, dating back to ancient times when guests brought embers from their own home fires to put in the hearth of the new home of friends or neighbors. Eventually, gifts like bread and salt were offered to start new homeowners off with the staples of life, while sugar, introduced centuries later, was a "sweet" way to offer best wishes for a happy future.

Today, the tradition lives on with parties that bring together new and old friends. More often than not, these are "open house" events with a buffet of simple food and drink for guests to enjoy as they admire your new abode and welcome you with gifts and good wishes. Hospitality is the name of the game, and no one does it better than our friends in the South! Full of sweetness and down-home comfort, this housewarming menu will bring delicious joy to every guest who arrives, from the first sip of traditional Southern Sweet Tea to the final bite of the rich, gooey Mississippi Mud Brownies. A casual cold buffet will allow you to mingle properly and give friends a tour of your home without worrying about the timing and reheating of hot food.

An early-afternoon lunchtime open house is the ideal setting for a housewarming, so that guests can clearly see the beauty of your new home (unpacked boxes and all) and feel comfortable in driving to a new location. It's also a great time for exclusively offering alcohol-free beverages, which are generally less expected than during the evening hours. Your invitations should indicate that casual food will be served and give a range of hours for guests to drop by. Welcoming yellow ribbons or balloons could be tied to trees and railings for a nice touch and to assist out-of-town guests in finding their way.

A Southern Hospitality Housewarming

MENU
Open House for Twenty

NIBBLES:
Cheese Crackers, Smoked Almonds, Celery and Carrot Sticks

COLD BUFFET:
Blue Cheese Deviled Eggs
Virginia Ham Muffuletta Sandwiches
Prize-Winning Potato Salad
Bread and Butter Pickles

DESSERT:
Mississippi Mud Brownies
Shortbread Cookies

BEVERAGES:
Southern Sweet Tea
Ginger Mint Juleps
Filtered Coffee

WELCOME

Tips on Purchased Ingredients

Replenishable bowls of nibbles are a must at a party such as this, especially if guests will be dropping by with small children. Small, savory *cheese crackers* are a great choice for little nibblers, while *smoked almonds* add a special touch and go well with the sweet drinks you're providing. *Celery and carrot sticks* are great for kids as well and can be cut up that morning or the night before, then kept cold and crisp in a bowl of ice water until ready to serve.

Sweet and crunchy *bread and butter pickles* are the perfect complement to your muffuletta sandwiches. You could also add a jar of pickled vegetables, called *gardiniere*, for added color and variety on your relish tray. Although its not necessary, you can certainly add to your cold buffet by purchasing some coleslaw and macaroni salad from a local deli, or prepare some yourself if you have a favorite recipe. But try not to overload your cooking agenda, especially if you have some straightening and housecleaning to do in preparation for your party. Sometimes, it's a good idea to keep extra food items in the refrigerator, such as additional salads, blocks of cheese, or cold cuts that can be quickly assembled, in case your buffet starts to look skimpy after an hour or two of entertaining. With open-house events, it's often hard to predict just what will go and when, so be prepared with items on hand in case you need to touch things up for the next round of guests.

For those who prefer something light, simple *shortbread cookies* are a great addition to the dessert table as a small, sweet bite to go with coffee. Other good purchased cookie choices are peanut butter, molasses, or oatmeal raisin.

No matter the time of day, the welcoming aroma of fresh-brewed coffee can make any house feel like a home. The best way to handle coffee service is to brew your *filtered coffee* in the kitchen, then pour it into thermos-type pitchers from which guests can help themselves out in the dining room, along with milk and sugar. Check the pitchers periodically and brew more coffee as needed. For those who request decaf or tea, be hospitable and bring them into the kitchen as you prepare a special cup just for them. It will give you a chance to show off your new kitchen as well as spend some quality time with a few of your guests.

Ingredients:

1½ cups granulated sugar

3 cups water

¼ teaspoon baking soda

4 family-size or 12 regular-size tea bags

Cold water

Lemon slices

EASY DOES IT: If time or space in the refrigerator doesn't allow advance preparation, consider buying a variety of single-serve, flavored iced teas for guests to help themselves. Arizona® even makes a Southern Sweet Tea variety. Keep them on ice in a large chilling bucket on the porch for easy access, next to a bin for recycling.

Southern Sweet Tea

Just about any meal is unthinkable in the South without a tall glass of Southern Sweet Tea. For those unfamiliar with its taste, it may seem oversugared, but I have known many a Northerner who has been won over by this traditional, thirst-quenching drink. You'll want to make at least a gallon and keep it well chilled. Double or triple the recipe if you think your sweet tea will be a particularly big hit. To serve, pour into a decorative pitcher with plenty of ice and a few lemon slices.

The secret ingredient in Southern Sweet Tea is a bit of baking soda, which darkens the tea and presumably removes any bitterness. A simple syrup of water and sugar, also called tea syrup, is the key to sweetening without ending up with undissolved grains of sugar at the bottom. Most Southerners recommend Lipton® or Luzianne® brand teas in the family-size bags, equivalent to three regular-size tea bags. And they also suggest storing it in a "huge pickle jar." Of course, if you don't happen to have one of those handy, an empty gallon-size water jug will do the trick!

Ingredients:

1 cup fresh mint leaves, washed and all stems removed

1½ cups granulated sugar

2 cups boiling water

¾ cup fresh lemon juice (about 4 to 6 lemons, squeezed)

1½ quarts ginger ale, chilled

Mint sprigs for garnish

Ginger Mint Juleps

Classic mint juleps speak of the South as nothing else does. We'll be making a close cousin to them, without the typical bourbon, by introducing the flavor of ginger, which will add the perfect amount of refreshing tang. Like the Southern Sweet Tea, it has a hefty amount of sugar, but the addition of lemon juice helps balance out the sweetness. Fresh mint sprigs are a must for flavor. "Muddling," or crushing the mint leaves with sugar and a little water, is the classic method for julep-making. The word "julep" stems from medieval times and means a type of sugar syrup used in medications.

This recipe will yield half a gallon and can easily be doubled or tripled. You can make extra amounts of the "julep," keep it chilled in the refrigerator, and make up extra pitchers as needed with the lemon juice and ginger ale. Diet ginger ale can be used to cut back a bit on the sugar if you prefer.

1. In a medium-size saucepan, bring the sugar and 3 cups of water to a boil and stir until the sugar has dissolved. Remove from the heat, add the baking soda and tea bags, cover and steep for 15 minutes.

2. Remove the tea bags from the pot and pour into a gallon jug or pitcher. Add enough cold water to make a gallon, shake or stir, and keep chilled in the refrigerator. Serve with ice and lemon slices.

Serves 20

1. Make the julep by placing the mint leaves, ½ cup of the sugar, and a few tablespoons of water in a small mixing bowl. "Muddle" together using a pestle or the end of a wooden spoon, until the mint leaves are well crushed and the ingredients are combined.

2. Pour in the boiling water and the remaining sugar, and stir until the sugar has dissolved. Allow to steep for 30 minutes. Strain through a fine sieve into a pint-size container and chill until ready to use. This "julep" will keep in the refrigerator for up to 3 weeks.

3. When ready to serve, mix together the julep, lemon juice, and ginger ale in a large pitcher. Pour into ice-filled glasses and garnish with a mint sprig.

Serves 20

Blue Cheese Deviled Eggs

Ingredients:

1½ dozen large eggs

¾ cup mayonnaise

2 teaspoons yellow mustard

2 tablespoons sweet pickle relish

Freshly ground pepper

½ cup crumbled blue cheese

1 tablespoon finely chopped, fresh parsley leaves

When cold buffets are called for, deviled eggs almost always make an appearance. Here, we'll be adding a delicious twist by folding in creamy, crumbled blue cheese. You can buy containers of pre-crumbled cheese to save a step. I've also made these with Roquefort and crumbled feta flavored with herbs to rave reviews. Feel free to experiment according to taste.

Making hard-boiled eggs is one of those kitchen tasks that people seem to struggle with quite often, resulting in eggs that are either undercooked or overcooked with a greenish-gray tinge. The perfect hard-boiled egg can sometimes be a difficult thing to master. After trying many different methods, I've found that the following one yields perfection every time. One and a half dozen large eggs will do nicely for about 20 people, estimating one to two per person, as well as a few losses in the cooked egg-white department. Don't worry if you end up with only 30 or so solid egg-white halves to fill — you'll be able to mound more of the delicious filling into each one.

Serving Alcohol: Hospitality or Liability?

Even though you may not be a drinker yourself, there may be occasions when you want to offer an alcoholic beverage to a guest. I know many sober people and light drinkers who keep a small supply of wine, beer, or spirits in the house for just such an occasion. If having alcohol around and hospitably serving it to others does not pose a problem for you, it's certainly fine and legal to do so. However, you should know that as the host you may have certain responsibilities under the law.

Although laws vary from state to state, in general, if someone leaves your house drunk and gets behind the wheel of a car, you could be held liable for any ensuing accident that occurs. In fact, you may even be responsible for the safety and behavior of your guests until they sober up – however long that takes. Many states have cracked down severely in this regard, particularly because of underage drinking, and the legal limit for blood-alcohol levels has been reduced quite drastically from

what it was years ago. One stiff drink could easily put someone over the limit, so be aware before you pour. A recent study by the Alcohol Research Group at the Public Health Institute has shown that for the most part, home-poured drinks are not the "standard" serving amount that bars, restaurants, and police use to gauge "number of drinks" consumed. Your "two drinks" could easily be the equivalent of "four or five," and even if your guests appear completely capable and sober, their blood-alcohol level will register quite differently if they happen to be stopped by the police.

The best thing to do if you decide to serve alcohol when entertaining is to keep someone who is sober (a professional or friend) in charge of the alcohol, offer plenty of food to eat, and provide designated drivers or cab service for those who may be in need. When being hospitable, being responsible is also a must.

1. Place the eggs in a large saucepan, add enough water to cover, and over medium-high heat, bring to a low boil. Immediately cover the saucepan with a tight-fitting lid and turn the heat off. Time the eggs for exactly 13 minutes. Then transfer with a slotted spoon to a large bowl of ice water to stop the cooking. When the eggs are cool, carefully peel off the shells, cut in half lengthwise or crosswise, and scoop the yolks into a medium-size mixing bowl. Place the whites on a large baking sheet or tray and discard any broken ones.

2. Add the mayonnaise, mustard, relish, and pepper to the egg yolks, and using a pastry blender or the back of a fork, mash together until well blended. Fold in the blue cheese and mound spoonfuls into the egg-white halves. Sprinkle the parsley over all, transfer to a deviled egg platter or decorative plate, and serve immediately, or refrigerate until ready. Can be prepared up to one day ahead.

Serves 20

Virginia Ham Muffuletta Sandwiches

Ingredients

Olive Salad:

1½ cups pimiento-stuffed green olives, drained, brine reserved

1 cup marinated artichoke hearts, drained

¾ cup pickled cocktail onions, drained

2 large garlic cloves, peeled and roughly chopped

1 large celery stalk, trimmed, peeled, and roughly chopped

2 tablespoons capers, drained

2 teaspoons dried oregano

Freshly ground black pepper

¼ cup olive oil

Other Ingredients:

Two 24-inch-long French baguettes, sliced in half horizontally

2 pounds thinly sliced Virginia ham

¾ pound sliced Genoa salami (optional)

¾ pound sliced provolone cheese (optional)

Muffuletta is a hero-type sandwich that originated in New Orleans. Its characteristic "olive salad" is what sets it apart from other sandwiches. It's usually made with salami, ham, and provolone cheese, but here, the smoky, delicious Virginia ham is the star of the show. If you would like a more authentic, not to mention heartier sandwich, feel free to include the salami and cheese. Similarly, you can substitute smoked turkey for the ham, or make a vegetarian version using sliced mozzarella or fontina cheese. When purchasing the ingredients for your olive salad, be sure to avoid cocktail onions spiked with vermouth or other alcoholic beverages used in martini-making.

Although the traditional bread for muffuletta is the large, round *boule*, we'll instead use long baguettes, which make the sandwiches easier to slice. You'll need party picks to hold the sandwich slices together for cutting. If these are prepared the morning ahead, wrap the entire unsliced loaf in foil and refrigerate until you're ready to cut individual portions. A long, narrow tray that fits the entire length of the muffuletta is great for presentation. Otherwise, simply arrange the slices on a large serving platter. Be sure to provide plenty of napkins.

1. Make the olive salad: Place all the ingredients, except the reserved brine, in a food processor fitted with a sharp blade and pulse until the mixture is well combined, but still slightly chunky. Drizzle in some of the reserved brine until the consistency is spreadable. Transfer to a bowl and allow to sit at room temperature for 1 hour. If not using immediately, store, covered, in the refrigerator. Can be prepared up to 1 week ahead.

2. To make the muffuletta: Spread ½ cup of the olive salad on each of the four cut sides of bread (you can use all of it if you like, or save the extra for another dish). Layer the ham (and salami or cheese, if desired) over the bottom half of each loaf and cover with the top halves. At this point, you may wrap the sandwich tightly in foil and chill until ready to serve.

3. To slice the sandwiches, insert 10 party picks into each loaf about 2½ inches apart to hold the muffuletta together. Using a serrated knife, make slices between each party pick. Transfer to a large platter and serve immediately.

Serves 20

Prize-Winning Potato Salad

There are as many recipes for potato salad as there are cooks, but this one, I must say, really takes the prize. The key lies in marinating the potatoes before adding the mayonnaise and sour cream. This gives them a chance to develop real flavor from the seasoning, often missing from homemade versions.

Red potatoes will hold up best for salad, but you can also make this with buttery Yukon Golds or everyday white potatoes. Baking potatoes will crumble and are best left to mashed potato recipes. Five pounds of potatoes will yield a sufficient amount, but you can always double the recipe if you feel it necessary. With other offerings on the buffet table, it's unlikely you'll need much more, although given its "prize-winning" taste, you may be pleasantly surprised! If sweet onions such as Vidalias are available, by all means use them, as they add a lovely, mild flavor to the salad. I like a bit of crunch, so I always add chopped celery too. You can substitute a light mayonnaise and sour cream to cut back on calories and fat. If you make this the night before, it will definitely need a splash of milk to "loosen" it up before serving.

1. Wash and place the potatoes in a large saucepan, add a good pinch of salt, cover with cold water, and bring to a boil over high heat. Reduce the heat to medium and simmer, partially covered, until the potatoes are fork-tender, about 30 minutes. Drain and allow to cool until they are easy to handle.

2. Using a sharp paring knife, remove the skins and any eyes or blemishes. Cut the potatoes in half and then into ⅓-inch-thick half-moons and place in a large mixing bowl. Sprinkle with the sugar and vinegar, season with salt and pepper, and using a rubber spatula, carefully toss the potatoes to coat. Cover and refrigerate until the potatoes are completely cold, about 2 hours.

3. Add the diced onion and celery, mayonnaise, and sour cream, and gently stir to combine. Taste for the addition of salt and pepper and refrigerate until ready to serve. When serving, stir in a splash of milk to "loosen" if necessary, sprinkle the top with paprika, and serve immediately.

Serves 20

Ingredients:

5 pounds red potatoes

1 tablespoon granulated sugar

2 tablespoons white wine vinegar

Salt and pepper to taste

1 large onion, peeled and diced

1 large celery stalk, trimmed, peeled, and diced

1 cup of mayonnaise

1 cup sour cream

Paprika for sprinkling

Mississippi Mud Brownies

What's more comforting and welcoming than chocolate, especially when used to whip up this gooey and delectable dessert? Mississippi Mud Cake fans will hum with pleasure as they enjoy this rendition in the form of personalized brownies. Make these the night before if you can to give them a chance to set for easier cutting. You'll need two square brownie baking tins to make enough to go around. To save cleanup time, buy disposable 8-by-8-inch aluminum pans. Whichever you use, be sure to grease the pan corners and crevices well before baking.

Purchased caramel sauce will make this a breeze to create, and store-bought, pre-chopped pecans also save a bit of time. Don't use an electric mixer in this instance, as it tends to over-beat the batter. You can, however, enlist the aid of a food processor on the pulsing mode to combine the ingredients. Otherwise, a good, old-fashioned pastry blender and wooden spoon will do the trick.

Ingredients:

2 cups all-purpose flour

2 teaspoons baking powder

1 teaspoon salt

2½ cups granulated sugar

1 cup unsweetened cocoa powder

1 cup (2 sticks) unsalted butter, cut into pieces

2 large eggs

1 cup water

2 teaspoons alcohol-free vanilla extract

1½ cups purchased caramel sauce

2 cups miniature marshmallows

1½ cups shelled pecans, roughly chopped

1½ cups semisweet chocolate chips

1. Preheat the oven to 350 degrees. Lightly grease two 8-inch-square baking pans.

2. Combine the flour, baking powder, salt, sugar, and cocoa powder in the bowl of a food processor and pulse to combine. Alternatively, whisk together the dry ingredients in a large mixing bowl. Add the butter and pulse until crumbly (or use a pastry blender). Add the eggs, water, and vanilla, and pulse or stir with a wooden spoon to combine. Divide the batter between the two baking pans and spread evenly to the edges.

3. Bake until set and a toothpick inserted near, but not in, the center comes out clean. Remove from the oven, spread the caramel sauce evenly over the brownies, and sprinkle the marshmallows and pecans over the top. Return to the oven and bake a further 7 minutes. Transfer to a wire rack and set aside.

4. While the brownies are still warm, melt the chocolate chips in the top of a double boiler or in the microwave for 1 minute, stirring until smooth. Drizzle the melted chocolate over the warm brownies and set aside to cool completely. Cut into squares, arrange on a platter, and serve.

Serves 20

For a celebration with close friends for a job "well done," nothing beats the opulence of a full-blown Greek dinner. Why venture out when you can create a memorable, luxurious dinner in the comfort of your home and play host to an authentic "Opa!"-filled evening? Let everyone know you're "in the pink" with this lavish affair, which offers the best of everything Greek without a splash of alcohol. From the delectable meze appetizer platter, full of traditional bites, to a pseudo ouzo creation to toast your success, congratulate yourself for throwing this sumptuous and festive bash!

A deceivingly easy-to-prepare array of true Greek dishes will just keep coming as your guests watch in amazement. Preplated servings of salads, entrées, and desserts add an elegant and stylish restaurant touch – enlist the help of a spouse or friend to serve as you plate up each remarkable course. By the time the Greek Coffee arrives, your friends will applaud your culinary expertise as well as your occupational success. Who knows – they may even throw a dish or two at your most deserving feet!

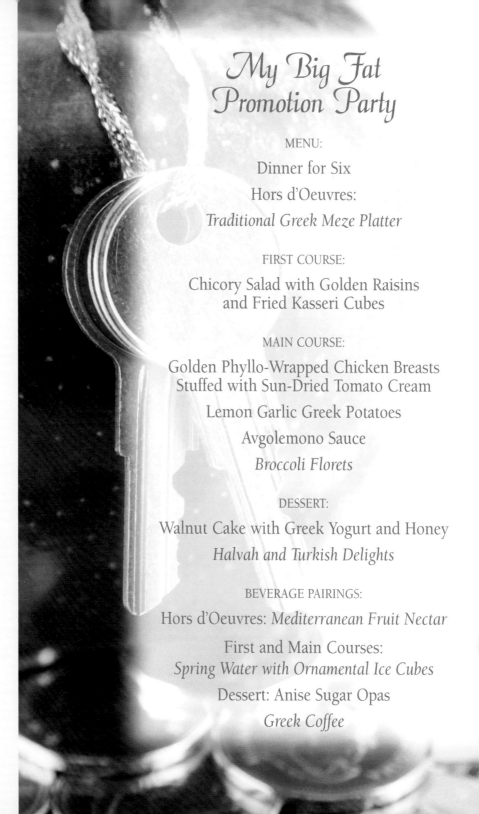

My Big Fat Promotion Party

MENU:

Dinner for Six

Hors d'Oeuvres:

Traditional Greek Meze Platter

FIRST COURSE:

Chicory Salad with Golden Raisins and Fried Kasseri Cubes

MAIN COURSE:

Golden Phyllo-Wrapped Chicken Breasts Stuffed with Sun-Dried Tomato Cream

Lemon Garlic Greek Potatoes

Avgolemono Sauce

Broccoli Florets

DESSERT:

Walnut Cake with Greek Yogurt and Honey

Halvah and Turkish Delights

BEVERAGE PAIRINGS:

Hors d'Oeuvres: *Mediterranean Fruit Nectar*

First and Main Courses: *Spring Water with Ornamental Ice Cubes*

Dessert: Anise Sugar Opas

Greek Coffee

Tips on Purchased Ingredients

*A **traditional Greek meze platter*** can consist of many different *mezedes*, or "little appetizers," served either in the afternoon or before dinner with a refreshing drink. Dating back to ancient Greek times, this delightful custom welcomes guests with thoughtful attention to their appetite and thirst. Any number of items can appear, from hummus to olives to tiny meatballs. When a lavish dinner like this one follows, small, tasty morsels are best. The ideal place to purchase ingredients for your mezedes is, of course, a Greek delicatessen, where many marinated olives, cheeses, and prepared appetizers can be found. However, large supermarkets and specialty food shops carry a full offering of these foods, so you should have no problem gathering a lovely selection. One of my favorite Greek cheeses is *manouri*. Soft, buttery, and mild in taste, it's often served with fruit, but I truly think it was made to accompany stemmed caperberries, a wonderful olive-sized nibble available in the pickle and olive section at better supermarkets and specialty food stores. There's no better way to start off a Greek-themed dinner than these two items, eaten together! Cut the manouri into bite-size cubes and pile them up on a serving plate, surrounded by the caperberries. Feta cheese cubes can substitute in a pinch. And another Greek cheese, *kefalotyri*, a sharp goat's-milk cheese similar to Asiago, could be added to the meze. Choose a variety of olives with different marinades, such as garlic, hot pepper, and herb, and serve these with little seeded crackers or small pieces of sliced pita bread. *Dolmades* (stuffed grape leaves) are probably the most famous of Greek appetizers and make a great addition as well. Look for cans of dolmades imported from Greece, pour off the oil they're packed in, and pat them dry with a paper towel; then, just before serving, squeeze fresh lemon juice over them liberally. Other mezedes you could choose from are *taramosalata*, a popular dip made from orange carp roe; giant beans, deliciously marinated in tomato sauce and dill weed; and, of course, traditional hummus – all of which require pita bread for eating. Remember that you have a huge meal coming, however, so make the meze platter small yet opulent in variety.

To accompany the appetizers, a sweet yet somewhat tart cordial is ideal to complement their richness. Unusual ***fruit nectars*** that recall the Mediterranean – sour cherry, pomegranate, or tamarind – served well chilled in fruit glasses are perfect. Greek delis will carry these beverages, but other ethnic grocers may also provide a good selection, as will Trader Joe's. For the dinner table, pitchers of cold ***spring water with ornamental ice cubes*** are all you need. Greek tradition dictates that water should "flow plentifully" at the dinner table, and it's considered rude if hosts don't offer it throughout the meal. With the multitude of flavors present in this menu, water is certainly your best choice, especially since you'll be offering your mock ouzo for toasting before long. You can embellish your water pitchers by making decorative ice cubes with fruit. Simply insert fresh raspberries, blackberries, or small grapes in ice cube trays before freezing for use in the pitchers.

To accompany your main course, *broccoli florets* are a simple, delicious choice, as they go extremely well with the lemon present in the potatoes and the avgolemono sauce. Make life easy and purchase a bag of precut florets that can be microwaved or quickly steamed. As an alternative, serve green beans or baby zucchini, but whichever you choose, leave them plain, as the avgolemono sauce will find its way to flavoring them on the plate. In this instance, the vegetable is really a type of garnish, merely adding a bit of color to the plate, so a very small amount is fine.

Greek coffee is generally thick and strong, not unlike Turkish coffee and Italian espresso. If you're able to find it, serve it the same way as its cousins – in a small cup with sugar on the side. Otherwise, plain black coffee or chamomile tea are very popular Greek choices for after-dinner hot drinks.

To continue the opulence, serve a small tray of sweets with the coffee, such as *halvah*, a sesame confection that is rich and delicious (chocolate-covered is particularly tasty), and ***Turkish delights***, a fruit-flavored gumdrop candy that adds color to any dessert tray. Some ethnic markets offer Turkish delights that are exotically flavored with rose water or *mastic*, an irresistible, aromatic spice that hints of pine and vanilla – a truly luxurious way to end the evening. Opa!

Substituting for Liqueurs: Adding More Than Flavor

When we come across recipes that call for alcohol in the form of a liqueur, chances are the liqueur in question is contributing a few things besides flavor. Its high sugar content is often part of the reason that it's being added, particularly in desserts, and its thick consistency may also play a role in the overall texture and body of the dish. Liqueurs such as Grand Marnier, kirsch, and amaretto are so intensely flavored that a simple one-on-one substitute of, for instance, orange juice for the sweet yet bitter orange, syrupy Grand Marnier cannot adequately do the job. For substitutions such as these, we need to provide a good general base to which we can add the needed flavor, and that base is simple syrup.

Simple syrup, essentially equal parts water and sugar that's been heated to dissolve the sugar granules, is commonly used in restaurants, bakeries, and many bartending recipes as well. Although some simple syrup recipes call for larger amounts of sugar (such as in the Anise Sugar Opas), for the most part, the basic one-to-one ratio is the most popularly used. Once the syrup is made, it can remain in your refrigerator for a few months in a covered container. We can get pretty close to duplicating the flavor, sweetness, and consistency of most liqueurs when we combine simple syrup with other flavorful ingredients. Fruit concentrates, flavored vinegars, teas, and alcohol-free extracts are among the things we can add to the simple syrup to turn it into a surprisingly good substitute. Flavored syrups made by Monin®, DaVinci®, and Torani®, used extensively in coffee bars, are great additions as well. Sometimes, it's worth adding just a dash of something tart or acidic, such as vinegar or lemon juice, to provide the piquancy and tang that the missing alcohol might have provided, and brewing a flavored tea in hot simple syrup will add mouth-puckering tannins we're often used to tasting in alcohol-containing products. Remember, however, that syrups and substitutes intentionally flavored to mimic brandy, whiskey, or rum, such as Irish coffee or butter rum, are not recommended for those in recovery, particularly the newly sober, whose taste buds may be acutely sensitive to recognizing alcohol characteristics, and for whom such dangerous triggers could set unwanted craving into motion.

Chicory Salad with Golden Raisins and Fried Kasseri Cubes

Mediterraneans love their bitter greens, and the Greeks are no exception. Chicory, which hails from the endive family, is a close relative of escarole, but generally lighter yellow in color with attractive, curly leaves. In this recipe, it takes center stage for an unusual salad that offers a variety of flavors and textures as the perfect first course for your lavish meal. A sprinkling of shredded carrots and golden raisins will add color as well as sweetness to balance out the chicory's slight bitterness. With an easy, delicious dressing to drizzle over it just before serving, you can compose the salad plates ahead of time and keep them in the refrigerator to chill until ready.

The real star, however, may be the crispy cubes of kasseri cheese topping this salad, which ooze with richness when eaten. Not unlike cheddar in flavor, Greek kasseri is often fried in a round pan and served almost like a raclette or fondue, but here, it will garnish the salad like warm croutons with a surprise inside! Called *saganaki*, these fried cheese cubes are sometimes also made with Greek kefalotyri cheese, or Italian Parmesan or Asiago. Fry them just before serving; they'll take no time at all.

Ingredients:

⅓ cup extra virgin olive oil

2 tablespoons red wine vinegar

Salt and pepper to taste

3 tablespoons golden raisins

1 medium-size head chicory, outer leaves and core removed, rinsed, dried, and torn into bite-size pieces

½ cup shredded carrots

Olive oil for frying the cheese

10 ounces kasseri cheese, cut into ¾-inch cubes

1. Prepare the dressing by whisking together the olive oil, vinegar, salt, and pepper in a small bowl. Stir in the raisins and set aside.

2. Distribute the prepared chicory on six salad plates, sprinkle with the shredded carrots, and set aside. When ready to serve, spoon the raisin dressing evenly over each plate and begin to fry the cheese.

3. Pour enough olive oil into a medium-size, heavy-bottomed, nonstick skillet to come ⅛ inch up the sides, and heat over medium high until very hot. Add the cheese cubes in a single layer and fry until the bottoms are golden, about 1 minute. Turn and continue to fry until the cubes are completely browned, 2 to 3 minutes more. Remove with a slotted spoon and drain on paper towels. Garnish the salad with the fried kasseri and serve immediately.

Serves 6

Avgolemono Sauce

Ingredients:

1 cup low-sodium chicken broth

3 large eggs

¼ cup freshly squeezed lemon juice

Salt and pepper to taste

This is a classic Greek sauce for everything from chicken to vegetables. Its perky lemon flavor wakes up food with delicious lavishness. It's a great alternative to common white wine sauces often used in restaurant presentations. The acidity of the lemon replaces that of the wine, while the richness of eggs adds substance normally contributed by loads of butter. Avgolemono soup, a lemon and egg-drop variety with rice or orzo, is popular in Greece and often served to awaken an appetite in the unwell.

I've had great success making this a few hours ahead and keeping it warm in a thermos, which will alleviate any trepidation you might have in putting the components of this meal together. Having the sauce ready to pour (give it a good shake first) saves a lot of time and worry. Or you can just keep the sauce in a warm place for up to 30 minutes, whisking well before pouring.

Lemon Garlic Greek Potatoes

These just might be the best potatoes you'll ever taste! Crispy on the outside and creamy on the inside, they're so full of amazing flavor, you'll no doubt be whipping them up on a regular basis. Greek-style potatoes are a staple with many meat and poultry dishes – the garlic, fresh oregano, and lemon all combine to complement just about any dish they accompany. It's okay to use russets or Idahos here – contrary to usual roasting suggestions, for some reason they're well suited to this dish. I've also made these with Yukon Golds, and the result was equally outstanding.

Surprisingly, you can bake these potatoes a few hours ahead and then recrisp them in the oven, adding a touch more water if necessary. Given the amount of time they take and the high temperature they require, you may want to do that if you're limited to one oven, since your chicken breasts need a cooler oven temperature. The amount of lemon you add is up to you. Greeks love lemon with just about everything and will generally add quite a bit here. Taste as you go (you won't be able to resist!), and add more if you like.

Ingredients:

6 medium-size russet, Idaho, or Yukon Gold potatoes, peeled and cut into wedges or 1-inch cubes

3 garlic cloves, peeled and minced

1/3 cup olive oil

3/4 cup water

2 teaspoons finely chopped, fresh oregano leaves

Juice of 1 or 2 lemons

Salt and pepper to taste

1. Preheat the oven to 425 degrees.

2. Combine all the ingredients in a large, heavy roasting pan and stir well. Bake, stirring occasionally, until a golden crust begins to form on the potatoes, about 40 minutes. Add up to 1/2 cup more water if the pan appears dry, and continue baking, stirring often, until the potatoes are crisp and golden brown, about 30 minutes more. Taste for the addition of salt, pepper, and lemon, and serve immediately.

Serves 6

1. Heat the broth in a medium-size saucepan to just boiling, then remove and set aside.

2. In a medium-size mixing bowl, beat the eggs until somewhat frothy. Whisk in the lemon juice until well combined. Continuing to whisk, slowly pour the hot broth into the egg-and-lemon mixture. Pour back into the saucepan and over low heat, cook, whisking gently until the sauce has thickened, 8 to 10 minutes. It should be thick enough to coat the back of a spoon, but still a bit thin and pourable. Remove from the heat, season with salt and pepper to taste, and set in a warm place until ready to serve, or pour into a thermos and set aside.

Serves 6

EASY DOES IT: Avgolemono sauce for our purposes is not unlike a lower-fat hollandaise sauce. You can substitute a prepared hollandaise (or make from a packet), but add extra lemon juice to replicate the appropriate flavor.

Golden Phyllo-Wrapped Chicken Breasts Stuffed with Sun-Dried Tomato Cream

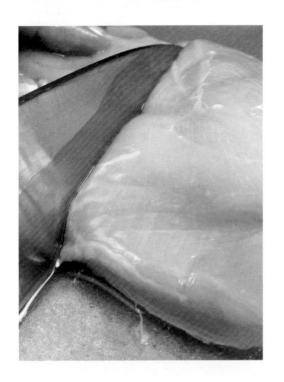

While making this dish is not nearly as laborious as it sounds, the toughest part is working quickly with the phyllo sheets before they dry out. Greek phyllo pastry is thinner than paper and requires a bit of patience. Keeping the sheets moist with a dampened dish towel is the best way to prevent them from becoming too dry. And brushing with melted butter while layering will keep phyllo pliable, so keep your saucepan and pastry brush close at hand. Phyllo comes frozen and needs to be thawed unopened overnight in the refrigerator or a few hours at room temperature. Don't remove the plastic wrapping until you're ready to begin. If you work quickly, you may be able to rewrap and freeze the remaining sheets, as you won't need all of them.

You can make the phyllo-wrapped chicken breasts the night before and keep them in the refrigerator, well-covered with plastic wrap. Alternatively, you can freeze them for future use, so you may want to make a few extra. If they're frozen, don't defrost them before baking. Simply reduce the temperature to 325 degrees and increase the baking time by 10 to 15 minutes.

Remove the tenderloin (the thin piece of meat on the side) from each chicken breast before cutting and reserve for another use. It will pull away quite easily. Be sure to season the chicken well on both sides before wrapping and don't worry if the phyllo sheets seem uncooperative at first. Just remove a few until you get to a nice batch.

Ingredients:

9 tablespoons cream cheese, softened

¼ cup marinated sun-dried tomatoes, drained, patted dry, and chopped

6 boneless, skinless chicken breasts, tenderloin removed

Salt and pepper to taste

12 phyllo sheets

½ cup unsalted butter, melted

1. In a small bowl, stir together the cream cheese and sun-dried tomatoes. Divide into six equal portions and set aside.

2. Slice the chicken breasts lengthwise, not quite all the way through, and open like a book. Season both sides generously with salt and pepper. Place a portion of the cheese mixture on one half and fold the other half over to close.

3. Carefully place one phyllo sheet on a clean, dry work surface and brush liberally with melted butter. Place another sheet directly on top and brush well again with the butter. Place the chicken breast 2 inches from the bottom of one of the shorter ends and fold over the long ends on both sides. Now roll up the breast in the rest of the phyllo to make a neat package. Place seam side down on a parchment-lined baking sheet and brush all over with the butter. Repeat with the remaining five breasts. Leave at least an inch between each wrapped breast to allow for browning. You may stop at this point, wrap the baking sheet tightly with plastic, and refrigerate or freeze until ready to bake.

4. Preheat the oven to 350 degrees. Bake uncovered until the phyllo is golden and an instant-read thermometer inserted in the chicken reaches 165 degrees, about 45 minutes. Transfer each with a spatula to a warm dinner plate, ladle the avgolemono sauce over, and serve immediately with the potatoes and broccoli florets.

Serves 6

Walnut Cake with Greek Yogurt and Honey

Rather than serving the expected Greek baklava as your dessert, surprise everyone with this traditional cake that highlights three beloved Greek ingredients: walnuts, yogurt, and honey. Served warm or at room temperature, it's a delight to the taste buds and the perfect end to your authentic Greek menu.

It's possible to find packages of preground walnuts, which will make this simple recipe even easier. Greek yogurt is luxuriously thick and rich, traditionally made from sheep's milk, although "Greek-style" yogurt, made from cow's milk, is probably more readily available. If you can't find either, substitute a whole-milk yogurt, but be sure it's well drained before spooning. A dark, flavorful Greek honey is ideal, but any other, such as orange blossom, will do nicely. Traditional walnut cake is often made with a splash of brandy, one of those additions that in this case is easily eliminated without substitution. Similarly, a wine-and-honey syrup will often be poured over the cake to moisten it. Since this recipe is slightly more Americanized, using flour instead of cracker crumbs and a tad more butter, the result will be sufficiently moist and requires only the sweet enhancement of the honey drizzle before serving.

Ingredients:

1½ cups walnut pieces

1 cup all-purpose flour

1½ teaspoons baking powder

¼ teaspoon salt

12 tablespoons (1½ sticks) unsalted butter at room temperature

½ cup honey

¼ cup sugar

3 large eggs

1 teaspoon alcohol-free vanilla extract

To Serve:

⅔ cup walnut halves

1 cup honey

1 cup Greek yogurt

1. Preheat the oven to 350 degrees. Butter and flour a 9-inch round cake pan. Line with a circle of waxed or parchment paper to fit the bottom and set aside.

2. In the bowl of a food processor fitted with a blade, combine the walnut pieces and ½ cup of the flour, and process until very finely ground. Add the remaining flour, baking powder, and salt, and pulse a few times to combine.

3. In a medium-size mixing bowl, using an electric mixer on medium speed, beat together the butter, honey, and sugar until light and fluffy, 2 to 3 minutes. Beat in the eggs one at a time to combine. Beat in the vanilla. Add the flour and nut mixture in two batches, beating on high 2 to 3 minutes until the dry ingredients are well incorporated. Spread the batter in the prepared cake pan and bake 35 to 40 minutes, until a toothpick inserted in the middle comes out clean. Transfer to a rack to cool for 10 minutes, then invert the pan and remove the paper. Place the cake right side up on a cake plate.

4. In a small mixing bowl, combine the walnut halves and the cup of honey to make the drizzle topping. When ready to serve, cut the cake into six wedges, transfer each piece to a dessert plate, top with a generous dollop of yogurt, and drizzle with the walnut-honey mixture.

Serves 6

Anise Sugar Opas

In "big fat Greek" style, no celebration is complete without the opa of ouzo. This "ouzo no-boozo" copycat version is so deliciously similar in taste that your guests will be happily toasting – even without the oomph of alcohol. Greek ouzo is not unlike Italian anisette liqueur or the somewhat less sweet sambuca – intensely licorice-flavored liqueurs served at dessert time. This alcohol-free alternative is a great way to toast your personal success and add a special touch to an already sumptuous meal.

Anisette sugar is completely alcohol-free and often used in cookie-making and for flavoring coffees. The Victoria® brand of this sugar can usually be found at your grocery store; if not, several online flavored-sugar companies make it as well (see Resources). Make the syrup earlier in the day so it has a chance to chill. Carbonated water such as Perrier® or San Pellegrino® is best, but low-sodium club soda or seltzer will work fine too. Serve small amounts in champagne flutes, white wineglasses, or small Old-Fashioned glasses. After pouring and just before toasting, plop an ice cube into each glass to bring back the festive fizz. As with other copycat drinks, be aware that the taste, smell, and toasting ritual might create discomfort for those in early sobriety.

1. In a medium-size saucepan, combine the sugar and water and bring to a boil over medium-high heat, stirring occasionally. Reduce the heat and simmer for 1 minute until all the sugar has dissolved. Transfer to a container, cool, then chill well for several hours.

2. When the syrup has chilled, stir in the carbonated water. Pour into toasting glasses and drop an ice cube into each before serving.

Serves 6

Ingredients:

One 9-ounce jar Victoria®
anisette sugar (about 1½ cups)

¾ cup water

1 cup carbonated water, chilled

Chapter 9

Pomp, Circumstance, and Poker

Grilled BBQ Chicken Pizzas

When the gang gets together, whether it's for a graduation bash or a night of serious poker-playing, good food is always a must. Make it great food instead by following these two hearty menus that are guaranteed to please every member of the crowd. No one will go home hungry after chowing down at these events, while refreshing, sober-safe drinks will keep everyone's thirst safely at bay.

In many ways, feeding teenagers and cooking for the guys are very much alike. The main goal is to provide basic, hearty foods that are easy to eat and familiar. Save the cutting-edge gourmet dishes for the elegant dinner parties – here, we're after good, solid eats! Grads will devour everything from the Zesty Chili Dip to Grilled BBQ Chicken Pizzas with gusto, while hungry poker players will more than appreciate some substantial grub when there's a lull in the action. Hey, you may decide to whip up these recipes to satisfy your own hunger pangs when comfort food is called for, regardless of any pomp or poker! Go on – any "circumstance" is fine when it comes to good eats!

When high school students finally reach that graduation milestone, it's a time for celebration! Why not make your grad's party one to remember by cooking up these fabulous dishes for everyone to enjoy? Turn your back yard into a delicious eating fest of all their favorite things, from chili to pizza to delectable s'mores cookies, and offer drinks that are safe and festive, like a novel keg of root beer for terrific floats and black cows.

To help build hearty appetites, you can organize backyard fun with games like badminton or volleyball, and let the kids' favorite music provide the background for mixing and mingling. Arrange something unique, like hiring a fortune-teller to let the grads see into their promising futures, or rent arcade games or karaoke. Show them how free-spirited a "spirits-free" party can be when it comes to really celebrating with friends and congratulating each other on a job well done.

You don't have to subscribe to the "myth of inevitability." Underage drinking, especially at graduation time, is not a given, and your hosting a fantastic alcohol-free party will make that clear. Kids have an ability to amuse and enjoy themselves. And as the hosting parents, you can easily create a lively atmosphere where fun and games are encouraged. Tap into that atmosphere and you'll have a successful graduation party that will not only win top grades from kids and parents alike; it will label you as the "coolest" parents around!

A Backyard Graduation Party

MENU

Party for Twelve

APPETIZERS:

Zesty Chili Dip
with Homemade Tortilla Chips

Raw Vegetables with Ranch Dip

MAIN SELECTIONS:

Grilled BBQ Chicken Pizzas

Wraps Times Two:

Tuna Salad BLTs

Grilled Veggie and Smoked Mozzarella

Coleslaw and Macaroni Salad

DESSERT:

Whoopie Pies

S'mores Cookies

BEVERAGES:

Bottled Water and Fruit Drinks

Keg Root Beer Floats and Black Cows

Tips on Purchased Ingredients

Supplement your chili appetizer with a store-bought platter of **raw vegetables** with a popular **dip** like ranch, or quickly throw one together with baby carrots and celery sticks, which are the most popular dippers for teens. Add some potato chips for good measure or a bag of crispy vegetable chips, which are also kid-friendly. Ask your grad to recommend any other appetizer snacks that friends will go for and have extras in the kitchen in case some unexpected partygoers arrive.

Traditional **coleslaw** and **macaroni salad** are welcome sides to your sandwich wraps. Order several containers from the local deli or favorite sandwich shop where teens hang out – they'll appreciate the familiarity. A bowl of tossed salad with some favorite bottled dressings for healthy eaters would be a good addition as well.

Water and soft drinks need to be plentiful, so arrange several buckets of ice with **bottled spring water, fruit drinks**, and any other soft drinks your grad recommends. **Kegs of root beer** can be ordered from your local liquor store or soda supplier. Have your kegs delivered and set up for you earlier in the day. For making **root beer floats** in large numbers, place scoops of vanilla ice cream in mugs or large plastic cups and have them ready in the freezer to fill with root beer from the keg. Some chocolate syrup for **black cows** is a fun touch. Don't forget long straws and spoons for slurping!

Ingredients

Chili Dip:

1 tablespoon canola oil

1 large onion, peeled and diced

1 large green bell pepper, cored, seeded, and diced

Salt and pepper to taste

1 jalapeño pepper, seeded and minced

2 pounds lean ground beef (sirloin or ground round)

3 tablespoons chili powder

1 tablespoon paprika

2 teaspoons ground cumin

½ teaspoon cayenne pepper

One 15-ounce can diced tomatoes in juice

Two 8-ounce cans tomato sauce

1 cup water

One 15-ounce can pinto beans, drained and rinsed

One 15-ounce can black beans, drained and rinsed

Chips:

One 12-count package corn tortillas

Vegetable oil spray

Salt to taste

To Serve:

1 cup sour cream

1½ cups shredded cheddar cheese

Zesty Chili Dip with Homemade Tortilla Chips

Who wouldn't love a flavorful chili with just the right amount of zip for dipping with hearty homemade tortilla chips? Start things off with this delicious hot appetizer and your grads will be totally impressed. It's true that chili tastes better the next day, so plan to make this ahead and reheat it just before the party. To keep it warm, a crockpot will be just the thing if you have an outdoor electrical outlet. If not, just bring the warmed slow-cooker out unplugged – I guarantee your chili dip won't be around for long anyway!

If you prefer, replace the ground beef with ground turkey (choose "lean" turkey, not breast meat – it's more flavorful and less dry). Small-sized beans such as pinto and black beans are best for dipping, so use one or the other, or a combination of both. The level of "heat" is really up to you. Eliminate the jalapeño pepper or cut back on the cayenne if you think the result may be a bit too "zesty" for most. Garnish with plenty of sour cream and cheese for a super finishing touch.

EASY DOES IT: If time is short, feel free to use premade tortilla chips in place of the homemade. Look for thick, sturdy dipping chips that will stand up against the chili.

1. Heat the oil in a large, heavy-bottom saucepan over medium-high heat. Add the onions and bell pepper, sprinkle with salt and pepper, and cook, stirring often, until the vegetables are softened, 5 to 7 minutes. Stir in the jalapeño pepper and cook a further minute. Add the ground beef and, breaking it up with a fork, cook until no longer pink, about 10 minutes. Stir in the chili powder, paprika, cumin, and cayenne, and cook 1 minute more.

2. Add the tomatoes in their juices, the tomato sauce, and water, stir well to combine, and bring to a simmer. Reduce the heat to medium-low and cook uncovered, stirring occasionally, until almost all of the liquid has been absorbed and the mixture thickens, about 35 minutes. Add the beans and cook until very thick, about 10 minutes more. Taste for seasoning, remove from the heat, and transfer to a storage container to cool somewhat before refrigerating. Can be made up to 2 days ahead.

3. Make the chips: Preheat the oven to 400 degrees. Stack three or four tortillas at a time on a cutting board and cut into quarters to make 48 wedges. Lightly spray two baking sheets with the canola oil and place the tortilla pieces on them in a single layer. Spray the tortilla pieces with the oil, and bake, turning once, until crisp and lightly golden, 9 to 11 minutes. Sprinkle lightly with salt and transfer to a large bowl lined with paper towels. Cool completely, then store in an airtight container or bag until ready to serve. Can be made a few days ahead.

4. To serve the dip, reheat gently in a saucepan, stirring often, and transfer to a heated crockpot. Spoon the sour cream in the middle and sprinkle the cheese around for garnish. Serve immediately with the tortilla chips.

Serves 12

Ingredients

Tuna Salad BLTs:

Three 6.5-ounce cans solid white tuna, packed in water, drained

1 large celery stalk, peeled and diced

½ cup mayonnaise

Salt and pepper to taste

6 large plain sandwich wraps

6 whole leafy green lettuce leaves, slightly smaller than the wrap, washed and dried well

2 medium-size tomatoes, sliced thin

12 slices bacon, fried crisply and roughly crumbled

Grilled Veggie and Smoked Mozzarella:

Oil for grilling

1 medium to large eggplant, peeled and cut into ¼-inch circles

2 medium-size zucchini, sliced lengthwise into ¼-inch pieces

1 large red bell pepper, cored, seeded, and sliced into ½-inch pieces

Salt and pepper to taste

6 large spinach-flavored sandwich wraps

6 whole leafy green lettuce leaves, slightly smaller than the wrap, washed and dried well

12 ounces smoked mozzarella, sliced thin

Fresh basil leaves

Wraps Times Two: Tuna Salad BLTs/ Grilled Veggie and Smoked Mozzarella

Sandwich wraps are great for parties, and these two versions will delight everyone. There are numerous varieties of wraps available in all flavors – the ones recommended here, plain and spinach, are just suggestions, so you can certainly choose other flavors or even whole wheat. Wraps can be made up the night before, provided the filling is lined with lettuce leaves to keep any excess moisture from leaking out and making the sandwiches soggy. Keep them tightly wrapped in plastic or foil until ready to serve.

Grilled veggies and cheese make a great vegetarian sandwich. Eggplant, zucchini, and bell pepper are the usual choices, but if your grads are a bit more adventurous, they may like portobello mushrooms and onion slices as well. Ask the deli to slice the smoked mozzarella into thin pieces, which will make these wrap sandwiches even easier to put together. Other types of cheeses would also go well, such as plain mozzarella, provolone, Muenster, or Gouda.

EASY DOES IT: Purchase grilled vegetables from the deli section of your supermarket to save time. Be sure to pat them dry with paper towels, however, as they are often packed in a marinade.

1. To make the tuna salad BLTs: In a medium-size mixing bowl, combine the tuna, celery, mayonnaise, salt, and pepper, and stir well with a fork. Cover and chill for 1 hour.

2. Place a plain sandwich wrap on a cutting board and lay a lettuce leaf on top. Spoon about ⅙ of the tuna salad across the middle, leaving a 1½-inch margin on either side. Top with the tomatoes and bacon. Fold the bottom of the wrap up to cover the filling. Fold in the two sides about 1 inch, then roll the wraps tightly away from you all the way up. Cut the sandwich in half on the diagonal and transfer to a piece of plastic wrap or foil. Tightly seal, and refrigerate until ready to serve.

3. To make the grilled veggie and smoked mozzarella wraps: Preheat a gas or charcoal grill to medium high. Lightly brush the grates of the grill and the slices of eggplant, zucchini, and bell pepper with olive oil. Sprinkle salt and pepper over the vegetables and grill until tender and browned, turning once or twice, 8 to 10 minutes. Transfer to a platter lined with paper towels to cool completely.

4. Place a spinach-flavored sandwich wrap on a cutting board and lay a lettuce leaf on top. Distribute ⅙ of the grilled vegetables across the middle, leaving a 1½-inch margin on either side. Top with a few basil leaves and the sliced cheese. Fold as above, cut, seal, and refrigerate until ready to serve.

5. To serve, remove the plastic wrap and place the sandwiches on a large, chilled platter.

Serves 12

Grilled BBQ Chicken Pizzas

Ingredients:

3 tablespoons olive oil

4 boneless, skinless chicken breasts

Salt and pepper to taste

1 medium-size red onion,
peeled and diced

Oil for the grill

12 individual premade pizza crusts
(like Mama Mary's® 7-inch crusts)

Two 16-ounce bottles
hickory barbecue sauce

4 to 6 cups shredded Monterey Jack
cheese (or a combination of
Jack and mozzarella)

It's no surprise that when teens were surveyed on their favorite foods, pizza topped the list by a landslide. And, believe it or not, barbecued chicken was not too far behind, which would account for the ever-increasing popularity of this combination in pizza parlors and frozen food aisles. Grilled on the backyard barbecue and whipped up to order, this dish will have everyone clamoring for a piece of the "pie."

Using premade pizza crusts makes this a snap to prepare. Although Boboli® makes the best-known version, there are others equally good, if not better. My favorite for grilling is Mama Mary's®, which comes in individual and large-size crusts and is found in the refrigerated section of your supermarket. When grilling, I like to use the small-size crust, and depending on the size of your grill, you'll be able to make two or three at a time. Count on at least one per person, maybe two (depending on who's coming), and prepare accordingly. (The following recipe makes 18 mini-pizzas.) The secret to these terrific pies is to have saucepan lids to cover the pizzas while they cook to ensure even heating and optimal cheese melting. Closing the lid of the grill instead can often result in too-intense heat, which will burn a premade crust such as this, so use the lid method and you won't be disappointed.

Having all the ingredients ready to go is important. Use your favorite BBQ sauce and pour it into a small bowl for easy application with a long-handled spoon. Be sure to keep the cooked chicken and cheese on ice packs, especially if it's a particularly hot day. Have handy equipment nearby like a wooden cutting board, large spatulas, and a pizza cutter for quick service. And feel free to keep a jar of pizza sauce and some shredded mozzarella around for the traditionalists, just in case.

1. Heat the olive oil in a large skillet over medium-high heat. Season the chicken breasts with salt and pepper, and fry in the skillet until the centers are no longer pink, about 5 minutes per side. Transfer to a cutting board and cut the breasts into ½-inch dice. Keep covered in a bowl in the refrigerator until ready to use.

2. Preheat a gas or charcoal grill to medium high. Brush the grates lightly with oil and place two or three pizza crusts on the grill. Cook until the crust begins to brown and grill marks appear, about 3 minutes. Turn the crust over and spread about ¼ cup of the barbecue sauce on top. Sprinkle with the cheese and add the diced chicken and red onion. Cover each pizza with a saucepan lid and continue to cook until the crust is lightly browned and the cheese has melted, about 5 minutes. Transfer with a large spatula to a cutting board, slice with a pizza cutter, and serve. Repeat for the remaining pizza crusts and toppings.

Serves 12

S'mores Cookies

Instead of the expected classic s'mores, serve up these chewy and delicious copycat cookies that will have everyone reaching for more! Purchase a box of graham cracker crumbs to make things easier, and look for bags of chocolate chunks to mimic the pieces of chocolate layers in traditional s'mores. Milk chocolate is the typical choice for s'mores, but feel free to use a semisweet variety, if you like. Poking the marshmallows into the tops of the cookies instead of mixing them into the batter will keep them from oozing onto the baking sheet, so be patient with this step.

You can make these cookies a few days ahead and store them in an airtight container. Although particularly delicious straight from the oven, they'll still be great at room temperature. If you like, however, you can heat them for a few seconds in the microwave before serving to get that authentic s'mores gooey texture. This recipe makes about 1½ dozen large cookies, but it can be doubled for a larger crowd or a dedicated "s'mores-loving" group.

Ingredients:

¾ cup (1½ sticks)
unsalted butter,
at room temperature

½ cup granulated sugar

½ cup packed light brown sugar

1 large egg

1 teaspoon alcohol-free
vanilla extract

1¼ cups all-purpose flour

1 cup graham cracker crumbs

½ teaspoon baking soda

½ teaspoon salt

2 cups milk chocolate chunks

1 bag miniature marshmallows

1. Preheat the oven to 375 degrees. Line two cookie sheets with parchment paper.

2. In a medium-size mixing bowl, using an electric mixer on high speed, beat together the butter and sugars until light and fluffy. Add the egg and vanilla and beat to combine. In another medium-size mixing bowl, whisk together the flour, graham cracker crumbs, baking soda, and salt. Add the dry ingredients to the butter-egg mixture in two batches, beating well each time to combine. Stir in the chocolate chunks.

3. Drop the cookie dough in heaping tablespoons onto the prepared cookie sheets, about 3 inches apart. Press three or four miniature marshmallows into the top of each cookie. Bake until the edges are browned and the marshmallows are gooey, 8 to 10 minutes. Remove from the oven and allow the cookies to sit on the sheets for 3 minutes. Transfer to a wire rack to cool completely before storing in an airtight container.

Makes 18 large cookies

Whoopie Pies

These chocolate cakes filled with fluffy marshmallow creme are a Pennsylvania Dutch tradition. They were supposedly invented when Amish mothers had leftover cake batter to use up, but you can be sure there'll be no leftovers after these arrive on the table. My local farmers' market has an Amish bakery stand where I got some tips on making whoopie pies. An ice cream scoop appears to be the secret for uniformity. A ¼-cup scoop measuring just under 2 inches in diameter is ideal for making about a dozen good-sized pies.

When it comes to the filling, traditional whoopie pies are often made with vegetable shortening, because it holds up well and lasts longer on the shelf. But here, we'll use a butter and marshmallow fluff filling that will be equally tasty, if not as durable. Not to worry – the pies will be eaten up before there's any chance of them getting stale! You can make these and store them, wrapped in plastic, in the refrigerator up to a few days before the party. Allow them to sit out briefly just before serving so the buttercream will soften up.

1. Preheat the oven to 350 degrees. Line two large baking sheets with parchment paper.

2. In a medium-size mixing bowl, using an electric mixer, beat together the butter and granulated sugar until light and fluffy, about 3 minutes. Beat in the eggs until well combined. Reduce the speed and slowly add the milk, then vanilla, beating 1 minute. In another medium-size mixing bowl, whisk together the cocoa, flour, baking soda, and salt. Add the dry ingredients to the wet in three batches, beating each time until smooth.

3. Using a medium-size ice-cream scoop, place mounds of the batter at least 2 inches apart on the baking sheets. Bake until the cake springs back when touched and a toothpick inserted in the center comes out clean, 10 to 13 minutes. Transfer with a metal spatula to a rack and cool completely.

4. Make the filling by beating the butter and confectioners' sugar to a light and fluffy consistency in a medium-size bowl with the mixer set on high speed. Reduce the speed and beat in the marshmallow creme until well combined. Chill the filling for 20 to 30 minutes.

5. To assemble the whoopie pies, spread a heaping tablespoon of the filling on the flat side of half the cakes and top with the remaining cakes. Serve immediately or wrap in plastic and refrigerate up to 3 days.

Makes 12 pies

Ingredients:

¾ cup (1½ sticks) unsalted butter, at room temperature

2 cups granulated sugar

2 large eggs, slightly beaten

2 cups whole milk

2 teaspoons alcohol-free vanilla extract

¾ cup cocoa powder

4 cups all-purpose flour

2½ teaspoons baking soda

1 teaspoon salt

Filling:

½ cup (1 stick) unsalted butter, at room temperature

1½ cups confectioners' sugar

2 cups marshmallow creme (such as Fluff)

Teenage Drinking in America: An Epidemic?

The most recent data from the National Center on Addiction and Substance Abuse (CASA) at Columbia University reveals some alarming statistics: 25 percent of the alcohol used in the United States is consumed by underage drinkers. And the age at which children begin to drink is dropping steadily, with 9- to 13-year-olds showing the greatest increase in alcohol consumption. It's a scary state of affairs, which has prompted much new research into the effects of early drinking habits and potential preventive measures that may help combat the epidemic.

We now know that the brain does not fully develop until age 25, so that any excessive drinking or drug-taking before then will definitely have long-term effects on mental functions such as learning and memory. Binge drinking, in particular, if accompanied by blacking out, can be extremely harmful to the developing brain's memory capabilities – far more so than in adults who experience the same thing. Also, early in life there is risk of permanent alteration of the brain's serotonin system, which can result in mental and emotional problems down the road, not least of which is alcohol dependence. It's been noted that drinkers under the age of 15 are four times more likely to become alcoholics. Addiction can occur more rapidly than in adults and perhaps with more permanency, creating formidable resistance to treatment.

Although concerns over illegal drug use continue, compared to other abused substances, alcohol is far and away the top drug of choice for America's teens. Unfortunately, adults may be contributing to that fact. Many parents consider drinking a "phase" that will pass and consequently don't enforce the same strict rules they apply to drug use. And it's in the homes of parents and friends' parents that teens obtain much of the alcohol they consume. Combined with the glamorization of drinking with which advertising bombards the American public, particularly youth, it's a tough battle to win. But research also tells us what can make a difference.

CASA's teen survey pinpointed the top risk factors for teen substance abuse. High stress, frequent boredom, and too much spending money can be a deadly combination for many kids, while family engagement is crucial to preventing potential problems. Being aware of and sensitive to the nature and intensity of the stress children experience in school and from peers is of utmost importance, while limiting funds and relieving boredom with healthy activities are critical. And family time together, particularly dinners at home, can create an opportunity for listening and discussion. In the fast pace of American life, this tradition has unfortunately fallen by the wayside, but indications are that frequent family dinners are significant in reducing underage drinking and drug use. Even in families where genetic tendencies toward addiction are at play, positive social interaction with parents and siblings on a regular basis, particularly at the dinner table, has been shown to make a significant difference.

No offense to the ladies, who these days are just as avid (and clever) poker players as the guys, but when the boys get together for their own night of cards, one thing is certain – they want some serious, quick grub and lots of it! Even the most kitchen-challenged boys will be able to whip up this hearty fare to keep everyone well fed into the wee hours. And with some terrific alcohol-free beverages on hand like Bluffing Bloody Bulls and microbrewed sodas, it'll be a lot easier to keep that poker face intact and sweep up the chips at every hand.

What better to serve than some stick-to-your-ribs Polish fare like pierogi with a spicy twist and satisfying Kielbasa and Kraut Sandwiches? And it's all so make-ahead easy that your poker buddies will think you've transformed yourself into the next Emeril. You've even got the coffee and dessert in perfect readiness for when a quick, late-night caffeine and sugar boost is required for a second wind. Hey, they may decide to make it a regular weekly event before the night is through ... Maybe next time you can even invite the girls!

Guys' Night In Poker Party

MENU
Party for Eight

APPETIZERS:
Ante Up Snack Mix
Buffalo Pierogi with Chunky Blue Cheese Dip

MAIN COURSE:
Kielbasa and Kraut Sandwiches
with Horseradish Mustard
Red Potato Salad, German-Style
Giant Relish Tray with Polish Dill Pickles

DESSERT:
Sour Cream Cinnamon Streusel Coffeecake
Refrigerator Ready-Bake Cookies

BEVERAGE PAIRING:
To Start: Bluffing Bloody Bulls
Throughout: *Assorted Microbrew Sodas*
Dessert: *Fresh-Brewed Coffee*

Tips on Purchased Ingredients

Microbrew sodas, like their beer counterparts, are not really new, just newly discovered. Small batches (less than 15,000 barrels) qualify for the designation and are usually far better-tasting than any mass-produced sodas you may be familiar with. This is because they're made with pure cane sugar instead of high-fructose corn syrup and tend to be smoother and less fizzy on the tongue. Microbrews come bottled and are sold singly or sometimes in four packs. Virgil's®, Boylan®, and Reed® are just a few of the companies that make them, with flavors ranging from cane cola, black cherry, and cream to heady, alcohol-free ginger and apple beer. The newer Jones® brand makes some of the more unusual flavors (and colors), like blue bubblegum and green apple. Many of these can be found in the supermarket soda aisle or a specialty food store, and you can also order an extended selection online. Put a variety on ice in a big bucket, and for those who might enjoy some extra caffeine with their sugar buzz, throw in a few Red Bull energy drinks. For customized bottles of all descriptions, visit www.partysoda.com, where you can order soda, water, and other beverage-filled bottles with your own labels that say everything from "Joe Smith's High-Rollin' Root Beer" to "Frank's Lemonade – Refreshes After That Losing Hand!"

A **giant relish tray** is all you need to round out your main course. Huge **Polish dill pickles** are perfect, as are walnut-sized radishes, washed and trimmed. Throw in some large cherry tomatoes and colossal black olives, and you've got some terrific mouth-poppers that are easy and quick to eat. Spicy hot cherry peppers wouldn't go amiss either. Just stay away from anything marinated in oil to prevent anyone from "marking" the cards!

The best compromise between baking cookies from scratch and buying them ready-made is the handy refrigerator package of dough "to go." Even the least baking-inclined guys can plop these **ready-bake cookies** on a baking sheet and stick them in the oven. The result will be perfect every time, and your house will be smelling like a bakery when everyone arrives. Chocolate-chip cookies are a must, with whatever add-ins you like – Nestle's Toll House Ultimates® offer a good variety.

If your game goes on into the wee hours, there's no doubt that your guests will ask for coffee more than once or twice. Consider their coffee-drinking habits and either make some **fresh-brewed coffee** on demand or borrow a medium-size urn and have it available all night. You can offer the usual milk, half and half, and sugar or sweeteners as well as some instant decaf for whoever is throwing in the cards and calling it a night.

Bluffing Bloody Bulls

The bluffing starts early with this alcohol-free version of a classic cocktail that's hearty and flavorful with a mean kick. Greet your poker buddies with this tangy mocktail over ice when they arrive. It will go great with the equally feisty buffalo pierogi.

This recipe will make one 8-ounce drink per person – double the quantity if you think you need it. You can make these up in pitchers earlier in the day and keep them chilled for serving. Have ready some washed and trimmed, long, crisp celery stalks to add as stirrers. Be sure to use the low-sodium beef broth, as most tomato juices are quite high in salt already. A tomato-based vegetable juice like V8® can be substituted for the tomato juice.

Combine all the ingredients in a large pitcher and whisk together to combine. Keep chilled and stir again before pouring into ice-filled Collins glasses. Insert a celery stalk in each glass and serve immediately.

Ingredients:

One 32-ounce bottle tomato juice

Two 14.5-ounce cans low-sodium beef broth

½ cup freshly squeezed lemon juice

1 tablespoon Worcestershire sauce

2 teaspoons Tabasco® sauce or more to taste

2 teaspoons celery salt

Ante Up Snack Mix

Although a variety of snack mixes is available in supermarkets, most unfortunately are loaded with excess oil, which can coat your hands and grease up your playing cards. This homemade version makes use of mainly baked and dry-roasted ingredients that will leave no residue on fingers and cards, so everyone can happily munch away all night without being accused of "marking" the cards!

There are many snack-mix varieties you can make – the following are just a few suggestions to get you started. If you'd like your mix to be more like a classic trail mix, add raisins and M&M's®, or clusters of sweet granola. Watch for ingredients, however, that might become sticky, like caramel-coated or honey-drenched snacks, which will create a similar residue problem while handling cards. Make the mix in a large bowl or pot, and provide plastic cups for players to scoop up servings and bring to the table.

Combine all the ingredients and store in a large zip-locked bag if not serving immediately. Can be made several days in advance.

Serves 8

Ingredients:

6 cups wheat cereal squares, such as Chex®

3 cups sesame stick crackers, such as Twigs®

3 cups baked reduced-fat cheese crackers

2 cups mini-pretzels

One 16-ounce jar dry roasted peanuts

1 cup raw whole almonds

Buffalo Pierogi with Chunky Blue Cheese Dip

Pierogi are Eastern European dumplings stuffed with any number of delicious fillings, usually a combination of potatoes and another ingredient like cheese, sauerkraut, onion, or spinach. Normally served as part of a dinner, pierogi also make terrific appetizers for pregame munching while you discuss the night's house rules and await the arrival of your guests. Prepared in Buffalo chicken wing fashion, these pierogi are served with a "kicked-up" classic blue cheese dip for a perfectly paired combination.

Look for frozen pierogi in your supermarket – occasionally, you may find mini-sized ones that would be fine to use as well; just reduce the cooking time slightly. Plan on three or more standard-size or twice as many mini-size pierogi per person. My first choice of filling is potato and onion, followed by cheese or roasted garlic, if available. Avoid cooking sprays that contain alcohol when baking the pierogi. Many sprays are now made without alcohol since its presence, as well as that of other unwanted chemicals and additives, has come under question. Serve the pierogi right away while they're still hot and crispy. You can prepare the dip up to a day ahead.

Ingredients:

3 tablespoons hot sauce or Tabasco®

2 tablespoons canola oil

1 teaspoon chili powder

24 frozen standard-size pierogi, or about 48 mini pierogi

Chunky Blue Cheese Dip:

2 cups store-bought blue cheese salad dressing

1 cup sour cream

1 cup crumbled blue cheese

Celery sticks (optional)

1. Preheat the oven to 400 degrees. Spray a large baking sheet with cooking spray.

2. In a large mixing bowl, whisk together the hot sauce, oil, and chili powder. Add the frozen pierogi and toss well to coat. Place in a single layer on the baking sheet and bake until puffed, crispy, and golden, about 20 minutes, turning them once after the first 10 minutes. Transfer to paper towels to absorb any excess oil.

3. Make the dip by whisking together the salad dressing and sour cream in a medium-size bowl. Stir in the crumbled cheese and chill, covered, if not serving immediately.

4. To serve, spoon the chilled dip into a bowl placed in the center of a large platter and arrange the buffalo pierogi and celery sticks, if using, around the edge.

Serves 8

Red Potato Salad, German-Style

This mayo-less potato salad, often served warm, is the perfect side dish for your kielbasa and kraut sandwiches. Delicious bites of potato engulfed in a bacon, onion, and vinegar dressing will provide a hearty accompaniment along with the select relish tray you're offering. It can be prepared in less than an hour on the day of the party and is super-easy – no potato-peeling involved! Thin-skinned red potatoes are the classic spuds to use. You can buy bags of baby reds or what are often called salad potatoes, or simply weigh out about four pounds of medium-size red potatoes from the supermarket bin. For easy bacon slicing, partially freeze the package, unwrap, then cut with a sharp chef's knife.

Be sure to dress the potatoes while they're still warm so they can marinate in the vinegar mixture for peak flavor. Use a sweet onion like Vidalia, when available, or a red or Bermuda onion in its place. Heat the salad briefly, if you like, with a quick zap in the microwave before serving, or simply bring out the platter at room temperature. Refrigerate any leftovers (very unlikely!) you may have.

1. Place the potatoes in a large saucepan, add cold water to cover and a large pinch of salt, and bring to a boil over high heat. Reduce to medium low and simmer until the potatoes are fork-tender, 15 to 20 minutes. Strain through a large colander and set aside.

2. In a large, heavy skillet, fry the bacon pieces until browned and crisp. Remove with a slotted spoon and drain on paper towels.

3. When the potatoes are cool enough to handle but are still quite warm, cut them into ½-inch-thick slices (if some of the skins come off, simply discard) and put in a large mixing bowl. Sprinkle with salt and freshly ground pepper, toss lightly, and set aside.

4. Pour off all but 2 tablespoons of the bacon grease and over medium-high heat, sauté the onions until they're soft and just beginning to brown, about 4 minutes. Stir in the sugar, vinegar, water, and celery seed, and bring to a boil. Cook for 1 minute, then pour the entire mixture over the potatoes, add in the crisped bacon, and toss gently. Taste for seasoning and additional vinegar. Serve warm or at room temperature, sprinkled with the chopped parsley.

Serves 8

Ingredients:

4 pounds small- to medium-size red potatoes

½ pound bacon, cut into thin strips

1 large Vidalia onion, chopped

2 teaspoons granulated sugar

⅔ cup apple cider vinegar

½ cup water

1 teaspoon celery seed

Salt and pepper to taste

2 tablespoons roughly chopped, fresh parsley leaves

Ingredients:

3 tablespoons canola oil

1 large onion, diced

Salt and pepper to taste

6 cups shredded white cabbage (about 1 medium-size head)

Three 16-ounce cans or bags of sauerkraut, drained and rinsed under cold water

2 teaspoons caraway seeds

½ cup apple juice

1 cup water

3 pounds smoked kielbasa, cut on the diagonal into 1-inch-long pieces

Two 8-ounce jars spicy brown mustard

¼ cup prepared horseradish

1 tablespoon mustard seed

18 to 24 small- to medium-size crusty rolls

Kielbasa and Kraut Sandwiches with Horseradish Mustard

Authentic kielbasa, also called Polish sausage, just may be the hands-down king of sausages. Made of pork, precooked and smoked (although sometimes available fresh), kielbasa makes a superb sandwich when paired with sauerkraut and mustard. Try to find the real thing – many supermarkets bring in kielbasa from local producers in large links that are vacuum-sealed. The taste is far superior to what you'll find in any of the common commercial brands and is well worth seeking out.

For Polish kielbasa lovers, kraut preparation is not simply opening a can of sauerkraut. It requires some serious doctoring, resulting in the most delicious sauerkraut you've ever eaten. And while you're at it, whip up the accompanying mustard, which is as tangy and flavorful as it is easy. Plan to buy the sandwich rolls the day of the party – look for small- to medium-size crusty rolls with soft interiors such as mini-kaisers, Italian ciabatta, or Portuguese rolls. These make sandwiches easier to handle and eat, and players can help themselves to seconds and thirds over the course of the evening. You can pre-cut them if you like and scoop out the moist interiors to make room for the kielbasa and kraut.

Gambling with Genetic Addictive Tendencies: Are the Odds Against You?

Is it possible to predict from people's specific genetic makeup whether they may become alcohol- or drug-dependent? And what are the "odds," if they choose to gamble with these tendencies, that the outcome is certain? Since the mapping of the human genome, researchers have been asking these questions with great interest and have determined, at least in part, what the answers may be.

Research at the Mayo Clinic in Rochester, Minnesota, has been focusing on the identification of human genes that contribute to vulnerability to alcoholism. Although scientists and behaviorists have known for years that dependence runs in families, identifying specific genes that are inherited is an important step to discovering how these genes interact in the overall picture. It's by no means a simple process, but links have been made and continue to be made through laboratory research. Numerous factors can influence brain function and its proclivity to addiction – hyperactive nervous systems, level of cravings, involvement of specific proteins, and neurotransmitters associated with a variety of addictive substances – all play a part and make it difficult to "crack the code." What is hoped for is that a sufficient number of significant elements can be identified so that researchers can develop personalized therapies and effective methods of prevention in the future.

So, what are the "chances" that your genetic background will result in addiction, and is it worth the gamble? Although the genetic connection is strong, it appears that nurture, rather than nature, is still the determining factor. Children of alcoholics may inherit certain genes, but they learn and develop attitudes about alcohol and drugs from the people around them, particularly their parents and siblings. A genetic tendency does not predict future dependence. Similarly, a lack of genetic markers cannot guarantee a life free from addiction. When long-lasting adaptations occur in the brain through heavy, chronic drinking, dependence is formed, regardless of genetic background.

Incidentally, it appears that gamblers, alcoholics, and other substance-dependent adults may share similar personality profiles consisting of impulsive, risk-taking behavior and rebelliousness. Indeed, many addictions, like gambling and drinking, are often observed together (co-morbidity). However, the cravings experienced couldn't be more different. The craving for alcohol is linked to the desire for relief from negative emotions, while gambling cravings are based on the desire for positive feedback and elation.

A large slow-cooker set to low is the ideal receptacle for keeping this dish warm throughout the night. Otherwise, serve in a large, covered casserole that can be popped into the oven or microwave for a quick reheat.

1. Heat the oil in a large, heavy-bottomed pot or Dutch oven over medium heat. Add the onion, sprinkle with salt and pepper, and cook, stirring often, until softened and lightly browned, about 6 minutes. Add the cabbage, sprinkle with salt and pepper, and stir well to combine. Cook, stirring often, until the cabbage begins to wilt, about 5 minutes. Add the sauerkraut, caraway seeds, apple juice, and water, stir well, and bring to a simmer. Reduce the heat to low and cook, covered, stirring occasionally, until the mixture has reduced and the cabbage is well cooked, about 1 hour.

2. Add the kielbasa pieces, cover, and simmer over very low heat an additional 15 minutes. Transfer to a heated casserole or slow cooker to keep warm.

3. In a small bowl, whisk together the mustard, horseradish, and mustard seeds. Cover and chill. Serve with the kielbasa, kraut, and rolls.

Serves 8

Ingredients

Streusel:

1½ cups roughly chopped walnuts

1¼ cups light brown sugar, firmly packed

1½ tablespoons ground cinnamon

1 tablespoon unsweetened cocoa powder

Batter:

¾ cup unsalted butter (1½ sticks), at room temperature

1½ cups granulated white sugar

3 large eggs

1 tablespoon alcohol-free vanilla extract

3 cups cake flour (not self-rising)

1½ teaspoons each baking soda and baking powder

½ teaspoon salt

One 16-ounce container sour cream

Sour Cream Cinnamon Streusel Coffeecake

Every good cup of coffee deserves a great piece of coffeecake, and this one will definitely fit the bill. Bake the day before and keep it well-wrapped in foil to retain its delicious moistness. A 10-inch tube pan or a 12-cup Bundt pan can be used and should be generously buttered and floured before adding the batter and streusel.

Cake flour will greatly enhance the texture – be sure to purchase the regular, not self-rising variety. Other nuts can be substituted for walnuts, such as pecans or hazelnuts. Use a full-fat sour cream for the best result, and don't omit the cocoa – it adds an indescribably delicious flavor.

1. Preheat the oven to 350 degrees. Butter and flour a tube or Bundt pan (see recipe introduction).

2. In a medium-size mixing bowl, stir together the streusel ingredients until well combined and set aside. In another medium-size mixing bowl, using an electric mixer, beat together the butter and white sugar until light and fluffy, 3 to 5 minutes. Beat in the eggs one at a time and add the vanilla. In a clean, medium-size mixing bowl, whisk together the flour, baking soda, baking powder, and salt. Alternately beat the dry ingredients and the sour cream into the butter-and-egg mixture in two additions, then beat the batter on high for 1 minute until well combined.

3. Pour ⅓ of the batter into the prepared pan, smoothing with a rubber spatula. Sprinkle with half the streusel mixture, being careful to stay within the edges of the pan. Spoon another ⅓ of the batter evenly over the streusel layer. Sprinkle on the remaining streusel and top with the remaining batter. Bake until golden and a toothpick inserted in the center comes out clean, about 1 hour. Cool the cake in the pan on a rack for 10 minutes; then, using a sharp knife, loosen the edges of the cake. Either invert onto a wire rack (if using a Bundt) or lift out the center section and remove the cake with two metal spatulas (if using a tube pan), allowing it to cool for 1 hour. While the cake is still slightly warm, wrap it well in foil and set aside to cool completely.

4. Serve on a cake platter at room temperature and slice with a serrated knife.

Serves 8 to 10

Chapter 10

Ladies Only

Tangerine Buttercream Cupcakes
with Candied Flowers

Some special occasions are strictly for the girls, and when planning a "ladies only" event, you'll want to be sure to cater to their distinctive styles and taste. Although no one would say that women don't love to eat, party-portion sizes can often be calculated a bit smaller, while variety is definitely the name of the game. By offering these innovative menus, you'll press all the right buttons when it comes to an unforgettable get-together for the ladies and be, without contest, the superior hostess of the day!

Forthcoming nuptials and anticipated baby arrivals are just two reasons that girls will gather, but they're two of the most important milestones to celebrate. Make each celebration a special one by planning the happiest, most convivial party possible. Turn a simple bride's luncheon into an afternoon at the spa and indulge the bride-to-be and her entourage in a perfect day of fabulous food, fun, and beauty. Eliminating the alcohol was never so easy as when beautiful skin and an overall healthy appearance are the goal. Host a baby shower like no other for the expectant mother with a healthy, creative menu that rivals the finest the culinary world has to offer. Focusing on the tea in "tea party" will result in a wonderfully delicious and unique get-together that your guest of honor will cherish for years to come. Pull out all the creative stops and give the girls the parties they really crave – who knew they could be so rowdy without the boys (and the booze)?

Turn a run-of-the-mill bridesmaids' luncheon into an event they won't forget with this outstanding spa buffet get-together. They'll love the pampering and soothing atmosphere you've created by turning your house into a miniature spa and restaurant with everything to indulge their senses, from refreshing Herb-Infused Spa Water to deliciously creamy Panna Cotta for dessert.

Many brides-to-be and their moms are turning to this unique type of event for the most important ladies of the wedding day, and your gathering will be the best of the best. Have a manicurist come in for the afternoon to take care of hands and nails, and a local massage therapist to apply the magic touch of relaxation. If the wedding is close at hand, you could even offer the services of a hairdresser – or any other type of beauty treatment you think the girls would enjoy. The best thing is that they'll be together, chatting and laughing the afternoon away while getting healthy and vibrant for the big day. Send the boys off to the movies, because this is for ladies only. When it's over, your guests will agree that this was a day at the spa like no other!

A Bridal Spa Buffet Lunch

MENU

Buffet for Eight

APPETIZERS:

Cucumber Rolls

*Sugar Snap Peas, Carrots, Bell Peppers,
and Rice Crackers*

Spicy Thai Peanut Dip

MAIN COURSE:

Grilled Chicken Fillets on Spring Mix
with Fresh Peach Salsa

Rotini Salad Niçoise with Lemon Mint Dressing

Lentil, Walnut, and Fennel Salad

Miniature Muffins and Scones

DESSERT:

Vanilla Buttermilk Panna Cotta with Berry Compote

Assorted Chocolate Truffles

BEVERAGE PAIRINGS:

Appetizers: White Tea Tonic

Main Course: Herb-Infused Spa Water

Dessert: *Assorted Herbal Teas*

Tips on Purchased Ingredients

Cucumber rolls, a favorite vegetable-only treat among sushi lovers, are light and tasty. Many supermarkets carry them in their fish department, and your local Japanese restaurant will, of course, make them. Absent any raw fish, they're fine for a buffet spread. One whole roll will usually yield six bite-size pieces, so depending on their popularity, you may want to purchase three or four. California rolls, containing avocado, cucumber, and imitation crab sticks, are also popular and would make a nice addition to the platter.

Crisp, raw vegetables are ideal for scooping up the Spicy Thai Peanut Dip. **Sugar snap peas**, which are entirely edible, can be purchased in small packages, stringless and ready to eat. If you buy them loose, simply remove the string by starting at the top of the pod and pulling down along the inside edge. To add color as well as crunch to the veggie tray, **carrot sticks** and strips of colorful **bell peppers**, red, orange, and yellow, can be cut early in

the day, chilled, and added to the platter. **Rice crackers**, crisp little savory nibbles available in the cracker or deli section of your supermarket, come in a variety of flavors, from sesame to seaweed. Any type would be delicious here, but avoid those made with mirin, a sweet Japanese wine, or tamari, a thick soy sauce that usually has alcohol as a preservative.

Miniature muffins and scones add a nice touch to the buffet table and you can certainly make them yourself if you like. Otherwise, supermarket bakeries offer a pretty good variety of the usual muffins, including bran, lemon poppy seed, and corn, while miniature scones are generally triangular in shape and flavored with lemon, orange, or raisins. Some specialty grocers like Trader Joe's® will offer more "healthful" varieties of muffins, like dried blueberry wheat bran, protein carrot raisin, and oat bran, which would fit even better with your spa theme. They usually also carry a better and more unusual selection of scone flavors to add to the basket. Offer some light, whipped butter and organic honey to go along with them.

Given the amount of nutritious and healthy food and beverages you're providing, surely it wouldn't hurt to throw in some chocolate! Miniature **chocolate truffles** would be a luxurious offering, as would dark chocolate-covered nuts, dried berries, and crystallized ginger. Read labels to avoid truffles that contain rum, brandy, or other types of alcoholic enhancement.

White Tea Tonic

Start things off with this refreshing and invigorating drink that combines the immune-boosting antioxidants of white tea and the anti-inflammatory properties of fresh ginger root. A splash of orange blossom water, a great alternative to alcohol-containing extracts, adds a touch of the exotic. Sweetened to your taste with honey, it's the perfect beginning to an afternoon of pampering.

White tea, like the more familiar black and green varieties, also comes from the *Camellia sinensis* plant, but the leaves are harvested before they have a chance to open, and the buds are covered in fine white hair. Its flavor is extremely subtle, so it's often combined with other flavors such as fruit and ginger. It should always be steeped below the boiling point to maintain its sweet delicacy. Look for white tea varieties such as white peony, golden moon, or silver needle. If you end up finding bulk loose tea instead of tea bags, simply substitute one teaspoon per bag.

1. In a medium-size saucepan, bring the water to a boil and add the ginger root. Remove from the heat and allow to steep, covered, for 3 minutes. Add the tea bags, cover, and steep a further 5 minutes.

2. Remove the tea bags, and strain and discard the ginger. Stir in the orange blossom water. Add honey to taste, and transfer the tea mixture to a pitcher. Chill in the refrigerator, covered, at least 2 hours or overnight. Pour into ice-filled juice glasses and serve.

Serves 8

Ingredients:

9 cups water

One 2-inch piece fresh ginger root, peeled and roughly chopped

12 white tea bags

2 teaspoons orange blossom water

Honey to taste

Spicy Thai Peanut Dip

Eastern cultures have long been aware that "spice" can be extremely healing, particularly in the form of chile peppers. In addition to anti-inflammatory properties, compounds found in cayenne from chile peppers can raise endorphin levels and flush out toxins. Consequently, everyone will feel not only cleansed and healthy, but quite happy as well!

Make this dip a day ahead so that all the flavors have a chance to marry. For the best consistency, choose a creamy-style peanut butter (not a fresh-ground or old-fashioned type). For heightened flavor, allow the dip to sit at room temperature at least an hour before serving. If the dip needs a bit of thinning, add a touch of water or broth, and stir well.

1. Heat the oil in a medium-size skillet over medium heat. Add the shallot, ginger root, garlic, and a small sprinkling of salt, and sauté, stirring often, until softened, about 3 minutes. Reduce the heat, if necessary, to prevent the garlic from browning. Stir in the curry powder and red pepper flakes, and cook for 30 seconds.

2. Whisk in the remaining ingredients and bring to a simmer over medium-high heat. Cook, whisking often, until the mixture is thickened, 3 to 4 minutes. Taste for the addition of salt and red pepper flakes, and transfer to a bowl. Whisk occasionally until cool, then cover and refrigerate for at least 2 hours or overnight.

3. Serve at room temperature in a dipping bowl, surrounded by the raw vegetables and rice crackers.

Serves 8

Ingredients:

1 tablespoon peanut oil

1 small shallot, finely chopped

One 1-inch piece fresh ginger root, peeled and finely chopped

2 garlic cloves, peeled and minced

Salt to taste

1 teaspoon curry powder

Pinch of crushed red pepper flakes, or more to taste

1 cup low-sodium chicken broth

¾ cup creamy peanut butter

1 tablespoon freshly squeezed lime juice

2 teaspoons soy sauce

1 heaping teaspoon brown sugar

Rotini Salad Niçoise with Lemon Mint Dressing

A light pasta salad is the perfect accompaniment for your grilled chicken. Here, inspired by the classic French *salade niçoise*, we'll be tossing the pasta with all its delicious and healthy ingredients sans the tuna. For other occasions, you can add two 6-ounce cans of solid white tuna in water, drained and flaked, to make a complete and satisfying lunch salad. If available, use the tiny, delicate French *haricots verts* (green beans) traditionally used for this salad, and look for *niçoise* olives in your grocer's condiment isle. These olives don't usually come pitted, so you'll need to press them on a cutting board with the blade of a large chef's knife, then remove the pits with your fingers. If this seems like too tedious a prospect, substitute pitted Kalamata olives, which are more readily available.

A tricolor rotini pasta would make this more festive, but you can certainly use a plain variety or even a whole-wheat version. Make this salad the morning of the party and serve it at room temperature for peak flavor. Garnish with the hard-boiled egg quarters just before serving.

Ingredients:

1 pound rotini pasta, cooked, drained, and refreshed under cold running water

A drizzle of olive oil

3 tablespoons finely chopped, fresh mint leaves

2 teaspoons grated lemon peel

1 garlic clove, peeled and minced

1 teaspoon brown mustard

¼ cup freshly squeezed lemon juice

½ cup extra virgin olive oil

Salt and pepper to taste

8 ounces French *haricots verts* (green beans), trimmed and halved

½ medium-size orange or yellow bell pepper, seeded and thinly sliced into 1-inch-long strips

1 small red onion, peeled and cut into thin circles

½ cup niçoise olives, pitted

1 pint cherry or pear-shaped tomatoes, halved

4 hard-boiled eggs, peeled and quartered (see page 171 for cooking tips)

1. Place the cooked, refreshed pasta in a large mixing bowl and drizzle a little olive oil over it. Toss to coat and set aside.

2. In a small mixing bowl, combine the mint, lemon peel, garlic, mustard, and lemon juice. Slowly whisk in the extra virgin olive oil, season with salt and pepper, and set aside.

3. In a pot of boiling, salted water, cook the green beans until crisp-tender, 3 to 4 minutes. Drain and submerge the beans in a bowl of ice water to stop the cooking. Remove and drain well on paper towels. Add the green beans, sliced bell pepper, onion, olives, and tomatoes to the pasta bowl, pour on the dressing, and toss well to coat. Refrigerate, covered, if not serving immediately.

4. Just before serving, bring the salad to room temperature, salt and pepper to taste, and transfer to a large bowl or platter. Place the egg quarters decoratively around the edge of the dish and serve.

Serves 8

Grilled Chicken Fillets on Spring Mix with Fresh Peach Salsa

Ingredients:

8 boneless, skinless,
thin-sliced chicken fillets

Salt and pepper to taste

Oil for coating the grill

Peach Salsa:

3 medium-size ripe peaches

½ cup Vidalia onion
(or another sweet onion), chopped

1 small jalapeño pepper, trimmed,
seeded, and finely chopped

2 tablespoons freshly squeezed
lime juice

1 tablespoon finely chopped,
fresh cilantro leaves

Salt and pepper to taste

To Serve:

One 8-ounce package spring mix or
mesclun salad greens

Cilantro sprigs for garnish

This spa cuisine-inspired dish is the ideal main course for your buffet lunch as it is grilled ahead of time and served at room temperature. Your spa guests can help themselves to this light repast in between treatments and satisfy any hunger pangs without the uncomfortable feeling of overindulgence. To cook the chicken, you can fire up your outdoor grill or use an indoor countertop grill. These thin-sliced fillets take no time at all to cook, so watch carefully and remove the chicken from the grill just after it's lost its pink hue to retain tenderness.

When peaches are in season, the accompanying salsa can't be beat. Since most weddings take place in summer, you shouldn't have any problem finding the sweetest and juiciest peaches in your local farmers' market or grocer. Nectarines, also in season, would be fine for the salsa as well. If good, ripe peaches or nectarines can't be found or are not in season, depending on the time of year, don't use inferior ones. Instead, substitute diced mango or fresh pineapple in their place. In any case, you'll need about 1¾ cups of diced fruit. You can make the salsa a few hours ahead and keep it chilled until ready to serve.

1. Prepare an outdoor gas or charcoal barbecue for medium-high grilling. (Alternatively, preheat an indoor countertop grill or stovetop grill pan.) Lightly coat the grill with oil to prevent sticking.

2. Season both sides of the chicken with salt and pepper, and grill the fillets until no longer pink, 2 to 3 minutes per side. Transfer to a clean plate and set aside.

3. To make the salsa, bring a medium-size saucepan of water to boil over high heat. Drop in the peaches and cook for 30 seconds. Using a slotted spoon, submerge the peaches in a bowl of ice-cold water to cool. Remove and drain on paper towels. Using a sharp paring knife, peel the peaches, remove the pits, and cut

into ¼-inch dice. In a medium-size mixing bowl, combine the peaches and the remaining ingredients, and using a rubber spatula, gently fold to combine. Taste for seasoning, cover, and chill.

4. To serve, spread the spring mix on a large oval platter, place the chicken fillets, slightly overlapping, across the middle of the platter, and spoon some of the salsa over each fillet. Garnish with the cilantro sprigs and serve.

Serves 8

Lentil, Walnut, and Fennel Salad

Legumes are a part of a healthy diet, and here, the delicious lentil plays the starring role in a splendid, flavorful salad. If you can find the tiny black lentils *du Puy*, you should use them here; however, the ordinary brown lentil will do quite well, provided it's not overcooked. Be sure to pick over the dry lentils before cooking, as there are often bits of dirt and pebbles present. In place of white balsamic vinegar, you can use regular white wine vinegar and add a pinch of sugar. Make this salad the day before so that the flavors are well incorporated, and serve cool or at room temperature.

Walnuts and walnut oil are two of the few nonfish sources of healthy omega-3 fatty acids, which offer numerous health benefits, including vibrant hair and skin. Fennel, long purported to be both a cleanser of bodily toxins (including alcohol) and an aid in drumming up courage (gladiators used to eat it before entering the arena), adds a delightful crunch to this most healthy of salads. Make sure the bride gets a good spoonful!

Ingredients:

2 cups dried brown or *du Puy* lentils, picked over and rinsed

1 medium-size carrot, peeled and quartered

1 medium-size onion, peeled and halved

1 bay leaf

2 cups low-sodium chicken broth

2 garlic cloves, peeled and minced

1/3 cup white balsamic vinegar

1/2 cup walnut oil

Salt and pepper to taste

1/2 medium-size fennel bulb, trimmed, peeled, and cut into 1/4-inch dice, fronds reserved

1 cup chopped walnuts

1. In a large saucepan, combine the lentils, carrot, onion, and bay leaf. Pour in the chicken broth and add enough water to cover. Over medium-high heat, bring the lentils to a boil, reduce to a simmer, and cook until tender but not mushy, 20 to 25 minutes. Add more water as necessary to prevent sticking. Drain the lentils, discarding the vegetables and bay leaf, and transfer to a large mixing bowl.

2. In a small mixing bowl, whisk together the garlic, vinegar, and walnut oil. Season with salt and pepper and pour over the warm lentils. Toss well to coat and allow to come to room temperature, gently stirring once or twice.

3. Stir in the chopped fennel and walnuts, cover, and refrigerate overnight. Just before serving, taste for the addition of salt and pepper (you can add a touch more walnut oil for flavor if you like), transfer to a serving bowl, and decorate the edges with the fennel fronds.

Serves 8

Herb-Infused Spa Water

In place of uninspired bottles of plain spring water, serve up pitchers of this terrific spa water to keep everyone hydrated and healthy. Subtle in flavor and highly refreshing, this special touch will delight your guests and make them feel truly pampered.

You'll need plenty to go around for a full afternoon of treatments, so be sure to have lots on hand in the refrigerator to replenish pitchers as necessary. Two to three gallons should be sufficient for eight people. The following recipe is per gallon – double or triple as appropriate. If you're making several gallons, you can infuse the water directly in a gallon container by pouring out a bit of the water, then cutting the cucumber and lemon slices into quarters to fit in the mouth of the jug. Serve well chilled, with or without ice.

Pour the water into a 1-gallon pitcher (or two ½-gallon pitchers) and stir in the cucumber, lemon, and herbs. Allow to chill at least 2 hours or overnight before serving.

Serves 8

Ingredients:

1 gallon spring or purified water

½ medium-size cucumber, trimmed and sliced thin

½ lemon, sliced thin and seeds removed

One 4-inch sprig fresh rosemary

Four 2-inch sprigs fresh mint

Women and Alcohol: What You Need to Know

We have known for a long time that men and women react differently to the effects of alcohol. With less water in their bodies, women achieve higher concentrations of alcohol in their blood than men, resulting in more rapid intoxication. Lesser amounts of stomach enzymes that metabolize alcohol also contribute to heightened reactions in women. And it has also been determined that fluctuating monthly hormone levels can make women more susceptible to the effects of alcohol at certain times. But recently, it has been found that in spite of these greater vulnerabilities, women appear to be less sensitive to the sedative qualities of alcohol – arguably, what both men and women most desire when they're drinking. Because of this, women may not be able to accurately assess their levels of impairment when they consume alcohol and consequently attempt to perform normal activities like driving. This may also make them more inclined toward binge drinking, in order to achieve a higher level of sedation. These findings are very similar to those discovered about adolescent drinkers, whose cognitive skills may drastically decrease without their feeling sleepy – a dangerous situation that has been described as "wide-awake drunks with poor judgment."

Additionally, the findings on long-term physical effects of alcohol on women are disturbing. Liver damage, heart disease, and brain shrinkage are more rapidly reached and more seriously life-threatening for women than for men. Although typically, chronic alcohol consumption occurs later in life in women, the quick progression of dependence and health-related problems make up for lost time, leaving them even more vulnerable than men.

Finally, we have known unequivocally since the 1970s that drinking during pregnancy is harmful to the unborn baby. Fetal alcohol syndrome (FAS), characterized by abnormal facial features, growth retardation, and damage to the brain resulting in learning, memory, and social problems, occurs in about 40,000 babies in the U.S. each year. Still, about 15 percent of pregnant women continue to drink. Recently, it's been found that moderate drinking during pregnancy can increase the risk of infection in newborns, and pregnancy risks even with light drinking have not been dismissed as a possibility. For moms-to-be, the message is clear: There is no safe amount of alcohol to drink while pregnant. With abstention, FAS and alcohol-related birth defects are 100 percent preventable.

Vanilla Buttermilk Panna Cotta with Berry Compote

Panna cotta, a classic Italian custard made with cream, gets a healthy makeover with the inclusion of low-fat buttermilk, adding a lovely tang that goes well with the sweet berry compote. Make these at least 5 hours ahead or the night before so they have a chance to set. Each portion is about half a cup, so choose an appropriate-sized glass to fit, leaving room for the berry compote topping. Medium-sized martini glasses are great for individual presentation and don't require the usual inverting so often used in panna cotta presentations when made in custard cups, although any similar type of glass, such as a wine- or parfait glass, would be fine. One large glass bowl to spoon from would also make a nice presentation.

Vanilla sugar is a terrific alternative for sober baking and is easily made by inserting a whole vanilla bean in a canister of sugar, and letting it work its magic for a week or two. The result is super-aromatic and can be used in place of unflavored sugar in recipes that call for vanilla extract. Maceration is a technique used to flavor fruit: An alcoholic beverage is generally used as the macerating liquid to help break down the fruit and allow it to develop its own natural sauce. Here, we'll be using a combination of tea and vanilla sugar as the liquid – tea being an excellent substitute in sober cooking for alcohol-containing ingredients because of its natural acidity and tannins. Combined with a sweet element, it mimics beautifully the qualities of a liqueur. Macerate the berries a few hours ahead and keep them well chilled.

Ingredients:

2 teaspoons powdered, unflavored gelatin

2 tablespoons water

1 cup heavy cream

½ cup vanilla sugar (or ½ cup granulated sugar and 1 teaspoon alcohol-free vanilla extract)

2 cups reduced-fat buttermilk (2 percent)

Berry Compote:

¼ cup vanilla sugar (see above)

½ cup water

1 blueberry, strawberry, or mixed-berry herbal tea bag

1 teaspoon fresh-squeezed lemon juice

1 cup each fresh blackberries, blueberries, and raspberries

1 cup strawberries, hulled and diced

Mint sprigs for garnish

1. In a small mixing bowl, combine the gelatin and water. Let stand until the gelatin has softened, about 10 minutes.

2. In a medium-size saucepan, combine the heavy cream and ½ cup vanilla sugar, and over medium heat, stir until the sugar has dissolved and the cream is hot but not boiling. Remove from the heat, add the gelatin mixture, and stir until well incorporated. Set aside to cool for 30 to 40 minutes.

3. Whisk the buttermilk into the cooled cream mixture and strain through a fine sieve. Pour mixture into a large glass bowl or divide equally among eight martini or other glasses, cover with plastic wrap, and refrigerate at least 5 hours or overnight until set.

4. Make the compote: In a small saucepan, combine $\frac{1}{2}$ cup vanilla sugar with the water and bring to a boil on medium-high heat. Stir until the sugar has dissolved, about 1 minute. Remove from the heat and add the tea bag. Allow to steep for 5 minutes, remove the tea bag, stir in the lemon juice, and set aside to cool.

5. In a medium-size mixing bowl, combine all the berries, pour the cooled tea mixture over, and using a rubber spatula, gently toss to coat. Refrigerate for at least 2 hours, stirring occasionally, until the berries have softened and a sauce has developed.

6. To serve, top the chilled panna cotta with a spoonful of the berry compote and garnish with a mint sprig.

Serves 8

Your guests may have been to many a shower and perhaps just as many teas, but I guarantee that they've never been to such a delightful baby shower "tea party" as the one you'll be hosting with this menu. Every dish, from hors d'oeuvres to dessert, has some type of tea as an ingredient. From green to herbal, citrus to floral, you'll be the quintessential queen of teas as you present these fabulous and fragrant dishes, each more outstanding than the one before.

Since moms-to-be, by necessity, must abstain, too often they feel left out of the usual celebrations. But here, no one will even blink an eye at the absence of alcohol – they'll be too impressed by your creativity to even notice. The Iced Apricot Tea Punch will keep everyone happily sipping, while an array of innovative dishes like Shrimp with Bergamot and Honey Glaze and Cardamom and Jasmine Tea-Scented Rice will have them intoxicated from the wonderful aroma alone! Decorate with any fancy tea-related items you have; fill pretty teapots with fresh flowers and offer china teacups for punch. It will be an afternoon that no one will want to end, and a party that will be talked about long after the little one arrives.

A Baby Shower "Tea Party"

MENU
Party for Twelve

HORS D'OEUVRES:
Baby Vegetables and Assorted Gyoza Dumplings
Green Tea Soy Dipping Sauce

MAIN COURSE:
Skewered Jumbo Shrimp with Bergamot and Honey Glaze
Cardamom and Jasmine Tea-Scented Rice
Peppermint Tea Cucumber Salad
Assorted Pita Breads

DESSERT:
Tangerine Buttercream Cupcakes with Candied Flowers
Seasonal Fresh Fruit Platter

BEVERAGE PAIRINGS:
Hors d'Oeuvres and Main Course:
Iced Apricot Tea Punch
Dessert: *Vanilla Chai, Herbal Teas*

Tips on Purchased Ingredients

Baby vegetables, cute little versions of their "parents," are perfect as part of a baby shower appetizer platter. In addition to the easily found baby carrots, look for miniature zucchini and patty pan squash, scallop-edged summer squash that's pale green or yellow in color and tenderly sweet. Some specialty grocers carry baby corn, bok choy, beets, and radishes, all of which would be nice here. You can also blanch thin asparagus spears cut into 2-inch pieces to add to the platter.

Gyoza, also known as pot stickers, are delicious little wonton packets that come filled with any of a number of ingredients, including chicken, pork, shrimp, or vegetables. Check the frozen food hors d'oeuvres section of your supermarket, or order them from a local Chinese or Japanese restaurant. Lightly steamed or simmered in boiling water, they're easy to heat. They can also be heated by sautéing in a bit of oil. Provide party pick forks or dessert-size forks for dipping.

Pita is the ideal bread choice for your main course. Purchase a few different flavors, like garlic, sesame, or whole wheat, and cut them into quarters. To serve warm, cover the bread with a damp paper towel and heat briefly in the microwave.

Something that's always welcome at any gathering is a **seasonal fresh fruit platter**. Many supermarkets have these pre-arranged and ready to go if you'd rather not take the time to peel and cut. Depending on the season of your party, you might include cantaloupe, watermelon, strawberries, kiwi, pineapple, and mango, to name a few. Even if you buy the prepared platter, before serving, you can arrange the fruit yourself on a decorative ceramic plate, then add one or two of

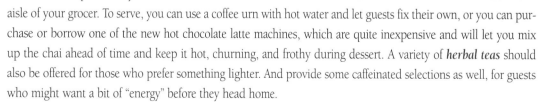

your own selections to make the presentation more attractive. Sprinkle fresh raspberries or blueberries over the platters, or add something unusual like persimmon or fresh figs. A drizzle of honey and mint sprigs to garnish would also enhance the dish nicely.

Chai is an ancient Asian beverage of tea mixed with milk, sugar, and spices. It's available in powdered or liquid form for reconstituting with hot water. *Vanilla chai* is particularly aromatic and can be found in the coffee and tea aisle of your grocer. To serve, you can use a coffee urn with hot water and let guests fix their own, or you can purchase or borrow one of the new hot chocolate latte machines, which are quite inexpensive and will let you mix up the chai ahead of time and keep it hot, churning, and frothy during dessert. A variety of **herbal teas** should also be offered for those who prefer something lighter. And provide some caffeinated selections as well, for guests who might want a bit of "energy" before they head home.

Iced Apricot Tea Punch

This light and not-too-sweet fruity punch will keep everyone refreshed as they enjoy every bite you've pre-pared. Apricot herbal tea gives this a tangy twist – you can substitute a peach tea if you prefer, or another variety, but be sure to choose herbal, so there's no caffeine present. Brew the tea ahead so you can make a couple of trays of ice cubes from it to keep your punch cool. This recipe will make enough for each person to have two full cups. However, you can double or triple the amounts if needed.

A pretty punch bowl and matching cups are the obvious choice for serving. You can get a little more creative if you like, instead serving the punch in a few large teapots and having your guests pour their "tea" into china teacups. Either way, everyone will agree that your iced apricot tea punch is nothing less than "tea-rrific!"

Ingredients:

15 cups water

20 apricot herbal tea bags

3 cups apple juice, chilled

3 cups white grape juice, chilled

6 cups ginger ale, chilled

1. In a large saucepan, bring the water to a boil. Remove from the heat, add the tea bags, and steep, covered, for 10 minutes. Remove the tea bags and pour into heat-proof pitchers or con-tainers to cool. Reserve 3 cups of the tea to make ice cubes.

2. To serve, pour the tea into a punch bowl (or a large saucepan to ladle from if you'll be serving in teapots) and stir in the apple juice, grape juice, and ginger ale. Add the prepared ice cubes as needed to keep cold.

Serves 12

Tea in the Kitchen: Thinking Outside the Cup

The next time you're looking for culinary inspiration, look no further than your kitchen tea cupboard. You won't be the only one. Chefs from all over the culinary world are turning to tea as the new darling of the kitchen, using it for such diverse purposes as a tenderizer in marinades or the key element of a fanciful dessert. It's not surprising – after all, tea contains many of the characteristics we seek in specialty ingredients, like aromatic infusibility and even tannic acid for breaking down proteins. And when alcohol-free cooking is on the agenda, tea can be your best friend in exploring substitutions.

Deliciously fragrant teas steeped in simple syrup (see page 177) can result in wonderful "liqueur-like" liquids that can be used in drinks, cakes, and sauces. You can even grind loose tea leaves and use them as a spice in rubs and stir-fries. A pinch here or there can add an exotic aroma and taste to everything from salads to steamed rice, while desserts can get a fabulous flavor boost from tea. Sugar takes to it like a charm and the result, whether a sorbet or a cookie, can be alluringly satisfying.

Green Tea Soy Dipping Sauce

This delicious dipping sauce, ideal for your gyoza and baby vegetables, will surprise everyone when you tell them the secret ingredient! Green tea makes a surprise appearance and adds a wonderful piquancy and aroma to a traditional soy sauce condiment. By steeping it with sugar, we get a close substitution for *mirin*, a sweet Japanese wine often added to dipping sauces such as this.

Seasoned rice vinegar already has salt and sugar added to it. Its extremely mild flavor, much less sour than other vinegars, is a good complement to the green tea. Also called sushi vinegar, it can be found in the Asian food aisle of your supermarket. You'll be using it for a few of the recipes in this menu, but if you have trouble finding it, substitute a white balsamic vinegar with a pinch of salt, or a plain white wine vinegar with a pinch of sugar and salt to replicate the flavor. Use a low-sodium soy sauce as the base, which is quite salty enough. You can prepare the sauce up to 2 days ahead and keep it chilled. Serve in a couple of Asian-style soup bowls and stir in the scallions just before setting out on the table.

1. In a small saucepan, combine the water and sugar and bring to a boil, stirring until the sugar has dissolved. Remove from the heat, add the tea bags, and steep for 5 minutes. Remove the tea bags and set aside to cool.

2. Stir in the soy sauce and vinegar and, if not serving immediately, pour into a container, cover, and refrigerate. Just before serving, stir in the sliced scallions and pour into bowls.

Serves 12

Ingredients:

¾ cup water

2 tablespoons granulated sugar

2 green tea bags

1½ cups low-sodium soy sauce

½ cup seasoned rice vinegar

½ cup thinly sliced scallions

With all the possibilities in the kitchen, it's easy to forget how wonderfully tea can be paired with food, especially when looking for an alcohol-free beverage to complement your menu. The Tea Council Ltd. and the Food and Wine Service in the United Kingdom (where else?) have come up with some recommended tea and food pairings to enhance your dining pleasure. Here are a few of their suggestions:

Darjeeling complements anything creamy, particularly desserts like cheesecake.

Lapsang goes well with chicken, Stilton cheese, and lemon sorbet.

Kenya holds up well with beef, horseradish, and rich chocolate cakes.

Earl Grey should be poured with paté and crème brûlée.

English Breakfast matches well with ham sandwiches and ice cream.

Finally, tisane-making, an old medicinal tradition of fresh herbal infusions, is enjoying a comeback. These light, aromatic drinks make for delightful accompaniments to many dishes, particularly when served in steeping teapots at the table to replicate the ritual of sharing a bottle of wine. And any leftover tisane could prove inspiring as an ingredient in your next dish. So, forget about the corkscrew – let's put the kettle on and start cooking!

Skewered Jumbo Shrimp with Bergamot and Honey Glaze

Ingredients

Glaze:

1½ cups strongly brewed Earl Grey tea

½ cup honey

½ cup orange juice

¼ cup seasoned rice vinegar

¼ cup low-sodium chicken broth

3 tablespoons soy sauce

One 1-inch piece ginger root, peeled and finely chopped

Shrimp:

3 pounds uncooked jumbo shrimp, shelled, deveined, with tails removed

Salt and pepper to taste

Jumbo shrimp, somewhere in size between colossal and large, usually come about 16 to 20 per pound uncooked. They make for a stellar presentation when skewered, as they still look quite large even after they're cooked. About four shrimp per person is the desired serving, so you'll probably need about 3 pounds. Have the shrimp shelled, tailed, and deveined to save yourself this chore later. You'll need 12 medium-size metal or pre-soaked bamboo skewers. For indoor cooking, simply line up the skewered shrimp on a baking sheet and cook them under the broiler. You can also grill them outdoors, but you'll have to allow time for the fuss of barbecue lighting and preheating. Either method is fine in this case, as it's the delicious glaze that really makes the dish.

In keeping with our "tea party" theme, we'll make use of the wonderfully fragrant Earl Grey variety, which contains the perfumed fruitiness of bergamot, a small, acidic orange famous for the oil extracted from its peel. Combined with ginger and honey, it produces an intoxicating aroma and superb glaze for the skewered shrimp.

Prepare the glaze ahead and reheat in a small saucepan while the shrimp is broiling. Be sure to have the rice ready and waiting on a large, heated platter to receive the skewered shrimp. Metal skewers will be quite hot, so use tongs to transfer, and wrap the ends in heavy foil or provide small potholders so your guests don't burn their fingertips!

1. Make the glaze: Whisk together all the ingredients in a medium-size saucepan and bring to a boil over high heat. Reduce the heat to medium and simmer about 10 minutes, stirring often, until the mixture has thickened and reduced by almost half. Remove from the heat and, if not using immediately, cool and store in a covered container until ready to use. Before cooking the shrimp, reheat the glaze in a small saucepan and have a pastry brush ready.

2. Line a large baking sheet with foil. Thread the shrimp onto 12 skewers, dividing evenly, and place in a single layer on the baking sheet. Season well with salt and pepper, and under a preheated broiler, cook on high until the shrimp are no longer pink, about 3 minutes per side. (Alternatively, grill over medium-high coals or on a gas grill for 5 minutes, turning once.)

3. Remove from the heat source, and immediately brush both sides of each skewer with the glaze. Carefully transfer to the ready rice platter and pour any remaining glaze evenly over the shrimp. Serve immediately.

Serves 12

Cardamom and Jasmine Tea-Scented Rice

Ingredients:

4 cups basmati rice

3 cups strongly brewed jasmine tea

4 cups water

8 whole cardamom pods

Pinch of salt

Jasmine has a hauntingly beautiful scent not unlike that of honeysuckle, and when brewed as a tea, it has an aroma that can permeate an entire room. Twinings® makes one of the only pure jasmine-scented teas that's not combined with green or white tea. Try to find it, as it will really enhance your rice. Cardamom, a member of the ginger family, is a popular spice used in Scandinavian and Indian cuisine, and comes either ground or in whole pods. It's wonderfully fragrant in its own right, exuding a sweet-spicy warmth that will remind you of Indian restaurants. Use whole cardamom pods to flavor the rice and add a touch of the exotic to its presentation. Basmati rice, also an aromatic ingredient, completes the trio of scents to make this dish the perfect match for your glazed shrimp.

Ingredients:

⅓ cup seasoned rice vinegar

1 teaspoon granulated sugar

2 peppermint tea bags

2 large English cucumbers, ends trimmed, sliced very thin, patted dry

1½ cups plain low-fat or nonfat yogurt, drained

Freshly ground pepper to taste

Mint sprigs for garnish

Peppermint Tea Cucumber Salad

Fresh mint, cucumber, and yogurt are a classic Middle Eastern combination, but here, in keeping with our theme, the main source of mint flavor will be provided by peppermint tea. Combined with seasoned rice vinegar and creamy yogurt, cucumbers never tasted so good! We'll be infusing the vinegar with the tea, a slightly different method than the ones used in the previous recipes. It's a great way to flavor plain vinegars, and in the future, you may want to experiment with different teas and vinegars for use in salad dressings and as additions to dishes where wine may be called for.

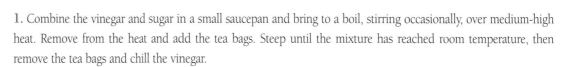

Use English seedless cucumbers, which will require no peeling unless you prefer to do so. Cutting thin slices can prove a bit labor-intensive, so by all means employ a Japanese *mandoline* or a food processor fitted with a slicing disk. Be sure to pat the cucumbers dry with a paper towel to avoid excess water in the final salad. Also, be sure that the vinegar tea is not hot, which could curdle the yogurt. Make this a few hours ahead and chill well until ready to serve.

1. Combine the vinegar and sugar in a small saucepan and bring to a boil, stirring occasionally, over medium-high heat. Remove from the heat and add the tea bags. Steep until the mixture has reached room temperature, then remove the tea bags and chill the vinegar.

2. Place the cucumber slices in a large mixing bowl. In a small mixing bowl, whisk together the chilled vinegar tea mixture, yogurt, and pepper. Pour this over the cucumbers and toss gently to coat. Keep refrigerated if not serving immediately. To serve, transfer the cucumber salad to a chilled platter and garnish with the mint sprigs.

Serves 12

Although this rice could be made ahead of time and reheated in the microwave or by steaming over a pot of simmering water, it's just as easy to make it before serving. Basmati rice takes much less time to cook than long-grain rice and requires very little attention until you are ready to fluff and serve. It also does not expand as much as long-grain varieties, which is why you'll want to make 4 cups' worth. A pot with a tight-fitting lid is the perfect receptacle for cooking, or if you have a rice steamer and prefer to use it, just follow the manufacturer's directions for the recommended method. Soaking and rinsing the rice beforehand will ensure optimal fluffiness by removing any excess starch.

1. In a large mixing bowl, soak the rice in cold water for 1 to 2 hours. Drain in a colander and rinse thoroughly with cold running water. Set aside to drain well.

2. In a large saucepan with a tight-fitting lid, combine the remaining ingredients and bring to a boil. Stir in the rice, cover, reduce the heat to low, and allow to cook until all the liquid is absorbed and the rice is tender, about 15 minutes. Remove from the heat and do not disturb for 5 to 10 minutes.

3. When ready to serve, fluff the rice with a fork and transfer to a heated platter.

Serves 12

Tangerine Buttercream Cupcakes with Candied Flowers

These moist, flavorful cupcakes are the perfect ending to your baby shower "tea party" and yet another treat to showcase the delicious use of tea in the kitchen, this time as a baking ingredient. Tangerine juice and tea are the secret ingredients for these delightful delicacies and will tempt your guests to go for seconds. It's okay if they do – this recipe makes 2 dozen!

Use pretty paper muffin cups to line the tins – white, yellow, or a baby or floral design would be great. Make the cupcakes and icing a day ahead if you like, but wait to frost them until the morning of the party for peak appearance. (If you've chilled the frosting, you'll need to let it sit out about 15 minutes to regain its spreadable consistency.) Little candied flowers can be bought at baking supply stores and used to decorate the tops – violets, daisies, or a "bouquet" of a few selections will really make these outstanding.

1. Preheat the oven to 325 degrees. Line two 12-cup muffin tins with paper baking cups.

2. In a medium-size mixing bowl, using an electric mixer, beat together the sugar and oil on medium speed until well combined, about 1 minute. Add the tangerine juice, grated rind, and egg yolks, and continue to beat until well incorporated, about 1 minute more. In another medium-size mixing bowl, whisk together the flour, baking powder, and salt. Add the dry ingredients to the wet mixture in two batches, beating on medium speed each time until well combined, about 2 minutes.

3. With clean beaters in a clean, medium-size bowl, beat the egg whites with the cream of tartar on high speed until stiff peaks form. Stir about one-quarter of the beaten egg whites into the batter, then gently fold in the rest. Pour the batter into the prepared muffin cups to three-quarters full. Bake until the cake tops spring back when lightly touched and a toothpick inserted in the middle comes out clean, 20 to 25 minutes. Cool on wire racks.

4. Make the buttercream: Steep the tea bags in the boiling water for 10 minutes. Remove the tea bags and refrigerate the tea until well-chilled.

5. In a medium-size mixing bowl, using an electric mixer, beat the butter on medium-high speed until light and fluffy, 1 to 2 minutes. Reduce the speed to low and add the confectioners' sugar (start with 3½ cups), chilled tangerine tea, and the grated rind. Beat until smooth and creamy, 2 to 3 minutes. If the frosting seems thin, beat in a little more confectioners' sugar until thick enough to spread. Add enough yellow food coloring to make the frosting lemony yellow.

6. Frost the cooled cupcakes with the buttercream and decorate the tops with the candied flowers. Refrigerate the cupcakes until 20 minutes before serving.

Makes 24 cupcakes

Ingredients
Cupcakes:

½ cup canola oil

1⅓ cups granulated sugar

¾ cup tangerine juice, fresh-squeezed or bottled

2 teaspoons grated tangerine or orange rind

5 egg yolks

2¼ cups cake flour (not self-rising)

1 tablespoon baking powder

½ teaspoon salt

8 egg whites

½ teaspoon cream of tartar

Buttercream:

3 tangerine tea bags

⅓ cup boiling water

1 cup (2 sticks) unsalted butter, softened

3½ to 4 cups confectioners' sugar

1 teaspoon grated tangerine or orange rind

Yellow food coloring

Candied flowers for decorating

Chapter 11

Celebrating Couples

Chocolate Mousse "Cordials"
with Monogrammed Chocolate Mini-Cakes

Whether it's their first day as husband and wife or a milestone of 25 years together, a couple celebrating is one of the most popular reasons for entertaining with style. Too often, we relegate celebrations such as these to professional cooks and caterers, thinking that large groups of friends and family may be too much for our talents. But there's nothing like the personal, loving touch that results from hosting an occasion like a wedding or anniversary in your home. For manageable groups of up to 30 guests, there's no better place. So, dispense with the trepidation and try your hand at these terrific party ideas, which will be long appreciated by the couple of honor.

When it comes to an event like a wedding reception, you may wonder how to address the question of serving alcohol. Today, quite surprisingly, many receptions are alcohol-free, primarily to save on expense, so rest assured that yours is not the first without it and most certainly won't be the last. With a stellar menu of outstanding food and refreshments, its absence won't even be noticed. And the same is true for important anniversaries where a toast is expected. Provided there's something refreshing and tasty in the glass, whether it contains alcohol or not makes little difference. More and more people are discovering the pleasure and worry-free atmosphere of alcohol-free entertaining, even at large events like these. Bet you didn't know you were a trend-setter!

Originally, the term "wedding breakfast" was an English one, referring to any meal eaten by the bride and groom to "break the fast" after taking their vows. And a wedding breakfast or brunch in America is traditionally referred to as the meal served the morning after the reception, just before the newlyweds depart for their honeymoon. But recently, wedding receptions that are indeed actual breakfasts or brunches are becoming more popular for a number of reasons: Expenses are far less, the couple can embark that afternoon for their honeymoon destination, and perhaps most important for our planning, alcohol is less expected as part of the menu. Although you'll certainly find breakfast receptions that offer up Bloody Marys and mimosas, a morning meal can certainly be considered complete and appetizing without them. Even the usual champagne for toasting can be easily replaced by an alcohol-free beverage like the Celebration Shampagne included in this menu.

If you decide to take on the challenge of hosting a wedding reception for a relative or friend (not as formidable as you may think!), you'll definitely need help. Either solicit the assistance of friends or, even better, hire professional workers for the day of the reception who can be relied upon to watch over every detail according to your instructions. Their experience is invaluable when it comes to keeping things moving at a steady pace, cleaning up debris and dishes, and generally seeing to the needs of your guests. Two pros are all you need, and you'll find they're worth their weight in gold, so don't skimp in this area. You'll also want to rent party equipment, and an experienced party store employee can help you tremendously in figuring out seating, serving tables, chafing dishes, and types of linen and china. Setting everything under a large canopy is a nice, intimate touch and a good precaution against the weather. As for flowers, candles, and other decorative details, farm out these tasks to trusted friends so you're free to focus on your menu.

Many of the breakfast dishes included here not only lend themselves to make-ahead plans, they actually require it, so there's little chance you'll be inundated that morning with time-consuming cooking. You'll be delighted at how smooth and easy this menu will be to serve, while your guests will be truly impressed by not only its creativity, but its deliciousness as well. Don't be surprised if someone gets ideas about "hiring" you for future festivities – your talented performance in and out of the kitchen will no doubt propel you to culinary stardom!

At a morning reception, you can be sure there's one thing every guest will be dying for – a good cup of coffee! Rent two large urns, one for caffeinated coffee and the other for hot water to prepare instant decaf, tea, or hot chocolate, and make sure they're ready to serve when guests arrive. All the usual fixings of milk, cream, sugar, sweetener, and lemon should be offered. In addition, have chilled bottles of spring water and a variety of individual-sized bottles or cans of juices and any other type of soft drink you think your guests will look for. However, don't overwhelm the drink station with too many varieties of beverage. Usually, people will make a quick choice when the options are limited, which will help create less delay. A party of this size without alcoholic beverages does not generally require a bartender, but if you'd like to have someone overseeing the drink station, replenishing ice, and keeping things neat, by all means put someone in charge. Eventually, when guests are seated and eating, you may want to have one of your hired pros go around with a coffeepot, offering to top up their cups and see to any other beverage requests.

A Wedding Breakfast Reception in the Garden

MENU

Breakfast Reception for Twenty-Four

APPETIZER:

Orange Blossom Cup

Pistachio Orange Breakfast Biscotti

MAIN COURSE:

Tricolor Roasted Pepper Frittata

French Toast Strata with Pure Maple Syrup

Rosemary and Sweet Onion Sausage Patties

Canadian Bacon and Hot Honey Mustard

Assorted Bagels and Sweet Buns

DESSERT:

Wedding Cake

Sweetheart Trays featuring

Nutella Mexican Wedding Cookies

BEVERAGE PAIRINGS:

Throughout Breakfast: *Coffee, Tea, Spring Water, and Juices*

For Toasting: Celebration Shampagne

Tips on Purchased Ingredients

Canadian bacon is an excellent choice for breakfast, as it's precooked and requires only a bit of moist heat to serve. There are usually about eight pieces in the package – allow for two pieces per person just to be sure you have enough. The best way to heat Canadian bacon slices is to layer them in a large skillet with a bit of water. Cover tightly with a lid and let them "steam" on very low heat while your sausages are cooking. When ready to serve, transfer them to one side of the same inner chafing-dish pan that you're using for the sausages. Mustard is a great accompaniment for both the sausages and bacon, and *hot honey mustard* is superb. Of course, you can offer a variety of mustards, some hot, some sweet, if you prefer. Watch for Dijon varieties and whole-grain mustards, however, which usually contain white wine in amounts easily detected by those who are abstaining. Obviously, bourbon, whiskey, and beer mustards are not a good idea either!

Although you're certainly preparing an adequate amount of food, it's a good idea to supplement with purchased ingredients that help make the buffet look plentiful and attractive. These items can be set out before you serve the hot selections to keep people occupied in case there's a delay in the kitchen. Place platters, baskets, and trays of cut *bagels* (mini-ones are nice) and *sweet buns* on each side of the chafing dishes on the buffet table to fill space and prevent crowded serving. Flavored cream cheeses and even smoked salmon, if you'd like to splurge, are great with the bagels.

Don't forget to provide little spreaders in each bowl and small serving plates and napkins for guests to carry goodies back to the table. As for sweet buns, remember that there'll be wedding cake coming, so try not to offer anything that might compete with its flavor and sweetness. Cinnamon raisin buns, slices of date nut bread, and miniature turnovers make a fine selection. Include whipped butter and jams if you're offering croissants, scones, or muffins. Whatever you choose, make the display look inviting and decorative by creating height (baskets and boxes placed under the tablecloth are a great trick). You can also garnish with fruit, such as bunches of grapes, sliced melon, and scattered fresh berries to add color and variety.

A *sweetheart tray* of delectable sweets on each table at dessert time is a special and impressive touch and one that you can prepare ahead quite easily. Surround your Nutella Mexican Wedding Cookies with heart-shaped chocolates and candies, chocolate or candy-coated almonds, and other deliciously sweet nibbles (watch out for chocolates spiked with alcohol). Cover the trays tightly with layers of plastic wrap and set them somewhere out of the way until the day of the reception. Just be sure to write yourself a note so you don't forget to serve them!

A word about chafing dishes: You'll need to rent three chafing dishes for this menu to ensure that your hot selections remain hot. In general, a standard-size chafer has an 8- or 9-quart capacity and measures about 22 by 14 inches. It comes with a warming pan, which is meant to contain hot water, and an insert pan, which is for the food. A depth of 2½ inches is what you want for the insert pans – not the deeper ones that your party-rental store might include instead, so be sure to state your preference. You will also want to be sure to ask for three half-pan inserts that measure about 11 by 7 inches so that you can bake the French Toast Strata in them and transfer it directly to the warming

pan. All chafers come with lids: some with a roll top, which is nice but more expensive, and others with a plain lift-off top. Either is fine here. There will be space for two Sterno cans in the frame. Remember to buy the cans of Sterno, as they're not included in the price. Sterno will burn for about 3 hours, which is plenty of time in this case, so fire them up half an hour before serving time. Have your helpers fill the warming pans with hot water from a teakettle or saucepan so the chafers are ready to receive the food when it arrives.

Orange Blossom Cup with Homemade Biscotti

Ingredients:

8 cups water

4 cups granulated sugar

8 whole star anise

3 tablespoons orange blossom water

18 oranges, chilled

Mint sprigs to garnish

Pistachio Orange Breakfast Biscotti
(see recipe that follows)

This impressive appetizer will start things off right. Forget the usual orange juice, mimosas, or fruit salad, and have this dish ready and waiting at each guest's table setting as a refreshing welcome to the reception. Delightful homemade biscotti accompany sweet, sliced oranges laced with a spicy floral syrup. Biscotti are often served for breakfast in Italy, and here, they're the perfect way to "break the fast" after the ceremony. Meaning "twice-baked," biscotti are really quite easy to make at home, and by doing so, you can create any flavor of your choosing. Pistachios go particularly well with orange and spice, but you can substitute other nuts, such as almonds or pecans. These biscotti can be made up to 2 weeks ahead and stored at room temperature in an airtight container to retain their crispness. You'll have extras (about 36 total), so don't worry if some are broken or misshaped (or eaten!).

The syrup for the orange slices should be prepared a day before so it has a good chance to chill and develop flavor. Whole star anise can be found in the Asian section of your supermarket – don't substitute ground star anise, which will discolor the syrup. Instead, use three or four cinnamon sticks and a couple of whole cloves. Orange blossom water, a popular alcohol-free flavoring extract used in Middle Eastern cuisine, can usually be found at ethnic delis and grocers. Slice the oranges the night before or early in the day (look for oranges with minimal seeds) and keep them covered and refrigerated until ready to use. Small glass bowls or wide-mouthed martini or champagne glasses are perfect for presentation.

1. In a large saucepan, combine the water and sugar, and over medium-high heat, bring to a boil, stirring often until the sugar dissolves. Reduce the heat to medium low, add the star anise, and allow the mixture to simmer and reduce by half. Remove from the heat and stir in the orange blossom water. Cool to room temperature, remove the star anise, and transfer to a covered container to chill in the refrigerator overnight.

2. Prepare the oranges: Using a sharp knife, cut off both ends of the orange, set it flat on a cutting board, and cut away the peel and white pith from the fruit. Make ⅓-inch-thick round slices, remove any visible seeds, and place on a platter. Cover and refrigerate until ready to serve.

3. To serve, distribute the orange slices evenly among the serving bowls or glasses, drizzle the syrup over the oranges (about 2½ tablespoons per serving), garnish with the mint sprig, and serve with biscotti.

Serves 24

Celebration Shampagne

Ingredients:

One 1-liter bottle club soda, chilled

One 1-liter bottle ginger ale, chilled

3 cups unsweetened white grape juice, chilled

One 6-ounce can pineapple juice, chilled

A toast to the bride and groom is one of the highlights of any wedding reception. It usually takes place when the wedding cake is served: Tall flutes of champagne appear at each place setting for guests to raise their glasses in celebration. For sober receptions, there are many bottled sparkling beverages available that you can choose from to replace the champagne, but why not create a unique "shampagne" of your own? It will be unexpected and definitely will make the reception more memorable and festive.

Rented champagne flutes tend to be small – about 6 ounces in capacity – so very little is needed to fill them for the toast. This recipe, prepared and poured in the kitchen and brought out on trays (by your handy hired pros), will more than adequately fill 24 glasses, but feel free to double the recipe if you think anyone might ask for seconds. Keep all the ingredients well chilled and mix them together just before serving to retain maximum fizz. The easiest way to quickly pour a number of glasses is to make the "shampagne" in a large pitcher and pour directly from it. Or you can mix everything in a punch bowl and use a ½-cup ladle to fill the glasses. Either way, timing is important. Be sure everyone has a glass ready and in place before the toasting begins.

Pour all the ingredients into a large pitcher or punch bowl and stir to combine. Distribute evenly among the champagne glasses and serve immediately.

Serves 24

Pistachio Orange Breakfast Biscotti

1. In a large mixing bowl, using an electric mixer on high speed, beat together the butter, sugar, orange rind, and vanilla until light and fluffy. Beat in the eggs one at a time until well combined. In a medium-size mixing bowl, whisk together the flour, baking soda, baking powder, cinnamon, and salt. Adding the flour mixture in two batches to the butter-egg mixture, beat on low speed until just combined. Stir in the pistachios. Cover and refrigerate for 1 hour.

2. Preheat the oven to 350 degrees. Butter and flour a large, heavy baking sheet.

3. Divide the dough in half, and on a lightly floured surface (flour your hands as well), roll each half into a log that measures 1½ inches in diameter. Carefully transfer the logs to the baking sheet, placing them 5 inches apart, and lightly flatten them to 2 inches in diameter, using flour as needed to prevent sticking. Bake until the logs are lightly browned and firm to the touch, about 30 minutes. Remove from the oven and allow to cool on the baking sheet.

4. Using spatulas, carefully transfer the baked logs to a cutting board. Using a serrated knife, cut diagonally into ¾-inch-wide slices. Place cut side down on the baking sheet, return to the oven, and bake until golden brown, 12 to 15 minutes. Transfer to wire racks to cool, and store in an airtight container at room temperature. Serve with the Orange Blossom Cup.

Makes about 4 dozen

Ingredients:

½ cup (1 stick) unsalted butter, at room temperature

1 cup granulated sugar

2 tablespoons grated orange rind

1 teaspoon alcohol-free vanilla extract

2 large eggs

1¾ cups all-purpose flour

½ teaspoon baking soda

½ teaspoon baking powder

¼ teaspoon ground cinnamon

⅛ teaspoon salt

1½ cups unsalted, shelled, and skinned pistachio nuts

French Toast Strata with Pure Maple Syrup

Stratas are popular breakfast selections that can be either savory or sweet, depending on their ingredients. They are composed of layered bread, eggs, and a variety of flavorings and fillings. The best thing about them is that they must be set up the night before so that the egg mixture has a chance to soak into the bread layers. This means that all you have to do the morning of the reception is stick them in the oven and wait for the wonderful wafting aroma of French toast and maple syrup to fill your house! As mentioned in this menu's "Tips on Purchased Ingredients," be sure to get three half-pan chafing inserts from the party supplier the day before so you can prepare and bake directly in them, saving an enormous amount of time and effort. And yes, you'll want three – this will be popular, so an extra tray to replenish is a must!

As with regular French toast, slightly stale bread works best, as it holds up nicely when drenched with the egg mixture. You can speed up the process a bit by cubing the bread earlier in the day and letting it sit out in a bowl on the counter. French bread in particular will dry out pretty quickly. Keeping the crusts on is fine, but remove the crusty ends of the loaves. Sizes of bread vary – usually a couple of large baguettes are more than enough to yield 12 cups, so err on the side of plenty to be sure. The cream cheese can be reduced-fat or light, but not fat-free – you need the fat for moisture. Most important, purchase pure maple syrup, not an imitation, as you'll be serving it alongside the strata on the buffet table. Make sure there's enough syrup – figure at least 1/4 cup per person to account for those guests who are heavy-handed pourers. Serve it in a couple of syrup pourers or small glass pitchers, or if the bottles themselves happen to be particularly gourmet or decorative-looking, simply place them on the buffet table for added visual appeal.

1. Generously butter three 11-by-7-inch chafing half-pans (or the equivalent). Distribute the bread cubes evenly in the bottoms of the three pans, and sprinkle the raisins and diced cream cheese on top.

2. In a large mixing bowl, using an electric mixer on high, beat together the eggs, milk, syrup, and vanilla until well-combined. Pour evenly over the bread and use a rubber spatula to press down and submerge the cubes. Place a piece of plastic wrap directly on top of each surface, cover the entire pan with foil, and refrigerate overnight.

3. Preheat the oven to 350 degrees. In a small bowl, stir together the sugar and cinnamon.

4. Remove the pans from the refrigerator, lift off the foil and plastic wrap from each, and discard. Sprinkle the strata tops with the cinnamon sugar and bake until puffed and golden so that a knife inserted in the center comes out clean, 40 to 45 minutes.

5. Before serving, use a serrated knife to cut suggested portions (10 or 12 per pan) and transfer two of the pans to a chafer. Cover the third pan with clean foil and keep warm until needed. Serve with maple syrup on the side.

Serves 24

Ingredients:

12 cups of 3/4-inch cubes French or Italian bread

1 1/2 cups golden raisins

Three 8-ounce packages cream cheese, cut into small dice

9 large eggs

4 1/2 cups whole milk

1 1/2 cups pure maple syrup

1 tablespoon alcohol-free vanilla extract

1/4 cup granulated sugar

1 tablespoon ground cinnamon

Tricolor Roasted Pepper Frittata

A great way to serve eggs for a crowd without worrying about last-minute scrambling or poaching is in the form of a frittata. And this one is even easier than most, as it's baked rather than prepared on the stovetop, and can be made a day ahead, chilled, and reheated. You'll need two 13-by-9-inch glass baking dishes. Once the cooked frittatas are well chilled, you'll be able to easily cut them into serving sizes before transferring to the inner chafing dish to reheat. Cut each into 16 pieces so that there will be enough for guests to have seconds. Layer them like fallen dominoes in the pan, cover with foil, and heat in a low oven while preparing your other dishes for serving.

Roasting your own peppers for this dish will really make a difference, as the result will be firmer and more flavorful. Jarred roasted peppers are generally a bit mushy and can add unwanted liquid to the frittata. In-store deli-roasted peppers are probably fine to use, except that you're usually limited to red, so plan to roast them yourself – a couple of days ahead of time is fine. Keep them refrigerated and wait to slice them until you are ready to make the frittatas. If you like, you can replace some of the peppers with sautéed mushrooms, blanched asparagus pieces, or cooked chopped spinach, squeezed dry. On another occasion, diced ham is always a nice addition, as is crumbled, cooked sausage. Embellish this basic recipe as you wish for future entertaining – it will always be a hit!

Ingredients:

2 large red bell peppers

2 large green bell peppers

2 large orange or yellow bell peppers

Olive oil to coat

20 large eggs

1 cup heavy cream

Salt and pepper to taste

2 cups (½ pound) shredded fontina cheese

1. To roast the peppers, lightly coat them with olive oil and place on a foil-lined baking sheet under the broiler set to high. Turn the peppers often so that all the sides become black and charred. You can also do this on an outdoor grill or one at a time over a gas burner. Transfer the peppers to a clean brown paper bag, fold to close, and allow to steam (helping to release the skin) until they are cool enough to handle. Using your hands and a dry paper towel, rub away the charred bits until all the skin of the pepper is removed. Refrain from running them under water, which will diminish their flavor. Cut the peppers in half, remove the core and seeds, and store in an airtight container in the refrigerator until ready to prepare the frittatas.

2. Preheat the oven to 350 degrees. Butter two 13-by-9-inch glass or ceramic baking dishes.

3. In a large mixing bowl, whisk together the eggs, cream, salt, and pepper until well combined. Pat dry the roasted peppers and cut into ⅓-inch-wide slices. Cut the slices in half, then stir all the peppers into the eggs. Evenly distribute the egg-and-pepper mixture between the two baking dishes and sprinkle 1 cup of the cheese over the top of each. Bake until the frittatas are lightly golden and set, about 30 minutes. Remove from the oven, and if not serving immediately, cool on racks, cover with foil, and refrigerate. If serving right away, cut into pieces and transfer to a chafing dish or warmed serving platter.

Serves 24

Toasting: A Timeless Tradition

People have been raising glasses in ritual celebration for centuries. And today, toasts at weddings, birthdays, anniversaries, and other special occasions are anticipated just as eagerly as in ages past. It's an opportunity for people to praise, congratulate, and express their best wishes for the honoree or event they're gathered to celebrate. Words are spoken, glasses are raised (and usually clinked), and a sip of solidarity takes place. Why has such an odd custom become timeless, and has it always involved the imbibing of alcohol?

The "toast" gets its name from the Roman custom of dipping a piece of burnt bread in a wineglass to remove any impurities and undesirable flavors that were often present. Not as far-fetched as you may think, since the basis of modern water filters is activated charcoal, which performs the same task. Since burning toast carbonizes its surface, the Romans were pretty darn clever. Unfortunately for them, the toast did not eliminate any poison that the host may have added to their wine – not an infrequent occurrence between rivals! And there you have the true derivation of the "raising of a toast" custom – if you raised your glass to your host (toast and all) with your right hand, it was unlikely that you would be raising your sword instead, which dangled from the right side of your waist. Toasting to one's health therefore meant you were not intending to poison or stab your dinner companion, and consequently, you'd both be happy to drink to that!

The clinking of the glasses seems to derive from more reassurances – the guest would pour part of his wine into his host's wine cup (just in case it was poisoned) and in the process, their glasses would "clink" together. If your host drank after the "clink," you could be assured that your wineglass was free of hemlock or some such poison. The fact that the toasting ritual involved alcohol can be pretty much explained by the fact that alcohol was what everybody was drinking back then, since the purity of water was dubious. As centuries passed, alcohol continued to be the chosen drink for toasting as well as general refreshment – men were the ones who drank alcohol and toasted, while women, for the most part, drank alcohol-free beverages like tea and were never included in toasts, although they were sometimes toasted *to*.

Today, of course, all these considerations have been forgotten (thankfully) and toasting is now a universally happy and carefree affair, punctuated by kind words, the occasional long-winded speech, or a limerick or two. What beverage our glass holds is far less important than the spirit in which we raise it in celebration and togetherness. Whether performed with a sparkling cider or a mock-champagne punch, alcohol-free toasts hold just as much celebratory cheer as a sip of Dom Perignon®. So, don't be reluctant to raise a glass in honor of your friends, whether you imbibe or not – good cheer doesn't come from the bottom of a glass, but rather from the bottom of our hearts.

Rosemary and Sweet Onion Sausage Patties

Jazzing up some ordinary breakfast sausage will win applause for taste and creativity, and here, fresh rosemary and sweet sautéed onion are the special touch. Purchase the sausage in bulk for easiest handling, or remove the casings from prepared links. Be sure to buy uncooked sausage, not precooked, and if you buy it frozen, allow time to defrost in the refrigerator (a couple of days). Make up the patties the day before and keep refrigerated on a baking sheet lined with parchment so they're ready to pop in the oven. You can also make these further ahead and freeze them uncooked (this pertains only to fresh sausage), by placing the patties on a flat sheet in the freezer and then transferring them to a freezer bag for storage. If you end up cooking them from frozen, add to the estimated cooking time and be sure they're thoroughly cooked. While baking, these patties give off quite a bit of grease, so use a baking sheet with a rim, and if necessary, pour off any excess grease as they're cooking.

Vidalia onions are the most famous of sweet onions and are perfect in this dish. Other sweet onion varieties, such as Oso sweet, are fine to use as well. If your knife skills are not up to the task, or you tend to "weep" while chopping, feel free to use the food processor to finely chop the onions. If oven space is limited, frying on top of the stove in a couple of large, heavy skillets is definitely an option, if you don't mind a few splatters here and there. Whichever method you employ, make sure the sausage patties are well cooked by cutting one open and checking that there's no sign of pink.

1. Heat the oil in a large skillet over medium-high heat. Add the chopped onions and a sprinkling of salt, and sauté, stirring often (reduce the heat if necessary to prevent over-browning), until lightly golden and translucent, about 10 minutes. Stir in the rosemary and cook a further minute. Transfer to a large mixing bowl and allow to cool.

2. Add the sausage, mustard, salt, and pepper to the onion mixture, and using your hands, mix well to combine. Form the mixture into 2-inch-diameter patties (about 40 in total) and arrange them on two baking sheets with rims, lined with parchment paper. If not cooking immediately, cover with plastic wrap and refrigerate for up to 1 day.

3. Preheat the oven to 450 degrees. Remove the plastic wrap from the baking pans and bake, turning once, until cooked through and lightly browned, 10 to 12 minutes. (For browner patties, drain the grease and place the pans under the broiler for 2 minutes.) Alternatively, fry the patties in a heavy-bottomed skillet over high heat, about 3 minutes per side. Transfer the cooked sausages to brown paper or paper towels to drain, then arrange in the inner chafing dish with the heated Canadian bacon, and serve.

Makes about 40 patties

Ingredients:

3 tablespoons olive oil

3 medium-size Vidalia onions, peeled and finely chopped

1 tablespoon finely chopped, fresh rosemary

Three 1-pound packages of uncooked bulk breakfast sausage or sausage links, casings removed

1 heaping tablespoon spicy brown mustard

Salt and pepper to taste

Nutella Mexican Wedding Cookies

Ingredients:

1½ cups (3 sticks) unsalted butter, at room temperature

½ cup granulated sugar

1 cup Nutella® or other chocolate-hazelnut spread

4½ cups all-purpose flour

2 cups ground hazelnuts, toasted or plain

2 cups confectioners' sugar

These little yummy morsels of goodness are a great way to end your successful reception as part of a sweet tray set on each table. They're unique and traditional at the same time, and the wonderful flavor of hazelnuts found in Nutella® will set them apart from the Mexican wedding cookies that guests may have tried in the past. Nutella® is the brand name for an Italian spread that consists of ground hazelnuts and cocoa – a spread that's as popular in Europe as peanut butter is in the U.S. However, other companies have created similar spreads under differ-ent brand names that you may come across in your search. If you do, they're fine to use in this recipe.

Finely ground hazelnuts, either toasted or plain, can sometimes be found in specialty food stores like Trader Joe's. If you come across them, this recipe will be a snap to prepare. But if you must begin with whole or roughly chopped hazelnuts, don't worry – a quick pulsing in the food processor will do the trick. Although toasting the nuts adds a nice roasted flavor, it's not necessary to do so, and in fact, I prefer the unroasted flavor in this recipe. Either way, they're delicious, so it's purely a matter of preference and convenience on your part.

Make these cookies up to a week ahead and keep them in an airtight container. This recipe will make about 6 dozen cookies, which will be a good amount for piling up on the sweet tray. A last-minute dusting of powdered sugar freshens them for presentation.

1. Preheat the oven to 350 degrees. Line cookie sheets with parchment paper.

2. In a large mixing bowl, using an electric mixer on high speed, beat together the butter and gran-ulated sugar until light and fluffy, about 3 minutes. On medium speed, beat in the Nutella® until well-combined. Begin adding the flour, beating on low speed until combined. After half the flour has been added, switch to a wooden spoon and stir in the remaining flour and ground nuts until just blended.

3. Form the dough into 1-inch balls and place 2 inches apart on the prepared cookie sheets. Bake until the cookies are set and just beginning to brown, 10 to 15 minutes. Remove from the oven and allow to cool on the cookie sheets for 5 minutes.

4. Place the confectioners' sugar in a bowl and roll the warm cookies in the sugar to coat. Place the cookies on a wire rack to cool completely. Roll again in the sugar, then store in an airtight container until ready to serve.

Makes about 6 dozen

A milestone of 25 years together deserves a special celebration, not only between the couple themselves, but in the company of family and friends who have known and loved them all these years. Often, it's the couple's children or siblings who wish to acknowledge the event with some type of grand gathering that requires careful planning and organization. But, even the prospect of getting a large group of people together for a restaurant dinner can sometimes prove time-consuming, not to mention expensive. That's why the sweetest of all plans is the newest at-home trend – a simple but stylish dessert party!

This type of entertaining, which focuses on only one aspect of a meal such as hors d'oeuvres or desserts, resolves many questions of time, budget, and most certainly, the serving of alcohol. A dessert-only party will usually take place later in the evening after most people have eaten – when coffee and dessert are uppermost in everyone's mind – and could even be turned into a surprise party for the happy couple when they return from an intimate dinner out. However you decide to arrange it, this menu is guaranteed to entice every sweet tooth in the room to nibble at the wondrous collection of delicacies you've presented in simple, elegant style. By the end of the night, everyone will agree that you've created the most outstanding, not to mention "sweetest," silver anniversary anyone has ever been lucky enough to taste!

A Silver Anniversary Dessert Party

MENU

Party for Eighteen

Chèvre and Fig Walnut Sauce with Crackers

Roasted Peaches and
Cream with Caramel Drizzle

Raspberry and White Chocolate Tiramisu

Chocolate Mousse "Cordials" with

Monogrammed Chocolate Mini-Cakes

Assortment of Cookies

Sugared Nuts and Fruit Jellies

Two-Tiered Anniversary Cake

BEVERAGE PAIRINGS:

To Start: Strawberry Daiquiri Fantasies
Throughout: *Coffee, Tea, Spring Water*
To Toast: *Mini-Souvenir Bottles of Sparkling Cider*

Tips on Purchased Ingredients

To complement the desserts you've prepared and create opulence on the buffet table, purchase an **assortment of cookies** from a favorite local bakery. Or look for unusual varieties at a specialty food store that carries boxes of imported cookies and sweets that your guests will be unlikely to find elsewhere. Lacy, chocolate-coated Florentines are always a pretty addition to a cookie platter, as are pirouettes, delicate tubular cookies often filled with a flavored cream such as hazelnut or chocolate. Most supermarkets carry the French cookie brand LU®, as well as the German-made Bahlsen®, both offering a variety of specialty cookies that make a nice presentation on a platter. If you'd like to do something extra-special, several websites offer completely edible "photo" cookies made from photographs you submit, such as a wedding photo of the celebrated couple from 25 years ago!

Sugared nuts and jellied fruits will contribute variety and color to your serving trays and table. Indeed, candies of any sort will add tremendously to your lavish presentation, either in bowls strategically placed around the room or as decorations on platters of cookies. Create an atmosphere of tempting delights, so that everywhere your guests turn, there's yet another delicacy to sample. Mints or chocolate-covered espresso beans are a nice touch at the coffee station, while silver-paper-wrapped hard candies will echo the theme. Be sure to include treats that your anniversary couple may be particularly fond of as a gracious personal touch – even if it's something as simple as jellybeans! As always, be careful to avoid selecting candies and chocolates that are laced with booze by reading labels carefully.

Look to your local bakery for the centerpiece of your buffet table. Explain what you're planning and how many people there will be, and ask the baker to make a simple **two-tiered anniversary cake**. To save expense, the icing decoration can be minimal – simply purchase white and silver silk flowers and ribbons to garnish the cake yourself. Set the cake up on a cake stand or other elevated platter and if possible, see if you can retrieve the original cake topper from the couple's wedding cake. Otherwise, stick with your silver theme and decorate the top with fanciful, glittery decorations and silver candles. Of course, you'll want to continue the silver theme in your choice of paper products and/or rented china and cutlery. And now's the time to pull your silver and silver-plated serving pieces out of the closet and put them to good use.

No dessert party would be complete without **coffee**. However, if the hour is late, you may decide to brew a large urn of decaffeinated coffee and prepare special requests for the real thing in the kitchen. A variety of **teas** would also be welcomed, so you may wish to have a second urn of hot water available. Flavored creamers and sugars are a nice touch, as well as chocolate-dipped stirring spoons or reception sticks. Keep plenty of **spring water** available and any other soft drinks you think your guests may want.

For toasting to the happy couple as they cut their anniversary cake, order **miniature personalized bottles of sparkling cider** (see Resources). These novel little servings of alcohol-free bubbly will double as souvenirs for your guests. You can choose from 150 different label designs, and include names, date, and any congratulatory wishes you like. These are definitely worth the expense and effort to make your party a truly memorable one. Keep the bottles well chilled until cake time, then bring them out with rented or plastic champagne flutes for a terrific grand finale.

Chèvre and Fig Walnut Sauce with Crackers

This is a wonderful addition to a dessert buffet, as it can pass almost as a savory appetizer for those who are not yet ready to dip into the more sugary selections. Creamy white *chèvre*, or goat cheese, combines with a delicious fig, walnut, and honey sauce to tease the palate into an evening of sweet delights. Look for Calimyrna dried figs (grown in California), which are lighter in color and a tad sweeter than the more common black mission figs. Be sure to cut off the stem before chopping them into small pieces, about the same size as the walnut pieces. You can make the sauce a day or two ahead and refrigerate, and bring to room temperature before serving.

The easiest way to cut goat cheese logs without mishap is with dental floss (unflavored). Do this just before setting up the platter. As for crackers, my first choice is the slightly sweet wheatmeal biscuits – a type of graham cracker from England available in some supermarkets and many specialty stores. They also go by the name digestives. If you buy a variety box of Carr's® or Jacob's® biscuits for cheese, you'll find a few digestives tucked inside along with several other types of crackers, all of which would go nicely here and make for an attractive presentation.

1. In a small saucepan, combine the figs, water, and honey, and over medium heat, stirring often, bring the mixture to a low simmer. Cook on medium-low heat until the figs are tender and the liquid has reduced to a syrup, about 15 minutes. Remove from the heat, stir in the vinegar and walnuts, and transfer to a container to cool. Cover and refrigerate if not using immediately. Bring to room temperature before serving.

2. Arrange the chèvre slices in a circle, slightly overlapping, on a medium-size platter. Spoon the fig and walnut sauce in the center and drizzle some of the syrup on the cheese. Serve with the crackers surrounding or on the side.

Serves 18

Ingredients:

1¼ cups chopped, stemmed, dried Calimyrna figs

1 cup water

⅓ cup honey

1 teaspoon balsamic vinegar

1 cup chopped walnuts

Two 5.5-ounce logs plain chèvre (goat cheese), cut into ⅓-inch-thick rounds

Crackers to serve

Strawberry Daiquiri Fantasies

Ingredients:

Five 16-ounce bags frozen strawberries in syrup, thawed and kept cold

2½ cups crushed ice

1⅔ cups liquid sweet-and-sour mix

5 teaspoons grenadine syrup

18 (or more) fresh strawberries with stems, washed, dried, and cut halfway up the center

As guests arrive, treat them to this delicious fruity mocktail to set the stage for a night of sweet delights. Traditional daiquiris contain lime juice, rum, and usually an added fruit of choice. Frozen whole strawberries will be the main ingredient here, with a touch of sweet-and-sour mix to cut the sweetness, and a dash of grenadine for vibrant color. Although many daiquiris are served frozen, this mock version is best served less like a slushy and more like an ice-cold punch. To that end, we'll be thawing the bags of strawberries beforehand – just keep them cold in the refrigerator. If you'd like the drink a bit thicker, add more ice to the blender. When fresh, sweet strawberries are available, you can certainly use them in place of frozen. Wash, hull, and trim away any bruises from the fruit, sugar to taste, and chill well.

You can use a bottle of prepared sweet-and-sour mix, or purchase a packet of concentrate and reconstitute it with water. In either case, keep it chilled for your daiquiri-making. Grenadine, an alcohol-free drink enhancer made from pomegranates, is great for mocktails as it adds a delicious tang as well as color. (Check the label to be sure, however, as a few brands contain alcohol.) When adding grenadine to the blender, don't overdo it, as the syrup is quite potent and strong in taste. You can either make up batches of the Strawberry Daiquiri Fantasies as needed or prepare ahead and keep them in a couple of pitchers in the refrigerator. Each bag of strawberries will make one batch in a large blender. Traditional daiquiri glasses are similar to margarita glasses, but any type of medium-to-large glass will work fine. A fresh strawberry garnish and a straw will finish the drinks beautifully before you present them.

Prepare the daiquiris in batches: Place one bag of strawberries, ½ cup of ice, ⅓ cup of liquid sweet-and-sour mix, and 1 teaspoon of grenadine in a blender. Purée until smooth. Pour into a pitcher to chill or serve immediately in glasses, garnished on the edge with a fresh strawberry.

Serves 18

Raspberry and White Chocolate Tiramisu

This version of the classic Italian dessert, translated as "pick-me-up," replaces the usual addition of liqueur and coffee with a layer of flavorful raspberries in sauce. Combined with a creamy white chocolate mascarpone cheese filling, it becomes a match made in dessert heaven and will prove a real hit at your dessert buffet table. Without the addition of eggs, it can safely sit out all evening, if it lasts that long!

You can make this dessert in one large oval gratin dish or two smaller ones, whichever you prefer. Two large glass bowls also work well, allowing everyone to see the decorative layers. Make this up to 12 hours ahead and serve well chilled. Wait to add the whipped cream topping and garnishes until just before serving.

1. In a medium-size saucepan, combine the thawed raspberries and syrup with ¼ cup of the granulated sugar and all of the vinegar, and cook over medium heat, stirring often, until the mixture has broken down and is spreadable, about 10 minutes. Taste for additional sugar, then set aside to cool.

2. In the top of a double boiler, melt together the chopped white chocolate and ½ cup of the cream, stirring occasionally until smooth. Transfer to a bowl and allow to cool to near room temperature.

3. In a large mixing bowl, with an electric mixer, beat the mascarpone and the remaining ½ cup granulated sugar on high speed until well combined. Gradually add the melted chocolate mixture, beating well until smooth. In a medium-size mixing bowl with clean beaters, beat the remaining cream until stiff peaks form. Fold into the cheese and chocolate mixture and set aside.

4. Line the bottom of the dish, or dishes, with half the split ladyfingers, flat side up. Spread half the raspberry mixture on top; then spread half the white chocolate cheese mixture evenly over that. Repeat with the remaining ingredients. Cover with plastic wrap and refrigerate until well-chilled, at least 2 hours and up to 12 hours.

5. Just before serving, garnish the tiramisu: Spread or pipe the sweetened whipped cream over the top. Arrange the fresh raspberries decoratively, sprinkle the shaved chocolate and sliced almonds over all, and serve immediately.

Serves 18

Ingredients:

Two 16-ounce packages frozen raspberries in syrup, thawed

¾ cup granulated sugar, divided

2 teaspoons raspberry vinegar

1 pound white chocolate, roughly chopped

1½ cups heavy cream, divided

Two 8-ounce tubs mascarpone cheese

48 ladyfingers, split (four 3-ounce packages)

Garnish:

1 cup heavy cream, whipped to soft peaks with 3 tablespoons confectioners' sugar

1 pint fresh raspberries

One 4-ounce white chocolate bar, shaved

½ cup sliced almonds

Roasted Peaches and Cream with Caramel Drizzle

Here's another delectable offering that teases the taste buds into sampling the sweet party's smorgasbord. Roasted peach halves topped with dollops of *crème fraîche* and a hint of caramel will elicit "oohs" and "aahs" from the very first bite. The key to this dessert is the peaches – they must be ripe yet firm, hopefully at peak season. Roasting them in the oven brings out even more of their natural flavor, while the skin, later removed, leaves behind its beautiful, rosy hue.

Crème fraîche is now available in most supermarkets and is basically a French version of our sour cream, which in a pinch can be used as a substitute. The caramel can be made a day ahead and gently reheated before drizzling.

Ingredients:

10 medium-size firm, ripe peaches

Canola oil

Sugar

1½ cups crème fraîche or sour cream

Mint sprigs for garnish

Caramel Sauce:

1 cup granulated sugar

2 tablespoons water

½ cup whipping cream

2 tablespoons unsalted butter

1. Preheat the oven to 400 degrees. Lightly coat the peaches with the oil and place them in a large roasting pan. Roast for 45 minutes, occasionally shaking the pan to brown all sides of the peaches. Remove from the oven and let cool until easily handled. Remove the skins with a paring knife and cut the peaches in half, removing the pits. Set aside.

2. Make the caramel sauce: In a medium-size saucepan, combine the sugar and water, and over medium heat, stirring constantly, cook until the sugar dissolves. Increase the heat to high and boil, without stirring, until the syrup turns dark amber, about 8 minutes. (Brush down the sides of the pan with a wet pastry brush to prevent crystallization and swirl the pan occasionally to evenly distribute the heat.) Remove the pan from the heat and carefully add the cream and butter (the mixture will bubble up vigorously). Whisk the sauce over low heat until it has thickened a bit more, about 2 minutes. Cool and store covered in the refrigerator if not serving immediately. Rewarm gently, stirring often, over medium-low heat.

3. To serve the peaches, place them cut side up on a foil-lined baking sheet. Sprinkle lightly with sugar and set under the broiler until the tops begin to brown slightly, 2 to 3 minutes. Shift the pan around to brown evenly. Transfer the peaches with tongs to a large serving platter, arrange in a single layer, and let cool for 5 minutes. Place a dollop of crème fraîche in each peach half, drizzle with the warm caramel sauce, and garnish with the mint sprigs.

Serves 18

EASY DOES IT: A jar of purchased caramel sauce can step in nicely to save time and effort. Warm it slightly in the microwave before drizzling.

Alcohol and Aging: A Growing Concern

As we get older, our bodies react to alcohol in different ways. Sensitivity to its effect increases primarily because, due to aging, the body has less water to dilute it, causing a higher blood-alcohol concentration. Gastrointestinal absorption changes as well, so, although an older person's drinking pattern may not have altered, the effects that person experiences from the same amount of alcohol can increase. This can be particularly worrisome, especially when several medications have been prescribed for various conditions. The potential of drug and alcohol interactions becomes more likely, and the hoped-for effect of the medication may be drastically altered, sometimes dangerously so.

According to the U.S. National Library of Medicine and the National Institutes of Health, there are more than 9,000 drugs, including prescriptions and over-the-counter brands, that carry alcohol warnings on their labels. There are also numerous medicines that contain alcohol in varying degrees. Possible interactions range from increased drowsiness to stomach bleeding to potential overdose, so it is important to check with your physician and pharmacist when you are taking any type of medicine and plan to drink alcohol, regardless of your age. Since the average adult over 65 takes between two and seven medications daily, it is of vital importance that his or her family knows about potentially harmful interactions and is able to recognize them if they occur. Sadly, recent statistics have shown a lack of public awareness in this area, and even more alarming, it appears that chronic drinking among seniors has increased. Loneliness caused by loss of a spouse, depression over the aging process, persistent aches and pains, and a general feeling of ennui are just a few of the probable causes. Physicians are often unable to recognize the usual symptoms of alcohol abuse because many age-related problems mimic the long-term effects of drinking, such as memory loss, balance disorders, and personality changes.

With an ever-increasing aged population in our future, we ought to give serious thought to how we can increase the quality of a long life – not just physically, but emotionally and spiritually as well. In many cultures, elders are revered and accorded much respect and attention. As a result, in those cultures, we find less age-related disease, depression, and substance dependence. Embracing our inevitable aging with reverence, if not enthusiasm, may make a difference in our health and well-being. In Okinawa, Japan, it is customary to lavishly celebrate one's 97th birthday – a milestone believed to bestow special powers upon both the honoree and everyone else present at the celebration. Upon reaching this age, one supposedly begins second childhood and is entitled to all the good things that go along with it, including an unabashed enjoyment of life, free of responsibility. Not a bad thing to look forward to after all, and certainly a great excuse for throwing yet another festive and celebratory party!

Ingredients

Chocolate Mousse:

8 ounces bittersweet or semisweet chocolate, broken into pieces

1 cup whipping cream

3 large egg whites

To garnish: small candied flowers or whipped cream

Chocolate Cake:

½ cup (1 stick) unsalted butter

½ cup water

3 tablespoons unsweetened cocoa powder

1 cup granulated sugar

1 cup all-purpose flour

½ teaspoon baking soda

¼ teaspoon salt

1 large egg, slightly beaten

⅓ cup sour cream

Chocolate Glaze:

¼ cup (½ stick) unsalted butter

½ cup water

½ cup unsweetened cocoa powder

3-3½ cups confectioners' sugar

1 teaspoon alcohol-free vanilla extract

Garnish:

Silver dragées

White cake-writing icing

Chocolate Mousse "Cordials" with Monogrammed Chocolate Mini-Cakes

What would a dessert party be without rich, dark chocolate? These adorable little "cordials" of chocolate mousse paired with miniature chocolate cakes will entice guests by their presentation alone. Cordial glasses are quite small, ranging anywhere from 1.5- to 3.5-ounce capacity, so each serving of mousse is modest. You can usually rent cordial glasses from a party supply shop, or for easier cleanup, purchase small-stemmed plastic glasses. Petite juice glasses will also work well, and you can certainly mix and match a variety of cordial and stemmed glasses if you have them. Demitasse spoons are the perfect size to provide for eating and can also be rented or purchased cheaply.

To add to your presentation and silver theme, look for little silver doilies to place on the saucers or small plates that will hold the individual "cordials." Silver foil cups can be used as well for the cakes, placed on the saucer or around the edge of the serving tray. A petite candied flower made from royal icing or a small dollop of whipped cream can top off the mousse, giving a lovely embellishment to your chocolate masterpiece.

Look for medium-size silver dragées to decorate the cakes. Many baking supply shops have them, as well as the candied flowers, foil cups, and doilies. Dragées are made from sugar and are completely edible, but their thin outer "metal" coating has prompted the FDA to put a warning on most dragée products. Whether to use them is really a matter of personal preference, but I know of no problems related to their use, and bakeries and pastry chefs use them all the time. They fall into the same category as edible gold leaf and glitter, also popular with bakers and chefs. For writing the monogram, ordinary tubes of white cake-writing icing are fine. Both the mousse and the cakes can be made a day ahead and kept refrigerated until ready to serve.

1. To make the mousse: Melt the chocolate in the top of a double boiler, stirring occasionally. Transfer to a large mixing bowl and allow to cool for 20 minutes. In a medium-size mixing bowl, using an electric mixer, whip the cream to soft peaks. In another medium-size mixing bowl, with clean beaters, whip the egg whites until stiff. All at once, add the whipped cream and beaten egg whites to the bowl of chocolate and whisk vigorously until well blended, about 1 minute. Spoon the mousse into cordial glasses and top with a candied flower. Cover with plastic wrap and refrigerate for at least 2 hours or overnight.

2. Make the chocolate cake: Preheat the oven to 350 degrees. Butter, flour, and line the bottom of a 13-by-9-inch baking pan with parchment or waxed paper.

3. Combine the butter, water, and cocoa powder in a small saucepan and cook over medium heat, whisking constantly until the mixture is smooth and begins to boil. Remove from the heat and set aside. In a medium-size mixing bowl, whisk together the sugar, flour, baking soda, and salt.

Using an electric mixer on medium speed, beat in the cocoa mixture until well combined. Add the egg and sour cream, and beat until well blended. Pour the batter into the prepared pan and bake 20 to 22 minutes, until a toothpick inserted in the center comes out clean. Remove from the oven and cool for 10 minutes. Invert the cake onto a wire rack, remove the paper, and cool completely. At this point, you may wrap the cake in plastic and freeze for up to 1 week.

4. Place the cake right side up on a cutting board and using a serrated bread knife, remove about ¼ inch from all four edges. (The cake will be easier to cut if partially frozen.) Cut the cake into twenty-four 2-inch squares and place them on a rack set over a rimmed baking sheet.

5. Make the glaze: Melt the butter with the water in a small saucepan over medium-high heat. Whisk in the cocoa powder, remove from the heat, and allow to cool for 15 minutes. Gradually add enough of the confectioners' sugar to the pan, whisking well after each addition until the mixture is thick yet pourable. Whisk in the vanilla. Spoon the glaze over the individual cakes, allowing it to run down the sides to coat them completely. Transfer the entire baking sheet with rack and cakes to the refrigerator and chill until set, about 1 hour. Decorate the cakes with the dragées and monogram each one with the white cake-writing icing. Transfer to foil cups and keep chilled until ready to serve with the chocolate mousse cordials.

Serves 18

Chapter 12

Celebrating the Joy of Food

Individual Baked Alaska

It's a remarkable fact: Even though as a nation we eat out more than ever before, cookbooks continue to be the most popular bookstore purchases. There's something about them, whether people actually use them or not, that continues to draw us into the creative realm of cooking. Perhaps it's the beautiful pictures or the delicious descriptions they contain, or maybe that interesting bit of history they offer us as we read page after page. Maybe it fulfills a secret desire to pack it all in and become a chef! Whatever it is, the joy of preparing food has captured our enthusiasm and attention for centuries and will no doubt continue to do so no matter how many fast-food stops we make along the way.

What better type of celebration is there than to applaud the wondrous ways that great food can enrich our lives? Preparing favorite dishes together, experimenting with new ones, or traveling back in time to enjoy the repasts of the past – all of these get-togethers in the company of those we cherish and care about give us excuse enough to celebrate. Isn't it really all about the food anyway? It brings us together, helps us nurture one another, and is the basis of every successful celebration, sober or not. When you make food the star of the show, you'll always be the host of a "spirited" party and the true master of lively entertaining.

It's not just about eating together anymore! Cooking clubs are becoming a popular trend among friends who share a passion for good food and its preparation. It can be a fun and often hilarious evening of camaraderie and cooking, resulting in a delicious meal shared by all. More often than not, however, bottles of wine are uncorked and flowing freely – not a particularly safe atmosphere for half a dozen people with sharp knives in close quarters! Not to worry here – this terrific alcohol-free menu won't pose a bit of peril as pairs of kitchen staff work together to create a magnificent three-course dinner without one drop of alcohol in the pot or in their glasses. A classic, time-honored Kitchen Staff Quencher that you've prepared to keep them refreshed will be just the thing for thirsty sous-chefs as they happily cook away. And sober makeovers of stellar dishes will leave everyone more than impressed with the outstanding results.

As the host, you'll have already prepared the main event the day before – a succulent and flavorful Oh So Buono Osso Buco. While it reheats in the oven (gaining even more flavor), its delicious aroma will be filling the kitchen as your friends chop and sauté to beat the clock and get the remainder of the menu on the table. Freed up for attending to any "staff" needs or questions, as well as putting any finishing touches on the dinner table, you'll feel like the executive chef of a five-star restaurant! By the end of the night, however, you'll all be receiving grand reviews for each incredible dish that's been prepared, with only one last, burning question – who forgot to invite the cleanup staff?

A Cooking Club Dinner Party

MENU

Dinner for Eight

APPETIZERS:

Kitchen Nibbles

FIRST COURSE:

Tuscan Five-Bean Soup with Pesto

Crusty Italian Bread

MAIN COURSE:

Oh So Buono Osso Buco

Wild Mushroom and Herb Risotto

Bibb Lettuce Heart and Radish Salad with

Cooking Club House Vinaigrette

DESSERT:

Miniature Tartufi:

Double Chocolate Cherry, Vanilla Toasted Almond, and Tropical Macadamia Snowballs

BEVERAGE PAIRINGS:

While Cooking: Kitchen Staff Quencher

Dinner: *Zinfandel Grape Juice*

Dessert: *Cappuccino*

Tips on Purchased Ingredients

Although everyone will no doubt be sampling and tasting as they cook, offering a few additional **kitchen nibbles** for hungry, hard-working chefs is a thoughtful touch. Bowls of mixed nuts, cheese crackers, or pretzels are the obvious choices. But a few hot snacks would also be welcome. For an easy hot canapé, cut the crusts off a few slices of firm white sandwich bread, top each with a thin piece of cheese, like American or Swiss, and four thin slices of plum tomatoes, and bake in a hot oven (about 425 degrees) on a cookie sheet until the bread toasts and the cheese melts – a mere 3 or 4 minutes. Cut each into four pieces and offer them to your hardworking kitchen staff to nibble on.

Castoro Cellars® of California has introduced a terrific *Zinfandel Grape Juice* made from unfermented juice saved at harvest. Fruity without being too sweet, it's an excellent choice for sipping with your meal. The important distinction about this product is that it's not one of those "de-alcoholized wines" we usually find in supermarkets (see page 55 on the disadvantages of "alcohol-free" wines), but rather a no-sugar-added juice made from vineyard grapes. As always, however, be mindful of serving to the newly sober (especially in a wineglass), who may find the association with the real thing too daunting. A good substitute drink for this meal is cranberry juice mixed with a cranberry-flavored seltzer.

A good **crusty Italian bread** is a must with this meal. Choose any type you like, from semolina to sourdough, and instead of butter, offer a shallow dish of some fruity extra virgin olive oil for dipping.

Although Italians wouldn't dream of serving *cappuccino* anytime after breakfast, here in America, we love it any time of day, and it would certainly cap off an excellent meal such as this. You don't need any fancy equipment. Just brew up some strong Italian roast coffee (decaf is fine) and use a hand-held milk frother to create the characteristic foam. You can find inexpensive electric or manual frothers that are easy to use – just heat up the milk and get pumping!

TIPS ON ORGANIZING THE COOKS: Each pair of workers should have their own workstation set up with a cutting board, knives, dish towels, and any other gadgets they may need. If you're short on supplies, ask guests to bring along some of their own tools of the trade. Depending on the size of your kitchen, space the stations comfortably apart and place people near the large appliances they'll be using most. For example, the ice-cream folks will want to be near the freezer and away from the stove, while the risotto makers should be closest to the burners. This menu works best with four workstations: soup, risotto, dessert, and one extra, for you or someone with a lull in the action to prepare the salad and pick up any slack. The eighth person can easily fit in by acting as a restaurant kitchen "trailer" – someone who goes from station to station to assist where needed or lends a hand with cleanup.

Kitchen Staff Quencher

Believe it or not, kitchen staff who nip at the bottle (one for the pot, one for me!) pose a centuries-old problem – one for which the famed French chef Auguste Escoffier found a solution in the 19th century. He had vats of refreshing barley water made up every day for his staff to drink as they slaved over a hot stove. A still-popular soft drink found in European supermarkets, flavored barley water is considered the ideal thirst-quencher and energy drink for everyone, from kids to professional athletes. The annual British tennis tournament at Wimbledon has served it since 1934, where it continues to be the choice of champions.

This version is flavored with orange and lemon and is lightly sweetened. You can prepare it the day of the party and serve it in pitchers, or for fun, in a big stockpot with a ladle. Make sure you have plenty of ice on hand as well as heavy-bottomed glasses, which will be less likely to topple over from quick movements by diligent cooks!

Ingredients:

2 cups pearl barley

1 gallon spring water

1 cup granulated sugar

Juice of 8 oranges, strained

Juice of 4 lemons, strained

Orange and lemon slices to garnish

1. Rinse the barley in a colander under cold running water until the water runs clear, 1 to 2 minutes. In a large stockpot, bring the spring water and sugar to a boil, stirring occasionally. Add the rinsed barley and bring to a boil again. Reduce the heat to low, cover, and simmer for 1 hour.

2. Remove from the heat, strain into a large pot or jug, and allow to come to room temperature. Stir in the juices and taste for additional sugar. Serve chilled, garnished with the fruit slices.

Serves 8

Tuscan Five-Bean Soup with Pesto

Here's a quick version of a delicious Tuscan soup that's perfect for a cooking-club night. No soaking of beans is required, so preparation is straightforward and swift. Lots of fresh garlic and sage will complement the variety of beans, while a dollop of freshly made pesto added on top just before serving will provide a classic restaurant touch.

A hand-held immersion blender is the ideal piece of equipment to bring the soup together with a few quick pulses at the end. Alternative methods are to remove about 3 cups of the soup and purée it in a food processor or blender and return it to the pot, or simply use a potato masher to break down some of the beans. A pesto garnish such as the one used here, also known as a *pistou*, is commonly added to bean and vegetable soups, as well as minestrone, for heightened flavor in both Italian and French cooking. A bowl of freshly grated Parmesan can be offered at the table for guests to sprinkle in their bowls. Serve piping hot and don't forget the crusty bread.

1. Heat the oil and butter in a large pot over medium-high heat. Add the onions, sprinkle with salt and pepper, and sauté until the onions are soft and translucent, about 12 minutes. Reduce the heat, if necessary, to prevent browning. Add the garlic and sage and sauté a further minute. Add the broth and all the beans and bring to a boil. Reduce the heat, cover, and simmer, stirring occasionally, for 15 minutes.

2. Remove the pot from the heat and using a hand-held immersion blender or other method (see recipe introduction), partially blend the soup to break down some of the beans. Taste for the addition of salt and pepper and thin, if necessary, with more broth or water.

3. Make the pesto by finely chopping the garlic, basil, and salt together in a food processor fitted with a sharp blade. With the machine running on low, gradually add the olive oil to form a paste. Add the cheese and pulse to combine. Transfer to a small bowl and add freshly ground pepper. Taste for additional seasoning and set aside until ready to serve the soup.

4. Ladle the hot soup into warmed bowls, place a dollop of the pesto on top, and serve immediately with additional Parmesan cheese on the side.

Serves 8

Ingredients:

3 tablespoons extra virgin olive oil

1 tablespoon unsalted butter

2 large onions, peeled and finely chopped

Salt and pepper to taste

5 garlic cloves, peeled and minced

1 tablespoon finely chopped fresh sage leaves

6 cups low-sodium chicken broth

One 16-ounce can each cannellini beans, Roman beans (or light kidney beans), black-eyed peas, and butter beans (or large limas), drained and rinsed

1 cup canned chickpeas, drained and rinsed

Pesto:

3 garlic cloves, peeled

3 cups packed, fresh basil leaves

Pinch of salt

6 tablespoons extra virgin olive oil

¾ cup freshly grated Parmesan cheese

Freshly ground pepper

Ingredients:

3 tablespoons olive oil, plus more as needed

2 tablespoons unsalted butter

8 large 1½-inch-thick veal shanks, tied securely with kitchen twine

Salt and pepper to taste

Flour for dredging

2 medium-size onions, peeled and roughly chopped

2 medium-size carrots, peeled and roughly chopped

2 celery stalks, roughly chopped

2 garlic cloves, peeled and smashed

2 bay leaves

1 small sprig fresh rosemary

4 sprigs fresh parsley

2 sprigs fresh thyme

Two 2-inch pieces of orange peel, white pith removed

One 2-inch piece lemon peel, white pith removed

½ cup unsweetened apple juice

3 tablespoons apple cider vinegar

3½ cups low-sodium beef broth

One and a half 8-ounce cans tomato sauce

Gremolata:

⅓ cup finely chopped, fresh parsley leaves

1 tablespoon freshly grated lemon zest

1 garlic clove, peeled and minced

Oh So Buono Osso Buco

Osso buco is one of those dishes that really benefits from being made ahead of time and reheating. The intricate layers of flavor have a real chance to develop, and the result is outstanding. Tender and flavorful with a sauce to die for, this osso buco will have your fellow cooks applauding with the first bite. Reheat the shanks, submerged in the finished sauce, in a casserole tightly covered with foil in a low oven (about 275 degrees) while the other dishes are being prepared. Wait to remove the twine until serving.

Osso buco cuts come in different sizes, depending on what part of the shank they're taken from. If you can, find a large cut for each person, which will be the perfect portion size. If you use smaller cuts, you'll need two per person. Tying the shanks is an important part of the process and will keep the meat attached to the bone, even after it's fork-tender. Use kitchen twine, tightly tying two or three times around the circumference of the shank to secure, and make a double knot at one end. The shanks will shrink during cooking and sometimes become untied by themselves, even if securely fastened, but do your best to keep them together by using large tongs when turning and transferring them. To remove the string at serving time, use kitchen scissors or a sharp paring knife.

Traditional recipes for osso buco call for deglazing the pan with wine. Here, we'll use a sober substitution in the form of unsweetened apple juice and cider vinegar, which will add another layer of delicious flavor to the sauce. I also like to add a couple of pieces of peeled orange rind and a fresh rosemary sprig for even more flavor. Finally, a traditional gremolata garnish is the finishing touch for this classic braised dish that will have everyone clamoring for the recipe before the night is through.

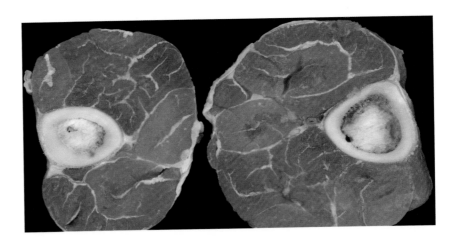

1. Preheat the oven to 350 degrees. Have ready a large roasting pan.

2. Heat the olive oil and butter together in a large, heavy skillet over medium-high heat. Season both sides of the veal shanks with salt and pepper, and dredge in the flour, shaking off the excess. Brown the shanks in batches, adding oil as necessary until golden brown, about 3 minutes per side. Transfer with tongs in a single layer to the roasting pan.

3. Drizzle a little more oil in the skillet and add the onion, carrot, celery, garlic, herbs, and orange and lemon peel; then cook over medium-high heat, stirring often, until the vegetables are slightly softened, about 4 minutes. Pour in the apple juice and vinegar and using a wooden spoon, stir as the mixture boils, scraping up any browned bits in the skillet. Transfer the entire mixture to the roasting pan. Add the broth and tomato sauce and stir to combine with the vegetables. Cover tightly with foil and braise in the oven for about 2 hours, turning the shanks with tongs once or twice, until the veal is fork-tender.

4. Using tongs and a spatula, transfer the veal shanks to a large casserole dish in a single layer. Strain the vegetables and pan juices through a medium sieve into a saucepan, pressing on the vegetables to extract as much liquid as possible. Bring the strained sauce to a boil and cook until it's slightly reduced and coats the back of a spoon, about 10 minutes. Taste for the addition of salt and pepper, and pour evenly

over the veal shanks. At this point, you may serve immediately with the gremolata or cool, cover with foil, and refrigerate for reheating (see recipe introduction).

5. Make the gremolata by mixing together the parsley, lemon zest, and garlic with a fork in a small mixing bowl. Sprinkle on top of the osso buco just before serving.

Serves 8

Wild Mushroom and Herb Risotto

Ingredients:

12 ounces fresh wild mushrooms such as chanterelle, cremini, oyster, and shiitake

4 cups low-sodium chicken broth (or 2 cups each mushroom broth and chicken broth)

1½ cups water

2 tablespoons olive oil

1 tablespoon unsalted butter

2 large shallots, peeled and finely chopped

Salt and pepper to taste

2 cups arborio rice

⅓ cup unsweetened white grape juice

2 tablespoons freshly squeezed lemon juice

1 tablespoon each finely chopped, fresh parsley, basil, and thyme

To Finish:

1 cup grated Parmesan cheese

2 tablespoons unsalted butter, softened

¼ cup heavy cream

Because there are a lot of hands on deck, risotto is the perfect cooking club dish. And this delicious version, with aromatic wild mushrooms and herbs, is a great companion dish to the osso buco. Constant stirring is required once the risotto making is under way, so cooking partners can switch back and forth as desired. Patience is key: The broth must be slowly incorporated into the rice for best results. And having all your preparations ready to go is important too.

Many risotto recipes call for wine in the earliest stage of preparation, as the acidity it contains balances the rice starch. Here, the acidity will be provided by a combination of white grape juice and lemon, which will add just the right tang to the risotto. Although this recipe calls for fresh mushrooms, wild varieties are often easier to find dried. If that's the case, soak them in warm water and save the flavorful liquid to add to the broth. Keep in mind, however, that one ounce of dried mushrooms is equivalent to four ounces of fresh. If you can find canned mushroom broth, use it in place of half the chicken broth for added flavor.

You can prepare the risotto up through step 2 and put it "on the back burner," continuing a bit later to time it for serving with the veal. Once it's ready, it should be served immediately, so in most instances it's better to wait for the risotto than the other way around. Having a party full of cooks is a real advantage: Here's one case in which there can never be too many cooks to spoil the broth! Take turns stirring while the soup is being served and you'll have perfect risotto when it's time for the main course. Have plenty of grated Parmesan cheese on the table for sprinkling, as well as a pepper mill for fresh grinding, which will really enhance the flavor.

1. Using a damp paper towel, wipe any dirt off the mushrooms. Remove and discard tough stems and cut the mushrooms into ¼-inch slices. Set aside. Heat the broth and the water in a medium-size saucepan and keep it on the back burner of the stove over the lowest heat. Place a ½-cup ladle in the pot for adding broth to the risotto in step 3.

2. Heat the olive oil and butter in a large, heavy-bottomed saucepan over medium heat. Add the shallots and salt and pepper, and cook, stirring until softened but not browned, about 3 minutes. Add the sliced mushrooms, sprinkle with salt and pepper, and cook, stirring often until slightly browned, about 3 minutes. Add the rice and stir well to coat the grains with the fat. Add the grape and lemon juice and over medium-high heat, stir constantly until all the liquid has evaporated. You may stop at this point and resume cooking 25 minutes before serving time, if necessary.

3. Begin adding the hot broth by the ladleful, stirring constantly and waiting to add the next ladleful until the previous one has been absorbed by the rice. Keep the heat at a temperature that will simmer the liquid gently and not boil it. Continue one ladle at a time, always stirring – the rice will become creamy and tender. When there are only one or two ladlefuls left, add the chopped herbs, and continue to stir and ladle until all the broth has been used. The entire process should take between 20 and 23 minutes.

4. Remove from the heat and finish the risotto by stirring in the Parmesan cheese, butter, and cream. Serve immediately with additional Parmesan cheese on the side.

Serves 8

Bibb Lettuce Heart and Radish Salad with Cooking Club House Vinaigrette

A rich meal such as this needs a side salad that's crisp and refreshing, and this one will definitely do the job. It's also very easy to prepare, so anybody with a free hand can jump right in and assist. The hearts of the Bibb lettuce are what we're after, so remove the outer leaves and reserve those for another use. Turn the lettuce upside down and remove the core of each lettuce head by using a sharp paring knife to cut around it on an angle, lifting out a small, triangular-shaped wedge. The inner leaves, which should be tightly joined, will require only a brief rinsing.

The delicious accompanying vinaigrette may become your cooking club's signature house dressing, once tasted. Whisk it up early in the evening and pour over the lettuce and radishes just before serving. Use a good-quality balsamic vinegar and a fruity olive oil for the best results. Any leftover vinaigrette can be kept refrigerated and used within three days.

1. Remove the cores from the Bibb lettuce hearts and gently open up the leaves without detaching them. Rinse under cold water and pat dry with paper towels.

2. In a small mixing bowl, whisk together the garlic, mustard, salt, pepper, and vinegar until well-combined. Add the olive oil in a thin, steady stream and whisk the vinaigrette until it has become emulsified (the oil and vinegar have blended together) and appears thick and satiny. Taste for additional salt and pepper, cover, and refrigerate until ready to use.

3. To serve the salad, cut the Bibb hearts into quarters and arrange on a platter. Scatter the sliced radishes over and drizzle desired amount of vinaigrette on top. Sprinkle the chives over all and serve immediately.

Serves 8

Ingredients:

4 heads Bibb lettuce, all soft outer leaves removed

1 bunch radishes, washed, trimmed, and sliced thin

1 tablespoon finely chopped fresh chives

Vinaigrette:

2 garlic cloves, peeled and minced

1 teaspoon honey mustard

Salt and pepper to taste

⅓ cup balsamic vinegar

⅔ cup olive oil

Miniature Tartufi

Tartufi are delightful little ice-cream balls named after the Italian word for truffle (tartufo). Popular in many Italian restaurants, they're typically made of chocolate ice cream with *amarene* (sour cherries in syrup) tucked inside, and an outside coating of shaved chocolate, but the possibilities for tartufi flavor combinations are only limited by your culinary imagination. Here, we'll make three delicious varieties of this dessert to end your cooking club party in style.

You'll want to use an ice-cream scoop with a thumb release, one that's no wider than 2 inches in diameter; otherwise, the tartufi will be too big and may not have enough time to freeze. A width of 1½ or 1¾ inches with a ¼-cup capacity is ideal. The easiest way to set up the assembly-line production is to use two 12-cup muffin tins with paper cupcake liners – enough for 8 servings – one of each flavor. As it comes time to roll each tartufo in its coating, simply remove them a few at a time so the others can stay well frozen. In order for you to work with the ice cream, it needs to be softened a bit, but not mushy. Particularly hard-frozen pints of ice cream can be microwaved for 10 or 15 seconds to make them scoopable. Work quickly with as light a hand as possible at all stages to avoid melting the ice cream.

Amaretti, cookies made by the famed *Lazzaroni di Saronno*, can be found in the cookie aisle of many supermarkets. Contrary to popular belief, they're not made with the liqueur amaretto, but rather a simple combination of sugar, apricot kernels, and egg whites, which give them a distinctive bittersweet almond flavor. Put them into a sturdy ziplock bag and use a rolling pin to crush them into coarse crumbs. If you can't find miniature cherry cordials (avoid those spiked with alcohol), substitute whole, pitted cherries from a can. Dried, whole cherries are also a good choice and can sometimes be found chocolate-covered. For the chocolate coating, use a vegetable peeler to shave a thick bar of chocolate, then toss lightly to create flakes.

1. Scoop out one portion of ice cream and level it with a knife. Insert the appropriate filling in the center, and turn out the scoop into a muffin tin lined with paper cupcake liners. Continue until you have a total of 24. Place the muffin tins in the freezer, and allow the ice cream to firm up for at least 30 minutes.

2. Spread the tartufo coatings on three separate pieces of waxed or parchment paper, and one by one, roll the ice-cream balls in the appropriate coating. Return them immediately to the muffin cups and place back in the freezer. Allow the finished balls to freeze for at least another 30 minutes or until firm.

3. To serve, place one each of the different tartufi on a chilled dessert plate, top with a dollop of whipped cream, and garnish with a mint sprig.

Serves 8

Double Chocolate Tartufi:

1 pint chocolate ice cream

8 miniature cherry cordials

1 cup flaked dark chocolate

Toasted Almond Tartufi:

1 pint vanilla bean ice cream

8 candy-coated almonds (such as Jordan almonds)

1 cup crushed amaretti cookies

Tropical Macadamia Snowballs:

1 pint peach ice cream

8 whole macadamia nuts

1 cup sweetened, flaked coconut

To Serve:

1½ cups sweetened whipped cream

Mint sprigs

Sobering Up Some Favorite Classic Recipes

If you're like most cooks, there's a messy little file tucked away somewhere with all your very favorite recipes accumulated over the years. Faded newspaper clippings, pages torn from magazines splotched with oil, or nearly indiscernible scribbles on kitchen napkins: They all hold a special place in your culinary memory of a dish worth remembering and repeating time and again. But what if they happened to contain alcohol in the form of wine or spirits, and now, for whatever reason, you're keeping a sober kitchen? Do not despair! By making use of terrific substitutions, you won't need to toss out any of your cherished recipes. With the help of the recommendations on pages 73 and 177, as well as the following tips, you'll be "sobering up" those classics in no time at all. Here are just a few ideas to get you started:

Bananas Foster:

A warm, gooey dessert made by sautéing bananas in butter, brown sugar, rum, and sometimes banana liqueur, served over ice cream.

Replace the dark rum with strongly steeped white tea and a spoonful of light molasses. Use banana-flavored syrup for the liqueur.

Cheese Fondue:

A mixture of melted Swiss Emmentaler and Gruyère cheeses combined with white wine and kirsch, served with French bread cubes for dipping.

Replace half the wine with low-sodium chicken stock and the other half with a sparkling white grape or pear juice. Substitute a dash of morello cherry juice for the kirsch (cherry brandy).

Shrimp Scampi:

Broiled shrimp flavored with garlic, butter, white wine, and parsley.

Replace the wine with equal parts lemon juice, white grape juice, and white balsamic vinegar.

Maryland She-Crab Soup:

A creamy soup made from crab meat and roe, flavored with sherry and Worcestershire sauce.

Replace the dry sherry with three parts apple juice, one part sherry vinegar, and a dash of balsamic vinegar.

Whiskey Cake:

A moist, dense cake of dried fruit, nuts and spices, soaked with a whiskey glaze.

Replace traditional glaze with Irish Breakfast tea heavily steeped in simple syrup (see page 177) with a dash of malt vinegar.

Re-creating a classic menu from the past is a wonderful way to celebrate our love of great food. It's also a terrific way to create a theme party, including not only the food of the day, but the type of entertaining that was popular at the time. You can even immerse yourself in the part by dressing up and planning activities that were popular during that era.

In this menu, all the glamour and hoopla of the Roaring Twenties sets the stage for an opulent supper. It was a time of lavish eating and drinking (in spite of Prohibition!), when friends gathered at ritzy hotels and restaurants for course after course of fine dining. Many rich dishes originated during this time, and no one worried about fat or calories. The only real concern was whether their dinner might be interrupted by a raid for illegal alcohol. Consequently, many supper clubs and speakeasies, such as the famous 21 Club in New York City, had their booze supply hidden behind impenetrable walls. And daring flappers kept personal flasks neatly tied to their legs, just in case!

There will be no chance of a raid here, however, as you serve mocktails of classic 1920s drinks to start things off and pour alcohol-free "bubbly" at the dinner table (sipped in true Twenties speakeasy style from teacups). Even Gatsby would envy this superb supper soirée, with everything from canapés to petit fours. Throw in a little jazz music, a 1920s-popular Ouija board, and of course, some faux pearls and red bow ties, and your guests won't care that temperance has taken hold. They'll be too busy enjoying the incredible ambiance you've created while happily eating their way through the glamorous past that was once the Roaring Twenties!

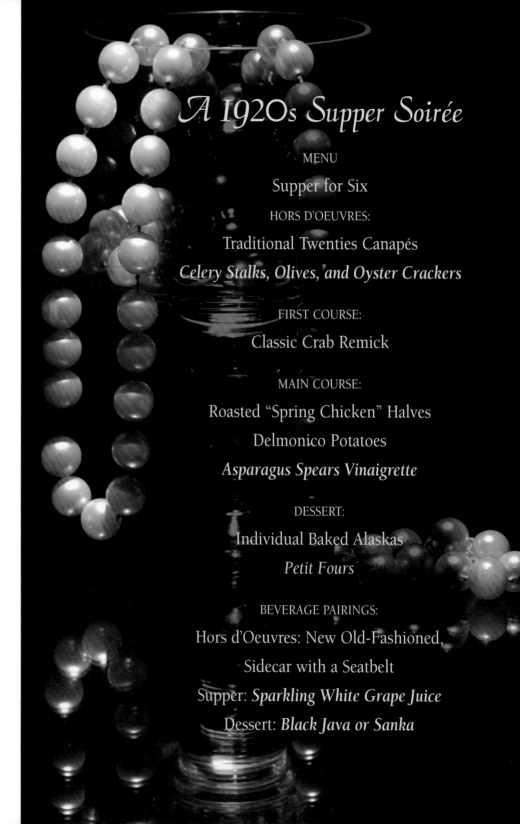

A 1920s Supper Soirée

MENU
Supper for Six

HORS D'OEUVRES:

Traditional Twenties Canapés

Celery Stalks, Olives, and Oyster Crackers

FIRST COURSE:

Classic Crab Remick

MAIN COURSE:

Roasted "Spring Chicken" Halves

Delmonico Potatoes

Asparagus Spears Vinaigrette

DESSERT:

Individual Baked Alaskas

Petit Fours

BEVERAGE PAIRINGS:

Hors d'Oeuvres: New Old-Fashioned, Sidecar with a Seatbelt

Supper: *Sparkling White Grape Juice*

Dessert: *Black Java or Sanka*

Tips on Purchased Ingredients

To complement your canapés, serve up some simple nibbles in the form of *celery stalks and olives*, two items that were never missing from a 1920s appetizer course. Whether plain or stuffed, raw celery was even listed on the menu as a selection! This is probably because tossed salads as we know them today were not often seen – relish trays were more the thing and included radishes as well as olives. Buy celery hearts, which require hardly any peeling and very little cleaning or trimming, and serve them with the leaves on, either as is or stuffed with a flavored cream cheese, pâté, or savory mousse. As for olives, the variety that we find today was not available back then – canned olives, mostly black, were the primary eating olives of choice, and in fact, it was at this time that the sizes we now know as jumbo, colossal, and mammoth were given their names in order to sell to the popularity of Cecil B. De Mille films, which were also described in this fashion. Choose some of these to add to your hors d'oeuvres. Little savory bites such as *oyster crackers* were popular nibbles and probably derived from the traditional Vermont common cracker, which dates back to early America. Speaking of oysters, they made an appearance at nearly all affairs, raw or cooked, but most often in the form of the oyster cocktail, freshly shucked and served "straight up" in a little cocktail glass of the same name. A dab of hot sauce and (when no one was looking) a bit of sherry were the usual condiments. If you and your guests enjoy oysters, by all means serve them as part of your hors d'oeuvres, without the sherry of course!

It's an odd fact, but during Prohibition, an enormous amount of champagne was consumed. Sometimes, especially in the speakeasies, it was sipped from teacups, as were many other drinks, to maintain the appearance of a "dry" establishment. For fun, serve up some bubbly, alcohol-free *sparkling white grape juice*, or another flavor of your liking, at the dinner table in just the same way.

The most popular vegetable served in 1920s-era supper clubs may very well have been *asparagus*. A number of asparagus serving platters and asparagus tongs, many in exquisite sterling silver, were made during this era to meet the demand. Often, it was served smothered in a cream or hollandaise sauce, or presented as a cold "salad." Trim and steam about 2 pounds of asparagus spears, then quickly submerge them in a bowl of ice water to stop the cooking and retain color. Lay on paper towels to dry and serve on a pretty platter with a drizzle of your favorite vinaigrette to accompany your chicken dish and Delmonico Potatoes.

No glitzy Twenties dinner ended without a tray of *petit fours*, those bite-sized, delicately decorated cakes most often seen at holidays. Many supermarkets carry them year-round, chocolate and vanilla being the usual flavors. French bakeries have them as well, where they're made onsite and where you may discover a greater variety of colors and flavors. Serve these little cakes after the Baked Alaskas, with coffee.

Many colorful slang terms appeared during the 1920s and *java* was one of them. Usually served up black or with a touch of cream, coffee was a necessary ending to a meal (occasionally spiked with a quick shot from the hip flask!). *Sanka*®, which made its first appearance at this time, was the decaffeinated coffee that virtually every American coffee drinker was familiar with, which is why to this day, many people still refer to a cup of decaf as a cup of Sanka®, regardless of the brand. Offer both for your guests, served up with this bit of historical trivia.

New Old-Fashioned and Sidecar with a Seatbelt

Ingredients:

Equipment needed: 1.5-ounce jigger or shot glass, cocktail shaker and strainer, ice bucket and tongs, 6-ounce Old-Fashioned glasses, 4- to 5-ounce cocktail glasses, a wooden pestle for muddling, measuring spoons

New Old-Fashioned:

Orange wedge, rind removed

Maraschino cherry, stem removed

1 sugar lump

2 jiggers water

2 teaspoons white balsamic vinegar

Cola, as needed

Garnish: orange slice and cherry

The Roaring Twenties didn't invent cocktails, but it was an age that definitely contributed to their popularity. One of the reasons was that the "bootleg" liquor that many speakeasies served was so vile in taste, fruit juices and sodas were often added to make many drinks more palatable. And that's exactly what happened to the Old-Fashioned. A "muddling" (mixing) of orange slice, cherry, and a sugar cube helped disguise the poor quality of the whiskey used, and eventually these masking flavors became the signature of the drink. For our mocktail, New Old-Fashioned, we'll be using the same flavors and replacing the alcohol with a bit of cola and balsamic vinegar for color and taste.

The Sidecar, an enormously popular drink in that period, was actually invented by a French bartender who arrived at work every day in the sidecar of a motorcycle. Brandy and the bitter-orange-flavored triple sec are the main ingredients, which may account for its popularity, since smuggled brandy was less likely to be adulterated, although it may have been watered down. In our mocktail version, we'll be using bitter lemon soda as the base for a refreshing, not-too-sweet taste, and some ginger-flavored tea for an added zing. A variety like lemon-ginger green tea would be excellent to use if you desire more depth of flavor.

The best way to present your mocktails is to set up a beverage area near the hors d'oeuvres where guests can either mix their own or have them concocted by an enlisted bartender. Provide the drink recipes and all the fixings, including ice and garnishes, and watch the fun begin!

Place the orange wedge, cherry, sugar, water, and vinegar in a 6-ounce Old-Fashioned glass and muddle to a paste. Add ice cubes, fill with cola, stir, garnish, and serve.

Makes 1 drink

Sidecar with a Seatbelt

Lemon and sugar for rimming the glass

1 jigger bitter lemon soda

1 jigger orange juice

1 jigger cold ginger tea

1. Run a lemon wedge around the rim of a cocktail glass and dip the rim in sugar.

2. Pour the soda, juice, and tea into a cocktail shaker, add ice, and shake well. Strain into the prepared glass and serve.

Makes 1 drink

Traditional Twenties Canapés

Although we don't often refer to them as such anymore, *canapés* are still popular offerings at cocktail parties and before dinner. Small pieces of bread or toast, topped with a savory spread or a bit of fish, meat, or cheese, these delicious bites were often served at Twenties soirées. Particularly popular were anchovy and sardine pastes, as well as dollops of caviar. Home cooks made them as well and usually had a set of canapé cutters in shapes like diamonds and hearts for special entertaining.

We'll make three classic selections that will wow your guests by presentation alone. The pinwheels can be made ahead (even 1 or 2 weeks) and frozen – a great convenience for spontaneous entertaining. The toasts and their shrimp topping can also be prepared ahead separately and put together just before serving, while the cheese canapés can be composed and refrigerated a few hours before.

Have your supermarket bakery slice a solid Pullman loaf lengthwise for perfectly even ¼-inch pieces and make the pinwheels and toasts that day before the bread dries out. Wrap and freeze the remaining slices to cut into squares on the day of the party. For variety, you can use one white and one wheat loaf, and freeze any extra bread that remains. With dinner to come, count on no more than five or six canapés per person. One average-size loaf, made into three types of canapés, will amply serve 6 guests.

Ingredients

Shrimp Toast Rounds:

Two ¼-inch-thick slices white or wheat bread (cut lengthwise), crusts removed

2 tablespoons unsalted butter, melted

1 cup frozen, cooked baby salad shrimp, thawed and roughly chopped

¼ cup mayonnaise

1 tablespoon milk

1 tablespoon small capers, chopped

¼ teaspoon dried thyme

Salt and pepper to taste

Chive sprigs, cut into 1-inch-long pieces, for garnish

1. Preheat the oven to 375 degrees.

2. Place the bread slices on a cutting board and using a 1½- to 2-inch round cookie cutter, make circles from the bread. Brush both sides of the bread rounds lightly with the melted butter and place on a baking sheet. Bake until both sides are lightly golden, turning once, about 8 minutes. Allow to cool on the baking sheet. If not using right away, place the toast rounds in an airtight container and store at room temperature (up to 1 day ahead).

3. In a medium-size mixing bowl, combine the shrimp, mayonnaise, milk, capers, thyme, salt, and pepper and stir well. Cover and refrigerate until ready to use (can be prepared a day ahead).

4. To serve, mound a tablespoon of the shrimp mixture on top of each toast round, garnish with two crossed chive pieces, and arrange on a serving platter.

Serves 6

1. Place the bread slices on a cutting board and using a rolling pin, gently but firmly flatten each slice.

2. In a small mixing bowl, combine the butter, dill, lemon juice, salt and pepper, and stir well to combine. Spread the butter mixture evenly over each bread slice. Arrange the salmon slices on top.

3. Beginning at the short end of the bread, roll up each slice, jellyroll-style, as tightly as possible. Wrap each roll in plastic and chill at least 2 hours before slicing. (Or double-wrap the rolls and freeze up to 2 weeks ahead.) Use a sharp knife to cut each roll into six pieces. Arrange decoratively on a serving tray and garnish with the dill sprigs.

Serves 6

Ingredients
Smoked Salmon Pinwheels:

Two ¼-inch-thick slices white or wheat bread (cut lengthwise), crusts removed

¼ cup (½ stick) unsalted butter, softened

1 tablespoon finely chopped, fresh dill

1 teaspoon fresh lemon juice

Salt and pepper to taste

4 ounces thinly sliced smoked salmon

Dill sprigs for garnish

Ingredients
Cheese and Cornichon Squares:

Two ¼-inch-thick slices white or wheat bread (cut lengthwise), crusts removed

Two 3-ounce packages plain cream cheese, softened

¼ cup (½ stick) unsalted butter, softened

⅔ cup finely shredded Gruyère cheese

2 teaspoons poppy seeds

1 teaspoon prepared mustard

6 to 8 cornichons or baby gherkins, cut into ¼-inch-thick circles

Parsley leaves for garnish

1. Place the bread slices side by side on a cutting board (if bread is partially frozen, it's easier to work with).

2. In a medium-size mixing bowl, combine the cream cheese, butter, Gruyère, poppy seeds, and mustard and stir well to combine. Spread the mixture evenly over the two bread slices and chill for at least 1 hour.

3. Cut the cheese-coated bread into bite-size squares and place a cornichon circle in the middle of each. Garnish with the parsley leaves, transfer to a serving platter, and keep chilled until ready to serve. Lightly cover the platter with plastic wrap to prevent drying out. Can be made up to 3 hours ahead.

Serves 6

Classic Crab Remick

Shellfish and creamy sauces went hand in hand during the Twenties. Popular since the advent of Lobster Newburg in the late 19th century, any kind of fish served in a rich sauce was the dish of choice for many. According to Arthur Schwartz in his superb book, *New York City Food*, Crab Remick was created in 1920 at a Plaza Hotel dinner in honor of the president of the New York Stock Exchange, William H. Remick. It made use of the growing popularity of ketchup by chefs who were looking for new ingredients, although here, as was often done later, chili sauce is used for a more intense flavor. Once the crash of 1929 occurred, I suspect Crab Remick fell out of favor for a while! Today, however, it's still a very popular dish in the South.

The ideal way to serve this is in ovenproof scallop-shaped shells, surprisingly cheap to purchase and handy for many other seafood appetizers. If you don't have any or can't come across them, small gratin dishes or ramekins will work just fine. Pick over the crabmeat carefully to remove bits of shell and cartilage. Jumbo lump or backfin crabmeats are the best choice for this dish. You can prepare the sauce ahead and spoon it on top just before you're ready to broil.

Ingredients:

1½ cups mayonnaise

½ cup chili sauce

2 teaspoons fresh lemon juice

1 teaspoon tarragon vinegar

1 teaspoon dry mustard

½ teaspoon paprika

¼ teaspoon celery salt

Dash Tabasco® sauce

1 pound crabmeat, in large chunks, picked over to remove shell and cartilage pieces

6 bacon strips, fried crisp and crumbled

1. In a small mixing bowl, combine the mayonnaise, chili sauce, lemon juice, vinegar, mustard, paprika, celery salt, and Tabasco® and stir well to combine.

2. Preheat the oven to 375 degrees. Divide the crabmeat among six scallop shells or gratin dishes on a large baking sheet. Bake until the crab is just heated through, about 10 minutes. Remove from the oven and turn on the broiler.

3. Sprinkle the crumbled bacon over the crab and spoon the sauce generously over the top of each serving. Place under the broiler until bubbly and lightly browned, about 2 minutes. Serve immediately.

Serves 6

Roasted "Spring Chicken" Halves

During the Twenties, chicken was considered a seasonal meat, and spring chickens (produced from spring eggs) were highly prized for their tenderness and freshness. They usually weighed no more than 2 pounds and were about 16 weeks of age, after which time they were no doubt considered "tough old birds." Today, we classify chickens by different means, the smallest usually being a broiler-fryer (up to about 3½ pounds), and the next size being the roasters (weighing up to 5 or 6 pounds). The closest thing we have today to a spring chicken in size would be the Rock Cornish hen, which is a hybrid of Cornish and White Rock chickens. Weighing up to 2½ pounds at most, these "miniature" chickens will fill in nicely for our Twenties spring chicken dish. If you'd prefer, the somewhat harder-to-find and more expensive poussins, or squab chickens, which were also very popular in the 1920s, could be substituted – although, because of their small size, you'll need one per person.

Cornish hens don't take long to cook through, but to gain a crisp and golden exterior, they will need extra roasting time. The best way to accomplish this is by buttering both on top of and underneath the skin, helping to keep the meat moist while crisping the outside. Little other than pan juices should be served with this dish, which you can quickly prepare by draining off the excess fat from the roasting pan and deglazing with a little chicken stock.

Rinse the hens under cold water and discard any giblet packets. Use kitchen shears or a sharp knife to cut along the small backbone, then halve between the breasts.

You can roast the birds ahead if you like and reheat them under the broiler for a fresh, crisp appearance at the table.

1. Preheat the oven to 425 degrees. Place the hen halves, cut side down, in a large roasting pan. Try to keep a little space between them.

2. In a small mixing bowl, combine the butter, shallot, zest, tarragon, salt and pepper, and stir well. Loosen the skin from the meat, including the legs and thighs, and rub half the butter mixture underneath the skins. Rub the remaining butter evenly on top of each hen half, and squeeze the juice from the cut lemon over all the pieces. Roast the hens in the middle of the oven until they're cooked through and the skin is crisp and golden, about 40 minutes. If making ahead, transfer the hens to a foil-lined baking sheet and set aside for warming under the broiler; otherwise, place the halves on a large, heated platter or individual dinner plates.

3. Pour off most of the grease from the roasting pan and deglaze with the chicken stock on top of the stove, scraping any bits up with a wooden spoon. Pour the flavorful liquid into a gravy boat or heat-proof creamer to reheat later, or spoon over the plated hens and serve immediately.

Serves 6

Ingredients:

Three 1- to 2-pound Rock Cornish hens, halved

½ cup (1 stick) unsalted butter, softened

1 medium-size shallot, peeled and minced

1 tablespoon grated lemon zest

1 tablespoon finely chopped tarragon leaves

Salt and pepper to taste

1 whole lemon, cut in half

1 cup low-sodium chicken broth

Delmonico Potatoes

Although New York's famous Delmonico's restaurant served its last meal in 1923, its signature potato dish lived on. After an alcohol raid in 1921 by federal agents, this 100-year-old landmark could no longer compete with the ritzy supper clubs and their well-hidden booze cellars, yet on the menus of many remaining hotel restaurants and clubs of that era, a version of these potatoes could be found. Its exact recipe is debatable, but in essence, it seems to borrow from the best of both French *dauphinoise* potatoes (cooked in cream) and potatoes au gratin (topped with cheese).

This version is somewhat akin to the familiar scalloped potatoes, though a good dose of cream, in keeping with the cooking style of the 1920s, has been added. Finely grated Parmesan cheese and a toasted, buttery bread-crumb topping will distinguish it, however, from its more commonplace cousin. Be sure to season the cream mixture generously with salt, as it's all the potatoes will be getting. These are at their best straight from the oven, with only a brief wait, so plan to have the dish ready to go into the oven 1½ to 2 hours before you'll be sitting down to eat. The potatoes can be made in one large baking dish, but for this occasion, two smaller ovals or gratin dishes will give a nicer presentation at the dinner table.

Ingredients:

8 medium-size Idaho or russet potatoes, peeled and thinly sliced, kept in cold water

1½ cups heavy cream

1 cup whole milk

1½ teaspoons salt or more to taste

¼ teaspoon ground nutmeg

Freshly ground black or white pepper

⅓ cup finely grated Parmesan cheese

1 cup plain, dry bread crumbs

2 tablespoons unsalted butter, melted

1. Preheat the oven to 325 degrees. Butter two 1½-quart oval baking or gratin dishes.

2. Drain the potatoes and dry them with paper towels.

3. In a medium-size saucepan, combine the cream, milk, salt, nutmeg, and pepper, and over medium heat, stirring often, bring to a boil. Remove from the heat.

4. Layer ⅓ of the potatoes in the bottom of the baking dishes and pour ⅓ of the hot cream mixture over it. Sprinkle ⅓ of the Parmesan cheese on top, and repeat twice more with the layering. In a small bowl, stir together the bread crumbs and melted butter, and distribute over the tops of the baking dishes. (You can prepare the dish a few hours ahead up to this point, cover with foil, and refrigerate.)

5. Bake, uncovered, until the potatoes are fork-tender and the tops are toasty and golden, 1 to 1½ hours. Remove from the oven and allow to stand for at least 10 minutes before serving.

Serves 6

Prohibition: When the Nation Went Dry and Drank Like Never Before

At the stroke of midnight on January 16, 1920, America went dry. The 18th Amendment, also known as the Volstead Act, prohibited the manufacture, sale, and possession of alcohol, and continued to do so for 13 years. Prompted by numerous temperance organizations and the hope that both crime and poverty would disappear, Prohibition went into full force. And for a short time, people did indeed drink less. But not for long.

It took only a year or two for rumrunners and bootleggers, who had already been prevalent in the South, to figure out a means of national distribution that could fool the Feds. Smuggling from Canada and Mexico became commonplace, while home distilling and wine-making skyrocketed. By the early 1920s, inhabitants of every city in America had access to numerous speakeasies and illegal taverns, as well as ample alcohol with which to drink themselves silly. In fact, it's estimated there were even more bars where alcohol was served (albeit on the sly) than before Prohibition. New York City alone may have had as many as 100,000. Both men and women (who had just received the right to vote and were feeling emancipated) gathered for all-night parties, music, and a "Roaring Twenties" good time. The occasional raid didn't discourage them; police were often bribed to keep things quiet or give advance notice of their arrival.

The most unfortunate side of what has been called the "noble experiment" was evident in the poorest parts of the nation, where adulterated whiskey, often cut with toxic substances, resulted in thousands of deaths, while the population that was already alcohol-addicted did not decrease. If anything, many alcoholics may have died unnecessarily from desperately drinking any form of alcohol they could get. "Bathtub gin" and other homemade concoctions were decidedly unpalatable and often just as dangerous to consume. Treatment facilities were rapidly closing their doors, with only a handful of places reserved for the very wealthy.

Interestingly enough, it was legal to obtain alcohol by doctor's orders for so-called "medicinal purposes" and, as you can imagine, a continuous string of sudden illnesses seemed to appear out of nowhere. Many medicines contained a good dose of alcohol, as well as other addictive drugs, which were prescribed for everything from headaches to fatigue. Little if anything was known about potential physiological dependence, and it was clear from temperance propaganda that those who drank too much were considered of low moral character. It was even suggested by hard-line prohibitionists that society should simply "let the drunks die out."

The only benefits of Prohibition were enjoyed by the black market, where mob-controlled liquor flourished and untaxed income poured in. Contrary to Prohibition's initial goals, homicide rates increased, as did arrests due to disorderly conduct and drunk driving, and alcohol consumption, in the end, grew by leaps and bounds. Why was this the case? It's been suggested that the idea of "forbidden fruit" simply increased the allure. But it's also likely that liquor sellers, seeing the potential profit, began marketing to nondrinkers, while many defiant Americans drank with an abandon rarely seen today. The "Iron Law of Prohibition," which states that the more intense the law enforcement, the more potent the prohibited substance becomes, played itself out well – spirits increased in strength, production, and consumption, while the demand for beer decreased because of its low-alcohol content and higher volume, which made it more difficult and costly to distribute. With more potent liquor available, intoxication no doubt became more frequent as well, fulfilling the old adage that "liquor is quicker."

After Prohibition was repealed in 1933, crime rates and alcohol-related deaths dropped. Jobs were created in distilleries, breweries, and other alcohol-related industries, prisons were less crowded, and alcohol consumption began to fall to pre-Prohibition levels. Alcohol production, overseen and taxed by the government, became safer, while moderation began to be preached rather than strict abstinence. Discussions of alcoholism were couched in terms of medical issues and societal compassion. A year later, in 1934, voluntary self-help groups began to appear. And in 1935, in Akron, Ohio, the most notable self-help group, led by Bill Wilson and Dr. Bob Smith, was born. It wasn't until 1939 in Cleveland, Ohio, however, that this "bunch of nameless drunks," as they called themselves, who gathered to help each other stay sober, officially took the name "Alcoholics Anonymous." Today, there are more than 2 million members in 150 countries.

Individual Baked Alaska

By far the most popular dessert of the 1920s was Baked Alaska, a spectacle credited to Chef Ranhofer of Delmonico's, who is often cited as the creator of many well-known dishes, including Eggs Benedict and Lobster Newburg. Although this dish had been around since 1867, when the U.S. purchased Alaska from Russia, it never lost its glamour and nearly always made an appearance at the dessert table during this time. Flaming Baked Alaskas, which were doused with brandy and set alight, fell a bit out of favor during Prohibition, but came back into style shortly after.

It's a simple thing really – ice cream on cake with some meringue on top. But what gives Baked Alaska its appeal is the contradictory combination of temperatures and flavors. There are now many different varieties of Baked Alaska, including the individual presentations we'll do here. They can actually be made ahead of time and popped into the oven before serving, so you may find yourself making these, with numerous ice cream and cake combinations, on a regular basis.

If you don't have giant muffin tins, you can use a large thumb-release ice-cream scoop to make a dome (not a rounded ball) to place on top of the cake. If you decide to make these far in advance (as opposed to the night before), you'll want to protect them in plastic wrap. Be sure that the meringue is well frozen and set before covering. If you have a kitchen butane torch (and are always looking for an excuse to use it!), you can add a few final touches to the meringue when the Baked Alaskas come out of the oven for a real show-stopping presentation.

Ingredients:

1 quart strawberry ice cream, softened

1 loaf marble pound cake

8 large egg whites

½ teaspoon cream of tartar

1½ cups granulated sugar

1 jar prepared chocolate sauce

1. Line a giant-size, 6-cup muffin tin with paper baking cups. Spoon the ice cream into each cup, almost to the top, and smooth over with a knife. Cover the surfaces with plastic wrap and freeze until firm, at least 2 hours or overnight.

2. Slice the pound cake into ¾-inch-thick pieces, and using a 3½-inch biscuit cutter, cut out six circles. Place them evenly apart on a foil-lined baking sheet. Take one of the frozen cups of ice cream from the freezer, tear off the paper lining, and place flat side down on top of the cake circle. Repeat with the other five ice cream cups. Cover each with plastic wrap and gently but firmly press the mound of ice cream onto the cake. Return the baking sheet to the freezer.

3. In a large mixing bowl, using an electric mixer, beat together the egg whites and the cream of tartar until foamy. Add the sugar, a little at a time, beating on high until the whites hold stiff and glossy peaks, about 5 minutes. Remove the baking sheet with the cake and ice cream from the freezer, and using a spoon or a pastry bag fitted with a large round or star tip, apply the meringue decoratively all over the ice cream down to the edge of the cakes, being careful to cover all spots. Return to the freezer until ready to bake.

4. Preheat the oven to 475 degrees. Place the baking tray with the Alaskas in the oven and bake until the meringue has lightly browned, about 4 minutes. Drizzle some of the chocolate sauce on the bottom of six dessert plates. Use a large metal spatula to transfer the Baked Alaskas to the plates, and serve immediately.

Serves 6

Bibliography

Aloni, Nicole. *Secrets from a Caterer's Kitchen*. New York: HP Books, 2000.

Amster, Linda, editor. *The New York Times Passover Cookbook*. New York: William Morrow and Co., Inc., 1999.

Augustin, J.; E. Augustin; R. Cutrufelli, et al. 1992. Alcohol retention in food preparation. *Journal of the American Dietetic Association* 92(4): 486-88.

Batali, Mario. *Holiday Food*. New York: Clarkson Potter, 2000.

Batra, Neelam. *1,000 Indian Recipes*. New York: Wiley Publishing Inc., 2002.

Cook's Illustrated Magazine Editors. *Italian Classics*. Brookline, MA: Boston Common Press, 2002.

Esposito, Mary Ann. *Ciao Italia: Traditional Italian Recipes from Family Kitchens*. New York: Hearst Books, 1991.

George, M.S.; R. F. Anton; C. Bloomer, et al. 2001. Activation of prefrontal cortex and anterior thalamus in alcoholic subjects on exposure to alcohol-specific cues. *Archives of General Psychiatry* 2001; 58(4): 345-52.

Good Cook Series. *Techniques and Recipes*. Chicago: Time-Life Books, Inc., 1982.

Herbst, Sharon Tyler. *The New Food Lover's Companion*. New York: Barron's, 1995.

Herbst, Sharon Tyler. *The Ultimate Liquor-Free Drink Guide*. New York: Broadway Books, 2003.

Hoffman, Susanna. *The Olive and the Caper: Adventures in Greek Cooking*. New York: Workman Publishing, 2004.

Kafka, Barbara. *Roasting: A Simple Art*. New York: William Morrow and Co. Inc., 1995.

Mooney, A. L.; Arlene Eisenberg; and Howard Eisenberg. *The Recovery Book*. New York: Workman Publishing, 1992.

Regan, Gary. *The Bartender's Bible: 1001 Mixed Drinks*. New York: HarperCollins, 1991.

Schuegraf, Ernst. *Cooking with the Saints*. San Francisco: Ignatius Press, 2001.

Schwartz, Arthur. *Arthur Schwartz's New York City Food*. New York: Stewart, Tabori & Chang, 2004.

Scott, Liz. *The Sober Kitchen: Recipes and Advice for a Lifetime of Sobriety*. Boston: Harvard Common Press, 2003.

Thomas, Frank, and Karen L. Brown. *The Mocktail Bar Guide*. New York: Meadowbrook Press, 2001.

Weil, Andrew. *Healthy Aging: A Lifelong Guide to Your Physical and Spiritual Well-Being*. New York: Alfred A. Knopf, 2005.

White, William L. *Slaying the Dragon: The History of Addiction Treatment and Recovery in America*. Bloomington, IL: Chestnut Health Systems, 1998.

Resources

These days, nearly everything we can imagine is available at the click of a mouse. Here are some helpful websites for numerous specialty items:

Alcohol-Free Extracts:

www.frontiercoop.com

Flavored Sugars:

www.faeriesfinest.com

Culinary Lavender:

www.jardindusoleil.com

Specialty Teas, including Kosher:

www.harney.com

Personalized Mini Bottles of Sparkling Cider:

www.foreverwedstore.com

Ethnic and Gourmet Food Items:

www.kalustyans.com

www.ethnicgrocer.com

www.chefshop.com

Specialty Cheeses:

www.igourmet.com

www.texascheese.com

Index

Cleveland Clinic Press

Cleveland Clinic Press is a full-line publisher of non-fiction trade books and other media for the medical, health, nutrition, cookbook, and exercise markets.

It is the mission of the Press to increase the health literacy of the American public and to dispel myths and misinformation about medicine, health care, and treatment. Our authors include leading authorities from the Cleveland Clinic as well as a diverse list of experts drawn from medical and health institutions whose research and treatment breakthroughs have helped countless people.

Each Cleveland Clinic Guide provides the health-care consumer with the highest quality, practical, useful, reliable, and authoritative information. Every book is reviewed for accuracy and timeliness by the experts of the Cleveland Clinic.

www.clevelandclinicpress.org